Entrepreneurship, Productivity, and the Freedom of Information Act

Entrepreneurship, Productivity, and the Freedom of Information Act

Protecting Circumstantially Relevant Business Information

William L. Casey, Jr.
John E. Marthinsen
Laurence S. Moss
Babson College

LexingtonBooks
D.C. Heath and Company
Lexington, Massachusetts
Toronto

Library of Congress Cataloging in Publication Data

Casey, William L.
   Entrepreneurship, productivity, and the Freedom of Information Act.

   Bibliography: p.
   Includes index.
   1. Government information—United States. 2. Public records—Law
and legislation—United States. 3. Business records—Law and legislation—
United States.
I. Marthinsen, John E. II. Moss, Laurence S., 1944-   . III. Title.
KF5753.C37   1983   342.73′0853   82-48609
ISBN 0-669-06349-5   347.302853

Published simultaneously in Canada

Printed in the United States of America

International Standard Book Number: 0-669-06349-5

Library of Congress Catalog Card Number: 82-48609

To Diana, Laraine, and Widdy

Contents

Figures and Tables

Preface and Acknowledgments

As this book goes to press, the news media are saturated with articles on a variety of topics surrounding the issue of business-information disclosure. We read of unions working toward reforms that require businesses to disclose all known chemical hazards in their work place. Governments of Western nations call for tighter controls on technology transfer to prevent the USSR from obtaining Western technology. In the United States, we witness the controversy surrounding Anne (Gorsuch) Burford, former chief administrator of the Environmental Protection Agency, and her attempt to withhold from Congress documents pertaining to the $1.6 billion superfund. With respect to the specific interests of business, we are informed of the theft of business documents from IBM by a former IBM employee and their subsequent unlawful sale to the Hitachi Company of Japan. Finally, we are alerted to the public disclosure of business trade secrets by government agencies whose job it is to collect sensitive business information. What these issue-laden episodes have in common is their concern with the timely disclosure of business information. In each case, we see an obvious group that would be hurt by disclosure and an obvious group that would be helped.

These particular disputes are the most recent variations of a broader theme that has reappeared over the long sweep of history in Western democracies. That theme concerns the extent to which an individual's right to privacy and the enjoyment of his or her property may be pre-empted by a more-far-reaching public interest. Can workers legitimately demand that a firm's chemical substances be disclosed to them when these disclosures may jeopardize the strategic position and value of that firm in the marketplace? Is there justification for censoring individuals and monitoring scientific activity around the world in order to uphold a strategic ideal of national security? Will these efforts result in severe limitations on international trade, a decline in world income, and the curtailment of individual liberty? Within the government, can an executive agency effectively manage its internal affairs when Congress and the public at large can access internal agency information? However, without the right to access information, can Congress detect malfeasance and corruption? When one business steals the entrepreneurial discoveries of another or when they are disclosed by government agencies, does this not promote the diffusion of invention and contribute toward lower prices for consumers? Or does this diffusion of stolen technology mostly dampen incentives to engage in entrepreneurial activities altogether? Thus, the newspaper stories surrounding the disclosure of information at the time this book goes to press touch on perennial questions of social and economic organization. We expect that different versions of these same questions will be in the news at the time this book is published—it is like old wine appearing in new bottles.

Our concern in this book is with one of these aforementioned themes—namely, the untimely disclosure of business information by government. Our focus is not on the illicit activities of departing employees but on the legal and apparently constitutional disclosure of business information after businesses have submitted that information to government agencies; that is, this book examines the Freedom of Information Act and its various amendments insofar as they affect the flow of business information.

This book grew out of the continued support and encouragement of Babson's Board of Research. That board, under the leadership of Professor Edward Handler, did more than provide us with research funds. The board encouraged the project, provided insights, and also pointed us in the direction of publishing our findings so that other scholars also might benefit from the research undertaken at the college. Babson's growing commitment to support scholarly research has been advanced not only by the Handler board but also by the active involvement of President William Dill and Academic Dean Melvyn Copen. All these people are building on a foundation established by our friend and colleague, the deceased former academic dean, Professor Walter Carpenter.

Outside our college, we extend a personal thank you to a prolific scholar, professor of law at the University of Cincinnati, and able legal counsel of the Procter & Gamble Company, James T. O'Reilly. O'Reilly's vast knowledge of the legal terrain of debates surrounding the disclosure of business records and his willingness to take time to share his insights with us are a rare and special combination from which we have benefited greatly. Other legal scholars such as Peter Rosenberg (U.S. Patent Office) and Russell Stevenson (George Washington University) were also helpful to us at various stages in our research.

A large number of Freedom of Information officers not only filled our requests for data and related information with considerable speed and accuracy but also shared their thoughts with us in a constructive manner. Among all those federal executives interviewed, we wish to single out George Chall and David Allen of the Office of Personnel Management, who helped us with our research and allowed us to have access to the libraries of the Executive Development Seminar Centers of Great Neck and Denver, respectively.

A large number of individuals outside government also provided us with various bits and pieces of information as well as lasting insights. We acknowledge the kindness of Kathryn Braeman (Department of Justice), Nancy Duff Campbell (National Women's Law Center), Diane Cohn (Freedom of Information Clearinghouse), Robert Cynkar (Senate Judiciary Minority Staff), Gerald Deighton (Food and Drug Administration), Charles Durr

(Machinery and Allied Products Institute), Grant Esterling (International Business Machines Corp.), David Elliott (Department of Commerce), Lester Grodberg (Digital Equipment Corp.), Robert Gelliat (Department of Defense), Robert Gelman (House Government Information Subcommittee), Peter Grace (W.R. Grace Co.), Joseph Levine (Department of Commerce), Edward Jones III (Department of Justice), W. Gregor McFarlan (Sterling Institute), James Nelson (Environmental Protection Agency), Jack Pulley (Dow Corning Co.), Robert Rice (Food and Drug Administration), Sheldon Rothstein (Polaroid Corp.), Tod Stevenson (Consumer Product Safety Commission), Thomas Susman (Ropes and Gray), and David Zoll (Chemical Manufacturers Association).

When deadlines were upon us and patience was short, a number of outstanding individuals helped us always with considerable aplomb and efficiency. Our two research assistants, Michael Crehan and Mary Ann Fabrizio, showed dedication to the project and made contributions beyond our expectations. Secretarial support was supplied graciously by Connie Stumpf and her staff at the Babson Word Processing Center. Kim Wells, who put the manuscript on the word processor, went beyond the call of duty to help us, and we remain immensely grateful. We extend our thanks to Ann Devlin whose meticulous eye for detail aided in the preparation of the footnotes and bibliography. The library staffs at Babson and Wellesley colleges were both helpful in locating documents and making copies available to us. Finally, our department secretary, Anita Clymas, was always there working when the twelfth hour struck. To these people, we acknowledge their indispensable help and offer our heartfelt thanks.

1 Introduction

The United States has been experiencing what many business analysts call an innovation slump. Traditional measures of innovative effort, like annual patents awarded to Americans, are registering historic lows, and when those same measures are compared to their foreign counterparts, it appears that the technological superiority of the United States is faltering. In the econometric work of Edward Denison, Robert Solow, and others, much of the outstanding gain in the per capita income of Americans over the last hundred years has been attributed to the "advancement of knowledge."[1] Changes in the size of the work force and capital-goods construction (and maintenance) have played a much less-significant role. These trends appear bleak because declines have become the rule rather than the exception. According to Denison, the rate of growth of national income per person employed declined by 0.5 percent between 1973 and 1976, a phenomenon that is unprecedented in the post-World War II period.[2] By way of international comparison, average U.S. labor productivity is greater than comparable productivity measures in the United Kingdom, Germany, France, or even Japan. Nevertheless, the rate of increase of U.S. labor productivity is slowing down. Clearly, this is a source of concern among business analysts.[3]

The U.S. Patent Office reported that, in the twelve-month period ending with September 1978, 70,292 patents were issued, down more than 4,000 from the previous ten-year average. Furthermore, patents of U.S. origin declined from 1945 to 1978 by 18.5 percent, while patents of foreign origin increased over the same period by 85.4 percent.[4] The National Science Foundation reported that, during the ten-year time span from 1968 to 1978, research and development (R&D), as a fraction of gross national product (GNP), increased by 20 percent in Japan, 16 percent in West Germany, and 15 percent in the USSR while it dropped 20 percent in the United States; that the share of the U.S. federal budget represented by R&D declined by 40 percent and that of basic research by 25 percent; that investment by U.S. companies in basic research, as a proportion of net sales, dropped 24 percent; and that the percentage of R&D scientists and engineers in the labor force rose by 62 percent in Japan, 50 percent in West Germany, and 13 percent in the USSR but fell by 13 percent in the United States.[5] As a percentage of gross national product, R&D expenditures declined from about 3 percent in the mid-1960s to a low of 2.2 percent by the end of the 1970s.[6] In 1980 and 1981, total R&D spending in the United States did rise by 4 percent and 3 percent respectively (in constant dollars), but these rates of increase continued to lag those of Japan and the major industrialized countries of Western Europe.[7]

In addressing the problem of low productivity in the U.S. economy, a number of economists have pointed to the historically high positive correlation between hourly productivity and R&D expenditures in various U.S. industries.[8] Thus, it is quite reasonable to identify the low rate of growth in per capita income with the faltering research commitment both on the part of industry and government during the Vietnam War period and continuing thereafter.

These economic trends have caught the eye of a wide spectrum of the public including several government agencies. For example, the Department of Commerce, as early as 1963, established the Civilian Industrial Technology program to encourage R&D in industries considered to be lagging but important to the U.S. economy. Former President Richard Nixon expressed concern with the alleged erosion in the technological leadership of the United States in the world. He made this issue a central part of his message to Congress and requested an ambitious research effort to assess R&D performance in the U.S. economy. In 1978 and 1979, the federal government, through the National Science Foundation and other agencies, continued to fund reviews and policy analyses about the waning of U.S. technological superiority.[9]

Quite naturally, a wide variety of explanations have been offered for the deterioration in U.S. productivity. A majority of these explanations, in one way or the other, have sighted the negative influence the government has had on productivity. This explanation is especially prevalent among business executives who blame the increase in government rules and regulations that reduce profitability.[10]

Environmental rules imposed by the government are cited frequently as a cause of the apparent deterioration in U.S. productivity. However, in this case, it could very well be that our index of productivity is defective. Pollution-abatement regulations are intended to be a way of forcing firms to recognize costs imposed on others that otherwise would not be accounted for in the market due to the high transactions costs associated with bargaining under current property and trading institutions. To the extent that regulations achieve lower transaction costs and thereby permit the internalization of external costs, they improve the quality of life.[11] The ability to breathe fresh air, drink clean water, and live in pleasant environmental surroundings is just as much a part of a good life as driving a new automobile. Indeed, a number of economists have offered a revised GNP accounting system to capture some of the hard-won benefits of environmental regulations.[12]

Yet, many economists feel that environmental regulations have gone too far and have imposed costs on the consumer in excess of the benefits.

Moreover, these controls may have stifled business investment and, in Mansfield's words "erected unnecessary obstacles to innovation."[13] For example, the jungle of waivers and contradictory standards that the Alaskan pipeline interests had to satisfy imposed severe disincentives to further oil development. In fact, these regulations were formidable enough to table the second important phase of the pipeline project. Did the costs justify the benefits? Consider how the environmentalists forced the private sector to spend millions of extra dollars to bury the pipeline at certain locations in order not to interfere with the migratory patterns of the caribou only to find later that the caribou welcomed the pipeline and bore and raised their families next to the warm, exposed pipes.[14] Clearly, at some point, the benefits of environmental regulations must be weighed against the costs, and one significant cost to consider is the potential decline in productivity. The search for cost-effective methods of environmental regulation is on the agenda for the 1980s as indicated by discussions in the scholarly journals and among the U.S. Council of Economic Advisors.[15]

Federal tax policy frequently is cited as another reason many risky research projects are abandoned and inventions not commercialized. Tax policy influences both the supply of funds available to finance R&D expenditures and also the type and nature of R&D conducted. New-product ventures are inherently risky, and with hefty taxation of corporate profits and capital gains, only the most lucrative of new-product developments can hope to offer investors a return on their involvement commensurate with the risk involved. Those ventures that cannot penetrate the tax net with a positive return are abandoned for less-risky (and sometimes less-innovative) investment projects. In 1979, the easing of the capital-gains tax produced a burst of venture activity, suggesting that the causal linkages among tax policy, the supply of capital, and innovative efforts are strong and immediate.[16] The recent trend is certainly toward an easing of an ill-conceived federal tax policy, a recommendation that first appeared in the "ponderous eighteen-month study" that former President Carter sponsored for the purpose of "revitalizing America's industrial base."[17]

The Carter initiative continued during the early part of the Reagan administration. For example, the Economic Recovery Act of 1981 had as its primary purpose the "shifting of the burden of taxation away from capital income . . . [in order to provide] substantially greater incentives for capital investment and personal saving."[18] While the accelerated depreciation of capital assets and the leasing provisions that together favor durable equipment-using industries may not encourage new innovations in the so-called high-tech industries and rather may concentrate on diffusing existing known innovation within the U.S. economy, clearly the common theme of both the Carter and Reagan administrations has been to improve the lagging trend in factor productivity and to reverse the innovation slump.

While tax policy and environmental regulations are important to the investment decision, of equal importance are the de jure and de facto rights given to inventors under our patent system. A patent is a limited monopoly designed to help an innovator to capture part of the sometimes enormous social return associated with useful innovations.[19] Part of this monopoly return is needed to recoup the sizable R&D investment that necessarily accompanies commercialization efforts. Equally important to the market process is the maintenance of an environment that is conducive to the type of entrepreneurial activity that promotes economic growth and development.[20] In short, public policy permitting elements of monopoly may be a small, short-term price to pay for an entrepreneurially dynamic form of capitalism.[21]

Until quite recently, federal district judges involved in patent-infringement cases seemed biased, in some commentators' views, toward the infringers of patents.[22] In addition, antitrust officials have been quick to link ownership of patents to anticompetitive practices even when the connection admittedly has been remote and difficult to document. Lately, many of the ominous trends seem to be turning around. In addition to the 1980 Supreme Court decision that microbiological inventions are not excluded from patenting,[23] the court also decided that a chemical manufacturer was not compelled to license his invention to a competitor found guilty of patent infringement.[24] These two developments in patent law have led one legal expert to declare that "patent lawyers [who are] distressed by lower courts whose patent decisions seem dictated by an antimonopoly bent can draw much comfort, and some quotes [that is, to use in their own litigation], from this case."[25] Thus, monopoly, when it results from patent ownership, is not by itself an incriminating act.

Also, the federal government has begun to support the awarding of exclusive licenses to companies that promise to commercialize inventions that were financed originally by government funds. The promise of exclusivity is needed to encourage risk capital or else those who pioneer a new product may find their investments wiped out by the rapid entry of so-called me-too competition. Only after the patent has expired may others enter with similar products. All of these efforts are turns on the road leading to more investment and may offset, to some extent, the innovation slump. But the environment of liberalized tax reform, a strengthening of patent monopoly rights, and the clarifying and ranking of environmental goals may not be enough. In fact, the hoped-for renaissance in the invention-commercialization process may succumb to yet another roadblock—the Freedom of Information Act.

The central purpose of this book is to analyze the impact of the Freedom of Information Act (FOIA) on U.S. manufacturing and marketing activity. We hypothesize that, because of the Freedom of Information Act, a legal form of industrial espionage has been encouraged, essentially involving damaging disclosures of the proprietary information of regulated firms by government agencies and causing deleterious changes in the entrepreneurial process. We further hypothesize that, because of the Freedom of Information Act, it has become increasingly more difficult for information-submitting firms to employ trade secrecy as a means of capturing sufficient returns on innovations to justify R&D costs. Neither patent protection nor trade-secrecy law is a potent remedy in this environment because what is being disclosed is a species of business information that we have termed *circumstantially relevant business information.* This information is neither patentable nor always regarded as a trade secret by government officials. Accordingly, we hypothesize that the Freedom of Information Act, by its insensitivity to circumstantially relevant business information, has become an independent cause of the innovation slump troubling the U.S. economy.

The Freedom of Information Act is a disclosure statute.[26] The intent of the legislation was to open the processes of government rule making to public scrutiny. As Max Weber explained early in this century, bureaucracies maintain their power by nurturing the notion of "official secrets."[27] The act can be described as an attempt to neutralize the power of large regulatory bureaucrats that often get co-opted by the industries they serve rather than regulating those industries in the public interest.[28] Ralph Nader and other investigative journalists who lobbied for the Freedom of Information Act may have made their greatest and possibly most valuable impact on the U.S. system of government.[29]

The purpose of this book, however, is not to measure or analyze the social benefits of this legislation, substantial as they no doubt are; our focus is on the impact of the Freedom of Information Act on the market process when that process is viewed as an engine of discovery and entrepreneurial activity. To what extent are the property rights of the information-submitting firms violated when such information is released by government agencies, and to what extent is innovation in U.S. industry discouraged if it becomes increasingly more difficult for innovating firms to guard against the erosion in their competitive market positions through the use of trade secrecy? To what extent do the particular financial losses of the firm owners result in a net decrease in dynamic competition to the detriment of the consumer? We shall address these questions in the chapter ahead.

This particular study is a logical extension of our earlier work, "Trade Secrecy and Patenting: Complementary or Substitutable Activities?" which was funded by the Babson College Board of Research in 1978.[30] In that working paper we hypothesized that, if patenting were becoming less effective in protecting the patentees' commercialization efforts, then the maintenance of secrecy should be relatively more popular. As a consequence of interviews with representatives of Polaroid, Gillette, Sylvania,

Digital, Data General, Galileo Electro-Optics Corporation, Burrows Research, Chemical Products Ltd., Damon, EGH Computer, Raytheon, Wang Laboratories, and Instron, we concluded (contrary to our hypothesis) that there was no obvious swing into trade secrecy as a means of keeping valuable innovative efforts from diffusing among rival firms. However, the firms did criticize the weakening of patent protection in recent federal court decisions.

After further research and reflection, we concluded that, while patenting efforts might be historically less effective in encouraging innovation, at the same time, secrecy also was becoming more difficult to maintain. We suspected that this had something to do with the formidable extent to which those companies in our sample depended upon government-contract work. Under such arrangements, it is almost impossible for a firm to protect proprietary information since any data generated as a consequence of government R&D funding belong to the federal government and not to the funded corporation. Another working paper, "The Relationship between Federally Sponsored Demonstration Projects and the Protection of Proprietary Information,"[31] explored the issues that revolve around the massive presence of federal-government intervention in the research process. The next logical step in extending this research focus was to examine the economic consequences of the business-disclosure features of the Freedom of Information Act.

The organization of this book is quite straightforward. In chapter 2, we trace the historical roots of FOIA legislation in some detail, including a summary and evaluation of the most significant legislative and judicial decisions in the trade-secrets area that have been made in recent years. Following the development of this historical framework, we construct an empirical framework in chapter 3. Using data gathered from sixty-four federal agencies, we measure the extent to which the Freedom of Information Act is being used by private companies to acquire business information from the government. We employ both visual and formal statistical analyses including the use of aggregated agency data in the testing of the central hypotheses of the book.

Chapter 4 is mostly descriptive and definitional, designed to prepare the reader for the major theoretical chapter in the book, chapter 5. We develop a system of categorizing different types of business information in chapter 4. Based on direct testimony from businessmen and on reverse-FOIA court cases, we identify the types of information that businessmen seek to protect from disclosure. We also define circumstantially relevant business information. The assumption is that such information, if disclosed, would compromise a firm's competitive advantage in some way. However, the compromise of competitive advantage is not always the same thing as impeding the entrepreneurial process. This distinction is most important in any normative analysis of the Freedom of Information Act and its impact on the U.S. economy, and we return to this issue in chapter 5.

Chapter 5 contains the central analytical core of this book. In it, we examine economic theories of information and trade secrecy and establish linkages between information flows and the imperatives of innovation and entrepreneurship. In examining competitive behavior in the economy, we draw distinctions between the requirements of static efficiency and those of dynamic efficiency. We consider the latter definition of efficiency most relevant to the policy debate surrounding the disclosure practices of government agencies. Within this context, we examine the importance of circumstantially relevant business information to those firms that are innovative and entrepreneurial.

The theoretical conclusions and observations of chapter 5 are used in chapters 6 and 7 to analyze company-specific data obtained from secondary sources and from personal interviews with representatives from U.S. chemical and pharmaceutical firms. The major findings and conclusions of the book, both theoretical and empirical, are then summarized in chapter 8. Policy recommendations based on such findings are also made. In our view, the single most important contribution of this book is to demonstrate the value of an important, but unfortunately overlooked, species of business information—namely, circumstantially relevant business information. We argue that a disregard for the proprietary nature of this information has been an important contributory cause of the innovation slump in U.S. industry.

Notes

1. Edward Denison, *The Sources of Economic Growth in the United States* (New York: Committee for Economic Development, 1962); and Robert M. Solow, "Technical Change and the Aggregate Production Function," *Review of Economics and Statistics* 39 (August 1957):312-320.

2. Edward Denison, "The Puzzling Drop in Productivity," *Challenge Magazine* 22 (May/June 1979):60-62. See also Edwin Mansfield, "Technology and Productivity in the United States," in *The American Economy in Transition,* ed. Martin Feldstein (Chicago: University of Chicago for National Bureau of Economic Research, 1980), p. 568.

3. Mansfield, "Technology," p. 581.

4. U.S. Patent and Trade Mark Office, *Patent Activity Profile, All Technologies: A Special Report by the Office of Technology Assessment and Forecast* (Washington, D.C., 1979).

5. National Science Foundation, *National Science Indicators* (Washington, D.C.: U.S. Government Printing Office, 1979); cited by

William N. Leonard, "Basic Research and Lagging Innovation" (Paper presented at the Eastern Economic Association Convention, Boston, 12 May 1979); also see Mansfield, "Technology," pp. 570-582.

6. Mansfield, "Technology," p. 582.

7. National Science Foundation, *National Patterns of Science and Technology Resources: 1981.* Report NSF 81-311 (Washington, D.C.: U.S. Government Printing Office, 1981), p. 1.

8. Mansfield, "Technology," pp. 364-368.

9. Ibid., p. 593.

10. Ibid., p. 572.

11. See Ronald Coase, "The Problem of Social Costs," *Journal of Law and Economics* 3 (October 1960):1-44; James Buchanan, *Freedom in Constitutional Contract* (College Station: Texas A&M Press, 1977); and Charles Wolf, Jr., "A Theory of Non-Market Failures," *Public Interest* 55 (Spring 1979):114-133.

12. See William Nordlaus and James Tobin, "Is Growth Obsolete?" in *Economic Growth Fiftieth Anniversary Colloquiere* (New York: National Bureau of Economic Research, 1972); and Paul Barkley and David Seekler, *Economic Growth and Environmental Decay* (New York: Harcourt, Brace, Jovanovich, Inc., 1972), pp. 43-47.

13. Mansfield, "Technology," p. 595.

14. "Where the Caribou Play," *Wall Street Journal,* 5 June 1979, p. 22.

15. Office of the Council of Economic Advisors, *Economic Report of the President [Reagan to Congress]* (Washington, D.C.: U.S. Government Printing Office, February 1982), pp. 30-33.

16. "Carter Plan to Spur Industrial Innovation Is Criticized for Its Lack of Proposals," *Wall Street Journal,* 1 November 1979, p. 3.

17. Advisory Subcommittee on Patent and Information Policy of the Advisory Committee on Industrial Innovation, *Draft Report on Information Policy* (Washington, D.C.: U.S. Department of Commerce, 1978).

18. Council of Economic Advisors, *Economic Report,* pp. 109, 117-126.

19. See Edwin Mansfield et al., "Social and Private Rates of Return from Industrial Innovations," *Quarterly Journal of Economics* 91 (May 1977):221-240.

20. For a discussion of this so-called Austrian view of competition, see Israel Kirzner, *Competition and Entrepreneurship* (Chicago: University of Chicago Press, 1973). For a complementary view of competition, see William J. Baumol, "Contestable Markets, Antitrust and Regulation," *Wharton Magazine* 7 (Fall 1982):23-31.

21. See also Harold Demsetz, "Information and Efficiency: Another Viewpoint," *Journal of Law and Economics* 12 (April 1969):1-22.

22. Jesse W. Markham, "Inventive Activity: Government Controls and the Legal Environment" in *The Rate and Direction of Inventive Activity: Economic and Social Factors,* vol. 1, edited by National Bureau of Economic Research (Princeton, N.J.: Princeton University Press, 1962), pp. 587-608. See also Arthur H. Guidel and Ronald L. Panitel, *What the General Practitioner Should Know about the Trade Secrets and Employment Agreements* (Philadelphia: American Law Institute, 1973), pp. 1-3; also see John J. Mahon, Jr., "Trade Secrets and Patents Compared," *Journal of the Patent Office Society* 50 (August 1968):540.

23. *Diamond v. Chakrabut,* U.S. 65 L. Ed. 2d 144, 206 U.S.P.Q. 193 (1980).

24. *Dawson Chemical Co. v. Rohm and Haas Co. U.S.,* 65 L. Ed. 2d 696, 206 U.S.P.Q. 385 (1980), summarized by Edward F. McKie, Jr., "Developments in the Supreme Court," in *Intellectual Property Law Review: 1981,* ed. Gerald Rose (New York: Clark Boardman, 1981), pp. 194-195.

25. McKie, Jr., "Developments," p. 198.

26. 5 U.S.C. §552; see also Robert F. Bouchard and Justin Franklin, ed., *Guidebook to the Freedom of Information and Privacy Acts* (New York: Clark Boardman, 1980).

27. Max Weber, *The Theory of Social and Economic Organizations* (New York: Oxford University Press, 1947), p. 339.

28. George Stigler, "The Theory of Economic Regulation," *Bell Journal on Economics* 2 (Spring 1971):3-21; Sam Peltzman, "Toward a More General Theory of Regulation," *Journal of Law and Economics* 2 (August 1976):211-240; and James Q. Wilson, "The Politics of Regulation," in *The Politics of Regulation* (New York: Basic Books, 1980), pp. 357-394.

29. See "The Short and Sad History of Freedom of Information," *Bureaucracy* 1 (Summer 1972):116-160; and Ralph Nader, "New Opportunities for Open Government: The 1974 Amendments to the Freedom of Information Act and the Federal Advisory Act," *American University Law Review,* Fall 1975, pp. 1-83.

30. William Casey, John Marthinsen, and Laurence Moss, "Trade Secrecy and Patenting: Complementary or Substitutable Activities?" (Paper presented at the Atlantic Economic Society Convention, Washington, D.C., 13 October 1978).

31. William Casey, John Marthinsen, and Laurence Moss, "The Relationship between Federally Sponsored Demonstration Projects and the Protection of Proprietary Information" (Paper presented at the Eastern Economic Association Convention, Boston, 12 May 1979).

2

The History of the U.S. Freedom of Information Act and Its Treatment of Business Information

The Intellectual Roots of the Freedom of Information Act

The intellectual roots of the Freedom of Information Act can be located in the centuries-old struggle to limit the power of the sovereign. The resolution of that struggle required that two conditions be met: first, the framing of a constitution imposing firm limits on the behavior of the executive branch of government; second, the institution of a system that enabled a broad participation of citizens in the decision-making process of government.

The purpose of this chapter is not to restate the historical development of the idea of designing government institutions that are consistent with a society of free and responsible individuals but to add an obvious and curiously overlooked dimension to this literature having to do with the information required by citizens to make rational decisions. How can a democracy that rests on the participation of an informed citizenry exist if it lacks a mechanism for becoming informed?

The public right to gain access to government information was an issue in both the United Kingdom and the U.S. colonies in the eighteenth century, and it remains an important issue today. In stark contrast to what is often thought to be the intellectual heritage of the United States, the early years of our colonies were not marked by open government debates and freely accessible records. In 1725, the Massachusetts legislature ordered the local newspaper not to print information about the proceedings of local government meetings.[1] What was the purpose of this secrecy? It seemed that legislators were fearful of exercising free speech since words uttered in debate might anger the British monarch, thereby leading to property expropriation or worse. This is an early historical example of the very strong link that continues to exist between the rights of the public to information and the privacy and property rights of individuals. The balancing of these two rights is one of the fundamental underlying problems of the intellectual and legal debate concerning information disclosure.

When Thomas Jefferson first learned that the members of the constitutional convention decided to hold their meetings in secret, Jefferson remarked to John Adams about the importance of opening the workings of government process to the public:

> I am sorry they began their deliberations by so abominable a precedent as that of tying up the tongues of their members. Nothing can justify this example but the innocence of their intentions and ignorance of the value of public discussion.[2]

Surely Jefferson would agree that the value of public discussion increases with the quantity and quality of information the public has about the issues involved.

One of the most ardent defenders of an open government, James Madison, echoed Jefferson's sentiments and stressed the hollowness of a popular government without the widespread dissemination of (accurate) information. Madison argued:

> Knowledge will forever govern ignorance, and a people who mean to be their own governors, must arm themselves with the power knowledge gives.
>
> A popular government without popular information, or the means of acquiring it, is but a prologue to a farce or a tragedy; or, perhaps both.[3]

Madison's views are consistent with John Stuart Mill's impassioned call for an unregulated marketplace in ideas.[4] Mill felt that a society's well-being could be measured by its inventory of uncontested truths.[5] Only through constant exposure and widespread debate can individuals familiarize themselves with arguments that lead to true conclusions. Debate also provides citizens with a basis for recognizing those arguments that are fallacious. An idea that does not survive the barrage of critical comment and analysis is an idea that ought not to have survived at all. Applying these ideas to the process of government, we can understand why the extension of voting rights does not ensure excellence in government unless the voters have open access to a substantial data base and a means by which to influence the content of that data base. Without knowledge, thought, and discussion, broad-based voting presents us with the illusion of self-government.

The history surrounding the rights to obtain public information is not only a struggle between private citizens and their government but also among the various branches of government. In particular, the legislative branch often complains about its lack of knowledge concerning the internal workings of the executive branch and especially concerning the various administrative agencies. The legislative branch must oversee the administrative agencies, and this requires firsthand accurate information about how the decision-making processes of government work.

Consider for a moment the enormous power of the Federal Trade Commission (FTC), one of the oldest and most controversial of the regulatory agencies. Part of the charter of this agency involves taking action to eliminate "unfair methods of competition."[6] What are unfair methods of competition? While a thousand citizens can agree that just behavior requires fairness, another thousand citizens are likely to have different definitions of what this fairness involves. Lacking an objective definition of the phrase *unfair methods of competition*, the Federal Trade Commission's criteria for enforcement is homemade and largely without congressional supervision. The Federal Trade Commission must request information from private business firms and, based on this information, issue regulations that result in the elimination or prevention of unfair competitive methods. The agency enforces these regulations by levying fines, holding hearings, and instituting criminal penalties if federal law subsequently is broken. Indeed, agencies in government have enormous legislative, judicial, and executive power. It is not surprising that they are often called the fourth branch of government.

Agencies like the Federal Trade Commission that have been created by Congress are subject to congressional review and are ultimately responsible to the Congress. However, Congress has little daily control over the agencies and can exercise its power only by amending the agencies' mandate or by abridging the agencies' budget appropriations. In either case, Congress requires accurate information about how these agencies conduct business, establish regulations, and monitor results. In the absence of a powerful information-disclosure act, agency personnel can withhold information from Congress, making its oversight responsibilities difficult.[7] Agency secrecy can insulate its activities from the checks and balances of an independent legislature and judiciary. As we shall see in the following section, the Freedom of Information Act emerges out of this concern on the part of the legislature to gain access to agency records. At the same time, the success of the legislature in opening government is met with the growing problem of how the property rights of information submitters can be protected in an era of open agency records.

History Leading to Passage of the Freedom of Information Act

The Housekeeping Act of 1789 was the earliest legislative act addressed to the management and disposition of information held in government agencies. Nothing in the language of that legislation suggested that agency[8] heads were authorized to keep information secret from the public, and certainly nothing suggested that agency heads could keep secrets from the legislators and their staffs. The act simply instructed agency heads to:

Prescribe regulations, not inconsistent with the law, for the government of his department [that is, agency], the conduct of its officers and clerks, the distribution and performance of its business, and the custody, use and preservation of the records, papers and property appertaining to it.[9]

Essentially, agency heads were given the authority by Congress to control the dissemination of information under their jurisdictions. Such a system is bound to give rise to a multiplicity of disclosure practices that vary with agency-head discretion and that may not always be in the public interest.

A rather Machiavellian pattern already forecast by Max Weber emerged. Weber predicted that bureaucrats would choose to augment their power by guarding the dissemination of that information legally entrusted to their care.[10] To point this out is simply to acknowledge that government cannot be viewed as Superman coming in to rectify market failures without introducing market failures of its own.[11] One of these failures is that agency personnel (like private-sector personnel) normally will act to serve what they perceive to be their personal interests. These personal interests may not coincide with the mission of the agency, especially when disclosure reveals the decision-making processes of that agency.[12] The possibility that a pattern of secrecy and nondisclosure of information might become a common pattern of agency behavior comes, therefore, as no surprise.

The 1930s was a watershed period in the history of federal regulations of the market economy. Due to the cataclysmic economic events surrounding the Great Depression, government regulations grew with astonishing speed. As a result of the growing number of laws and their complex rules and regulations, Congress passed the Federal Register Act of 1935.[13] This act required that all agencies publish their regulations in a single periodical, the *Federal Register*. By implication, the citizens (especially businessmen) were obligated to consult the *Register* in order to learn about regulations they were required to obey. While the act made headway in disclosing agency records and agency decisions at a reasonable expense, once again, very little information appeared in the *Federal Register* about the processes of agency decision making and the substantive bases for the decisions made. Moreover, the act did little to require the disclosure of contested information.

From its passage in 1935, there was glaring evidence that broader disclosure rules might be needed. A 1941 blue-ribbon committee highlighted the act's deficiencies and paved the way toward a more-comprehensive disclosure law.[14] In 1946, the Administrative Procedure Act (APA) was passed.[15] While the act was passed in large part to shed light on the government process, it also served to broaden public participation in agency rule making, to homogenize administrative actions, and to provide for judicial review of administrative actions.[16] In reporting this measure to the Senate, the Judiciary Committee stated:

> This Section has been drawn upon the theory that administrative opera-
> tions and procedures are public property which the general public, rather
> than a few specialists or lobbyists, is entitled to know or have ready means
> of knowing with definiteness and assurance.[17]

Rather than shed light on agency and departmental activities, the Administrative Procedure Act became a tool for nondisclosure. The act required
disclosure "except to the extent that there is involved (1) any function of the
United States requiring secrecy in the public interest or (2) any matters
relating solely to the internal management of an agency."[18] It also excluded
from disclosure final opinions or orders that were "required for good cause
found to be held confidential and not cited as precedents."[19] Finally, public
records were to "be made available to persons properly and directly concerned except information held confidential for good cause found."[20]

Nowhere in this act were the phrases *public interest, internal management, for good cause found,* and *persons properly and directly concerned*
defined. Moreover, attempts to use historical interpretations of such
phrases led to humorous ambiguities.[21] The Administrative Procedure Act
was cited in a 1966 House report "as the basic statutory authority for 24
separate terms . . . which federal agencies have devised to stamp on administrative information they want to keep from public view."[22] Another
commentator felt that, under the act, an individual's right to inspect a
federal nonjudicial record was "a mere matter of opportunity hanging
dependently upon the favorable and judicially unreviewable exercise of official grace, indulgence or discretion."[23]

The drive toward reforming the Administrative Procedure Act was
spearheaded by the press. Memories of the restrictions put on press
coverage during World War II and the tension surrounding the cold war
that followed gave media a predisposed bias toward a more-open government.[24] Ample evidence indicated that reform was needed. Both a Hoover
commission and the American Bar Association recommended changes to
the Administrative Procedure Act.[25] However, the real impetus for change
came with the publication of Harold Cross's report on agency disclosure
practices, entitled *The Public Right to Know.*[26] Sponsored by the American
Society of Newspaper Editors, the Cross report seemed to be the key to
spiriting congressional action.

At first, the House took an active lead in this investigation. In 1955, the
House Committee on Government Operations created the Subcommittee on
Government Information. Under the leadership of Representative John E.
Moss, this committee was to:

> [A]scertain the trend in availability of government information and
> scrutinize the information practices of executive agencies and officials in
> light of their propriety, fitness and legality.[27]

Cross's revelations spurred the Moss subcommittee toward its eventual eleven-year history of hearings regarding information-disclosure practices. Among the cases of agency nondisclosure reported by Cross and others were:

> The National Science Foundation's refusal to disclose competitive bids on the deep-sea Mohole Project when the winner happened not to be lowest bidder.

> The postmaster general's refusal to disclose either the names or salaries of federal employees.

> The Board of Engineers for River and Harbors' refusal to disclose the board's vote on issues brought before it.

> The State Department's Board of Review's refusal to disclose the rules and procedures it uses to determine the loss of an individual's nationality.

> The secretary of navy's refusal to furnish a copy of its internal-agency telephone book for public inspection.

> The refusal of a number of agencies to furnish the names and salaries of public employees.[28]

Apparently, the legislative branch of government was thwarted once again in its attempt to open the executive branch of government to either congressional scrutiny or that of the general citizen.

Passage of the Freedom of Information Act

Initially, the hearings before the Moss subcommittee focused on how information had been withheld from radio, television, newspaper, and communication specialists in general.[29] Several researchers, including academic historians, along with members of Congress, also testified about the difficulties of acquiring information. However, the memory of the Korean War, the loss of the atomic-weapons monopoly to the Soviets, and the subsequent change in the character of the cold war resulted in a dialogue about the impact of disclosure on national security. Should the United States rest its security on technological achievements fueled by the free flow of information between the government and the public or on the concealment of existing technological information? These were the important themes running through those congressional hearings, and they remain important issues today.[30]

As a consequence of their reluctance to disclose information that could jeopardize national security, agency heads indiscriminately classified information as secret. The obvious problem with this system was that agency heads became the sole interpreters of government-held facts. Dialogue and criticism were restricted because the information never got out into the general marketplace of ideas. One expert congressional witness restated the wisdom of John Stuart Mill's insights as follows:

> In our elective system, in the absence of public debate, there is no certainty that policymaking officials will possess the competence required for wise decisions or that they will even understand what elements of information are important. However, even assuming the wisdom of policymaking officials, sound policy results from the careful examination of the facts by the people of our nation in light of their diverse training and interest. Secrecy prevents the discussion necessary to such examination, and compartmentalization prevents proper evaluation even by trained specialists. . . . No adequate substitute can be found in internal intelligence, because information unevaluated by public debate lacks the convincing quality resulting from public review.[31]

Congressional battles to change the Administrative Procedure Act were waged in 1955 and 1957, but these efforts once again failed. In part, the failure was due to a jurisdictional issue. Most of the House activity on information disclosure was conducted in the Moss Subcommittee on Government Information. But Moss's committee had jurisdiction extending only as far as the Housekeeping Statute. Jurisdiction for the Administrative Procedure Act resided in the House Judiciary Committee. It is not surprising, therefore, that the first important change in the disclosure practices of agencies came in 1958 with the passage of the Moss-Hennings amendment to the Housekeeping Statute.[32] This amendment added new language to the 1789 statute, making it clear that the statute did "not authorize withholding information from the public or limiting the availability of records to the public."[33]

The Moss-Hennings bill did "produce some improvements with respect to the accessibility of Federal records,"[34] but agencies found that they could easily shift the basis for nondisclosure from the revised Housekeeping Statute to the Administrative Procedure Act. As a result, true reform awaited repeal of the Administrative Procedure Act, and that awaited action by the House Judiciary Committee and the (to date) relatively inactive Senate.

The process of overhauling the Administrative Procedure Act began to move forward in 1963 when two bills were introduced in the Senate, S. 1663 and S. 1666.[35] Debate on these bills was conducted under the auspices of the Subcommittee on Administrative Practice and Procedure of the Senate Committee on Judiciary. On 28 July 1964, the Senate passed S. 1666, but the act was not considered by the House.[36] S. 1666 was significant because it was the first version of the Freedom of Information Act introduced in the

Senate. Also, while its final version had a "trade secrets and confidential information" exemption,[37] the original bill did not. Only after strong urging by the National Association of Broadcasters was this exemption written into the act.[38] The Senate, in reporting the bill, stated the following:

> This exemption is necessary to protect the confidentiality of information which is obtained by Government through questionnaires or other inquiries, but which would customarily not be released to the public by the person from whom it was obtained. This would include business sales statistics, inventories, customer lists, and manufacturing processes. It would also include information customarily subject to the doctor-patient, lawyer-client, and other such privileges.[39]

In congressional debate, Senator Hubert Humphrey tried to amend this section to include all information gained "in confidence."[40] However, fearing that this language would give agency heads too much discretion in withholding information, the amended language was dropped. It is clear that even the most liberal-minded congressional representatives saw reason to protect the legitimate property rights of business. Apparently, during the 1960s, the struggle to open government to the public was not interpreted also as a struggle to gain access to privately held information—even corporate information.

Having passed the Senate but not the House, a compromise version of S. 1666 was introduced in 1965 as S. 1160. S. 1160 passed the Senate on 13 October 1965 and the House on 20 June 1966.[41] It was signed into law by President Lyndon B. Johnson on 21 July 1966 and became effective 4 July 1967.[42] One might hope that the nearly twenty years of debate on the Administrative Procedure Act would produce a significantly improved piece of legislation. That such is the case has been greatly disputed.

The Freedom of Information Act, S. 1160, opened identifiable agency records to any person, defined nine exemptions from disclosure, put the burden of proof for nondisclosure on the government agencies, and established that such access should be regulated by reasonable fees.[43] The nine enumerated exemptions cited were as follows:

1. Matters specifically required by Executive Order to be kept secret in the interest of the national defense or foreign policy;
2. Matters related solely to the internal personnel rules and practices of an agency;
3. Matters specifically exempted by statute;
4. Trade secrets and commercial or financial information obtained from a person and privileged or confidential;
5. Interagency or intra-agency memorandums;
6. Personnel and medical files, the disclosure of which would constitute a clearly unwarranted invasion of personal privacy;

7. Investigatory files compiled for law-enforcement purposes;
8. Matters contained in or related to examination, operating, or condition reports prepared by, on behalf of, or for the use of an agency responsible for the regulation or supervision of financial institutions;
9. Geological and geophysical information and data.

In spite of these exemptions, the courts have supported the legislature in its battle against stubborn executive agencies, claiming that the "Act was intended as a disclosure statute, not a withholding statute."[44] Notwithstanding this judicial reinforcement, however, the Freedom of Information Act proved to be an inadequate lever for prying open agency files from foot-dragging bureaucrats. True reform awaited legislative amendments to the act.

One significant part of the 1966 Freedom of Information Act was its exemption of the disclosure of trade secrets and confidential or financial information. This so-called trade-secrets exemption gave rise to varying interpretations and, in so doing, threatened confidential business information in agency files. This issue and those surrounding it occupy our attention for the remainder of this chapter.

The Definiton and Treatment of Confidential Business Information

Exemption 4 of the Freedom of Information Act states that administrative agencies may deny a request for information if that information consists of "trade secrets and commercial or financial information obtained from a person and privileged or confidential."[45] The ill-fated original Senate version simply exempted "trade secrets and confidential information," but this language was replaced in the House version by a phrase entirely obtuse in language and subject to varying interpretations. As the Department of Justice's 1967 attorney general's memorandum to all agency heads admitted:

> [T]he sentence structure makes [exemption 4] susceptible of several readings, none of which is entirely satisfactory. The exemption can be read, for example, as covering three kinds of matters: that is, matters that are . . . [a] trade secrets and [b] commercial or financial information obtained from any person and [c] privileged or confidential [bracketed initials added]. Alternatively, clause [c] can be read as modifying clause [b]. Or, from a strictly grammatical standpoint, it could even be argued that all three clauses have to be satisfied for the exemption to apply.[46]

During the period immediately following the passage of the Freedom of Information Act, a number of legal experts also sharpened their analytic blades on the intepretation of the trade-secrets exemption. Professor Kenneth C. Davis, writing in the *Chicago Law Review*, concluded the following:

> [B]ecause the first conclusion is that the law apart from the [Freedom of Information] Act continues, and because the second and third conclusions are that the law apart from the Act overrides the Act whenever non-commercial and non-financial information is privileged or confidential, combining these three conclusions produces this remarkable observation: *The Act is a nullity with respect to all commercial or financial information, and with respect to all non-commercial and non-financial information which is privileged or confidential.* The only information whose disclosure is governed by the Act's provisions, instead of by considerations beyond the Act, is non-commercial and non-financial information which is not privileged or confidential. This means that the Act governs disclosure of only a small portion of all government information.[47]

After concluding that the act "governs the disclosure of only a small portion of government information," a few pages later Davis admits that the new law "never protects privileged or confidential information from disclosure; it protects only from required disclosure."[48] Furthermore, the act does not require the agency to balance the interest of the party adversely affected by disclosure of privileged or confidential information. It also does not require the agency to take account of who is seeking the disclosure and why that party requires the information. Under these provisions, Davis was uncertain about the impact the Freedom of Information Act would have on the disclosure of confidential business information.[49]

The Ninety-second Congress of 1971-1972 conducted hearings about the implementation of the Freedom of Information Act during its nearly five years of existence.[50] The House subcommittee concluded after forty-one days of testimony that Congress's intent was "that all information, with some valid exceptions, was to be made available to the American people— no questions asked . . . and that . . . the exemptions were only permissive and not mandatory, but most of the Federal bureaucracy already set in its ways never got the message."[51] Bureaucratic obstacles delayed the processing of requests, thereby making the information-retrieval function useless to journalists with the usual deadline pressures. As we see later in this chapter, journalists were displeased with many of the disclosure aspects of the Freedom of Information Act, and there was broader-based dissatisfaction as well. A survey of 400 organizations revealed that numerous loopholes existed in the disclosure process.[52] Among the most often cited complaints were the ability of an agency to withhold disclosure of an entire document when only a few lines were confidential, the ability of an agency to fix varying fees for disclosure, and the arbitrary system of access to agency information. In short, a requester of agency information could not be sure of the fees he would be charged, the extent to which he had to identify the exact information held in agency files, the political connections that might be needed to extract othewise nondisclosed information, and if the request were denied, the extent to which an entire request was denied because of one or two confidential sentences within that document.

The lengths to which federal agency personnel would go to shoo away requesters inspired Ralph Nader's quip, "Anyone who denies that persons in the government are creative should examine the pattern of circumvention of the FOIA."[53] Clearly, in this environment, confidential business information that agency personnel cared not to disclose was safe from prying eyes. But the decision not to disclose such information was, in many cases, a fortuitous one for the business-information submitter.

The 1974 Reforms and Their Aftereffect

In spite of the recognition that government agencies held much information that should be exempted from disclosure, there was also a clear need for the public to be able to gain access to information that belonged in the public domain. Among the most ardent supporters of open government have been journalists and people associated with communication media. Consider the following words of James Russell Wiggins who insisted that a rigid trade-off exists between secrecy and freedom:

> Each added measure of secrecy, however, measurably diminishes our freedom. If we proceed with more secrecy we shall one day reach a place where we have made the choice between freedom and secrecy. We shall pass a point beyond which we cannot go without abandoning free institutions and accepting secret institutions. No man can say with assurance where this point is, but we move toward it.[54]

The concern over the public's right to gain access to agency information came to a head during the 1960s. Spawned by an unpopular war and civil protests, U.S. citizens became sensitive to rumors that personal data were being collected by the Federal Bureau of Investigation (FBI) and Central Intelligence Agency (CIA)—information the public could neither identify nor corroborate. These civil-liberties issues, coupled with the widespread findings of consumer-advocate groups that certain government agencies were being run to protect the interests of select client-business groups, created a powerful coalition dedicated to opening executive-agency files for public review in a timely and inexpensive manner. While the Freedom of Information Act was passed in 1966, the drive toward a truly liberalized disclosure statute was not accomplished until enactment of the 1974 amendments to this act. It is not a coincidence that these liberalized amendments were passed in the year of President Nixon's impeachment proceedings, brought on by the events surrounding the Watergate break-in of the Democratic head-quarters.[55]

The pursuit of a more-liberal information-disclosure law was aided also by many public-interest groups. Consider Ralph Nader's group, Public Citizens Inc., the purpose of which is to help citizens learn how to protect themselves against private industry and government bureaucrats. Another organization, Common Cause, targets "politicians who ignore the people, unresponsive bureaucrats and behind-the-scenes betrayals of public interest."[56] These groups battle for laws prohibiting secret meetings of public bodies and for the registration of lobbyists and middlemen. Naturally, among the enthusiasts of public-interest groups we find the strongest friends of open government.

Ralph Nader's researchers, after three months of study, found that "government officials at all levels in many of these agencies [Nader's people had studied] systematically and routinely violated both the purpose and specific provision of the law. Thus, the Act, designed to provide citizens with tools of disclosure, has been forced into a shield against citizen access."[57]

Just as the media and public-interest groups constitute two of the most vigorous prodisclosure interests, agencies constitute some of the most ardent critics of increased disclosure. It is reported that between 1955 and 1959, when the Subcommittee on Government Information held public hearings, 105 recalcitrant agency representatives testified in opposition to the Freedom of Information Act.[58] In the 1972 oversight hearings, no agency representative provided testimony in favor of the proposed amendments.[59] This executive-branch distrust of congressional inroads and its displeasure over many of the provisions of the 1974 amendments led President Gerald R. Ford to veto them on 17 October 1974. The House overwhelmingly overrode the veto (371-31), and the Senate narrowly gained the two-third vote needed for the override (65-27). It is obvious that the executive agencies have not been strong advocates of disclosure.

The amendments attempted to improve the speed of disclosure, to expand the breadth of the information release, and to facilitate public access to government information. Specifically, Congress broadened the list of agencies that were covered by the Freedom of Information Act and required all agencies to respond to reasonable requests for information within ten working days (twenty working days for appeals and a ten-day extension was permitted for unusual circumstances). For a request that had confidential information within it, agencies were required to segregate the confidential from the nonconfidential information and to disclose the nonconfidential contents. Moreover, the agency could charge only for the copying and search costs and not for the time spent disentangling the proprietary information.

To provide improved public access, agencies were required to report annually to Congress on FOIA matters and to prepare a quarterly index of their FOIA decisions and statements. Furthermore, it provided for accountability in government. Federal employees denying a request had to state the reason for the denial and identify themselves as the source of the denial. In cases where this decision was considered to be arbitrary or capricious, the Civil Service Commission was to investigate and recommend disciplinary action to agency heads (see figure 2-1). While the amendments to the Freedom of Information Act were in many respects far reaching, the trade-secrets exemption, with its obvious ambiguities and defects, was left untouched. Despite the fact that proposals were made to protect noncommercial and nonfinancial information,[60] to define more specifically "confidential information,"[61] and to protect internally generated data that might have commercial value,[62] these proposals were not enacted. Several reasons could be advanced, including that agreement could not be reached on this vital issue, the exemption was working sufficiently well not to warrant a change, or the significance of this exemption had not been realized fully at the time of the change (1974). Regardless of the reason, in the drive to open government-agency files to the public, especially in the post-Watergate period, inadequate attention was paid to the protection of business information that found its way into agency files as a by-product of either regulatory reporting (voluntary and mandatory) or by special government investigation.

The last amendment to the Freedom of Information Act was passed in 1976 (enacted in March 1977). The Government in the Sunshine Act (or the Sunshine Act as it was called)[63] clarified what information could be exempted from disclosure by exemption 3 (that is, information exempted under other laws). Originally, nondisclosure was permitted if the information was "specifically exempted from disclosure by statute," but the word *specifically* was defined broadly by the Supreme Court,[64] and congressional dissatisfaction with this interpretation culminated in the name Sunshine Act. The act underscored the fact that information could be withheld only when specific legal criteria existed for withholding it.

In line with this prodisclosure attitude, the 5 May 1977 letter of Attorney General Griffin Bell to agency heads ordered agencies not to withhold information "even if there is some arguable legal basis for doing so," and he committed the Department of Justice to defend "FOIA suits only when disclosure is demonstrably harmful to the public."[65] Examples of information that would be exempted were patent applications, income-tax returns, and the results of nuclear military testing.

A number of businesses felt that their confidential information was protected by the Trade Secrets Act of 1948.[66] However, the Justice Department's position was (and continues to be) that this act was too oceanic and ill defined to qualify under exemption 3, especially since Congress narrowed it in the

Reporting Requirements	Disclosure Requirements	Miscellaneous
Broaden agency disclosure practices,	Reply to requests within ten working days and to appeals within twenty working days;	The Civil Service Commission would investigate and recommend penalties for federal employees charged with arbitrary and capricious withholding of information.
Publish a quarterly index of FOIA decisions and related information,	Segregate confidential information from nonconfidential information and to disclose only the nonconfidential information;	*In camera* review by the courts was permitted to determine if the disputed information fell within any of the nine exemptions.
Prepare an annual report to Congress on FOIA-related information.	Respond to reasonably accurate requests for information;	Exemption 7 was narrowed by defining six specific harms that could be used as grounds for nondisclosure.
	Charge only for copying costs and search time in complying with FOIA requests;	Expand the number of agencies required to follow FOIA disclosure provisions.
	Pay court costs and legal fees for court-reversed denials for information (that is, payment is made only when so ordered by the court).	

Figure 2-1. Main Features of the 1974 Amendments to the Freedom of Information Act

Sunshine Act.[67] Thus, businesses desiring to stop an executive agency from giving out information to third-party requesters could not rest their case easily on Exemption 3.

In the first year following the 1974 amendments, FOIA requests quadrupled. Requests made to the Food and Drug Administration (FDA), for example, rose to 13,000 in 1975 from 2,600 in 1974.[68] In the early 1970s, a number of information-requesting corporations sued government agencies to acquire documents that the agencies decided fell within one or several of the nine exemptions. Similarly, a number of information-submitting corporations sued the government to stop it from giving their confidential business records to third parties—the so-called reverse-FOIA suits about which we shall have more to say in chapter 4.

The legal standing for these reverse-FOIA suits varied from case to case and injected considerable confusion into the proceedings. In general, three statutes were used, at different times and in different situations, as the basis for these suits: the Trade Secrets Act,[69] the Administrative Procedure Act,[70] and the Freedom of Information Act.[71] It was not until 1979, when the Supreme Court decided the *Chrysler* v. *Brown* case, that most of the confusion was resolved.[72] We will return to the *Chrysler* case later in this chapter.

Since the federal district courts have original jurisdiction over all disputes arising under federal laws, they were relied upon to adjudicate these disputes. The federal courts emerged as a singularly independent and important institution affecting both the theory and implementation of business-disclosure practices. They were asked to decide whether or not to furnish a requester with information. This is significant because under the Freedom of Information Act, no document was considered to be secret as a matter of law. In the early years of the Freedom of Information Act's history, the courts were willing to apply a subjective test to decide if indeed an information submitter had supplied an agency with confidential information.[73] Relying on the House interpretation of the provisions in the Freedom of Information Act,[74] the courts based their decisions on whether or not the contested information met the "promise of confidentiality test."[75] The court exempted business information from disclosure that was:

> [G]iven to an agency in confidence, since a citizen must be able to confide in his government. Moreover, where the government has obligated itself in good faith not to disclose documents of information which it receives, it should be able to honor such obligations.[76]

This test was opposed by many proponents of open government because it gave submitters carte blanche in deciding which information was confidential, and these decisions may not be in the public interest.

The courts soon realized that the promise not to disclose information was an inadequate guide for the confidentiality treatment of information. Such a criterion was too subjective and ignored the issue of what information deserved such a promise. Thus, the new standard became the "expectation of confidentiality test."[77] Based on the Senate reports on the Freedom of Information Act,[78] confidentiality was to be based on whether information would have "customarily not been released to the public by persons from whom it was obtained."[79] The not-customarily-released criterion gave way to a consideration of whether that release of information would be "harmful to the private interest" of the submitter.[80]

While this test provided a more-objective criterion in FOIA cases,[81] it still skirted the issue of whether a categorical definition of confidential information could be developed. A further move toward objectivity was accomplished in 1974 when the District of Columbia Circuit Court of Appeals decided the *National Parks* case.[82] From that landmark case, the legal test for confidential business information was whether such disclosure would (1) "impair the government's ability to obtain necessary information in the future, or . . . (2) cause substantial harm to the competitive position of the person from whom the information was obtained."[83] The test pointed to the court's intention to limit the discretion of both agency heads and information submitters, but it left many important questions unanswered, such as When is competitive harm substantial? If a product has not been marketed and therefore has no competition, can substantial competitive harm be shown? What are the legitimate property rights of nonprofit institutions that discover new products or processes?

The move toward an objective test for confidentiality has met with strong opposition.[84] Attorney James T. O'Reilly felt that such objectivity is without justification in terms of "the legislative history of the Freedom of Information Act and is in fact contrary to both the express terms and the legislative history of the [fourth] exemption."[85] He went on to state that such a test establishes too rigorous a standard for submitters of information, imposes an almost insurmountable burden on companies to prove competitive harm within ten days, forces courts to speculate on future competitive harm, ignores other types of harm having nothing to do with competition, and finally, discriminates against small companies that cannot afford expert witnesses (and the like) to prove harm.[86] More recently, the courts have signaled a trend away from the *National Parks* decision. In the *Worthington* case, the court decided that information, even if it was already in the public domain, could not be released if the cost of duplicating this information was substantial.[87] This decision is important to this book because in chapter 4 we will introduce a type of information called circumstantially relevant business information that is vital to the entrepreneurial process. *Worthington* illustrates that the information gains value not merely by creating a new product or process invention but by rearranging or combining various bits and pieces of dispersed facts in one place.

In 1979, the Supreme Court clarified still another area of disagreement about the workings of the Freedom of Information Act. In order for a company to sue a government agency to enjoin disclosure of their information, the company had to appeal to a statute that allegedly was being violated. We have already mentioned that in these reverse-FOIA suits, the Trade Secrets Act, the Administrative Procedure Act, and the Freedom of Information Act variously were cited.[88] In *Chrysler* v. *Brown*, the Supreme Court decided, initially, that neither the Trade Secrets Act nor the Freedom of Information Act was grounds for enjoining government agencies from disclosing submitted information.

The Freedom of Information Act, the Supreme Court ruled, was passed as a disclosure statute, and it would be up to Congress to amend this act so as to allow information submitters to enjoin disclosure under its provisions. Until that time, the exemptions of the Freedom of Information Act were held to be voluntary exemptions that were valid only to the extent that they were endorsed by the agency. Even if information clearly fell within one or several of the exemptions of the Freedom of Information Act, its confidentiality was assured only so long as the agency agreed it should be confidential. What makes this decision confusing is that it seems to be a clear move by the court away from the protections envisioned by the Congress in its deliberations leading up to the passage of the Freedom of Information Act in 1966. To some observers, the *Chrysler* decision represents a retrogression away from the idea that open government and safeguarded business information can coexist.[89]

The Administrative Procedure Act had rules forbidding "arbitrary and capricious abuse of discretion" by agency employees.[90] Under these rules, the Supreme Court decided, an information submitter could sue to protect against information disclosure. Furthermore, the Court saw violations of the Trade Secrets Act as being abuses of these arbitrary and capricious provisions of the Administrative Procedure Act.[91] The Trade Secrets Act did not constitute private grounds for action against the government but could be used as an independent means of prohibiting disclosure. Agency personnel could disclose information only if appropriate procedures for release existed and if there was a nexus between the information disclosed and some statute giving the agency the power to collect such information.

In a Department of Justice memorandum dated 21 June 1979 and sent to all agency general counsels, Assistant Attorney General Barbara A. Babcock outlined a procedure that all agency personnel were urged to follow when handling information requests. Following that procedure would protect those agency personnel against the charge of "arbitrary and capricious behavior."[92] Inasmuch as the Administrative Procedure Act required a

judicial review of only the agency record and not a review of the entire decision to release the information de novo, the agency need only follow a procedure designed to produce a trail of careful bureaucratic ritual. This practice, according to Attorney Babcock, will "maximize our [Department of
Justice's] ability to defend all government disclosure determinations in the
wake of *Chrysler*."[93] In short, now with the *Chrysler* decision, the chances
are small of ever stopping a government agency from disclosing business information when that agency decides the public interests will be served by
disclosure.

In 1980, Ronald Reagan was elected president of the United States in a
landslide victory over Jimmy Carter. Swept into office by a strong conservative public sentiment, Reagan pledged to reduce the level of government
intervention in the economy. In line with this philosophy, the Reagan administration sought to give greater assurances that business information
would be protected. On 4 May 1981, Attorney General William French
Smith revoked the previous (Griffin Bell) FOIA guidelines to the Department of Justice and began a policy of defending "all suits challenging an
agency's decision to deny a request submitted under the Freedom of Information Act unless it is determined that: (a) the agency's denial lacks a
substantial legal basis; or (b) defense of the agency's denial presents an unwarranted risk of adverse impact on other agencies' ability to protect important records."[94] Clearly, the thrust of the Reagan initiative was to begin
swinging the pendulum of information disclosure more toward protecting
the property rights of business-information submitters.

At present, the FOIA activities of the Department of Justice are handled
by the Office of Information and Privacy (formerly the Office of Information Law and Policy). This office and its predecessors have done an excellent job in centralizing, conducting, and organizing information relevant
to the Freedom of Information Act. It performs the clearinghouse function
of answering questions pertaining to the administration of the act.
Moreover, it publishes a periodic bulletin, *FOIA Update*, and holds cross-
country seminars explaining the act.

The Office of Information and Privacy also has led the way toward
making the procedures for handling FOIA requests more uniform among
agencies. In general, this office has promoted the rights of submitters to
notification prior to the release of information marked as confidential. In
its memoranda to department and agency heads in 1979 and 1982,[95] the office made it clear that it feels "business submitters are entitled, at a
minimum, to those basic rights of formal notice and full opportunity to object to the disclosure of this information."[96] However, because these
memoranda do not carry the force of law, agencies like the Food and Drug
Administration have disregarded them and true uniformity among agencies
awaits legislative reforms of the act.[97]

The 1980s and Beyond

Since 1980, the questions raised by the Freedom of Information Act have continued to be discussed in four major forums—the Administrative Conference of the United States, the various congressional committees given oversight responsibilities for the act, the American Bar Association, and the media. Within these forums, rather clear lines can be drawn among the various groups that are either supporting or opposing legislative reforms. In this section, we discuss these forums and then identify the combatants and the lines of demarcation that have been drawn separating the various group positions and the issues that have been (and that are likely to continue to be) debated.

The Forums

The Administrative Conference of the United States Forum. The Administrative Conference of the United States (ACUS),[98] established in 1964 as a permanent executive agency, was given the mandate of developing "improvements in the legal procedures by which Federal Agencies administer regulatory, benefit and other programs."[99] It achieves this purpose by providing "a Forum in which . . . continuing studies of selected problems involving these administrative procedures [are discussed] . . . in cooperative efforts toward improving fairness and effectiveness of such procedures."[100] With regard to the Freedom of Information Act, the Administrative Conference on Regulation of Business has been charged with investigating and making recommendations on the trade-secrecy exemption.

For this purpose, the Administrative Conference commissioned two important studies. The first, commissioned in September 1979, was completed by Russell B. Stevenson, professor of law at George Washington University.[101] Stevenson was asked to investigate "the practices and procedures used by Federal Agencies to resolve issues arising under exemption 4 of the Freedom of Information Act" and to "evaluate possible improvements in agency practices and procedures that may facilitate the protection of private interests while maintaining the public purposes that Act seeks to supplement."[102] The second study, commissioned in August 1981, was completed by James T. O'Reilly, professor of law at the University of Cincinnati and senior counsel for the Procter & Gamble Company.[103] O'Reilly's task was to investigate the substance of the trade-secrets exemption. Both reports were thorough and scholarly. While their philosophical outlook showed obvious differences, they have provided and will continue to provide grist for informed discussions on the Freedom of Information Act.

The Stevenson report was decidedly less critical than the O'Reilly report of the Freedom of Information Act and the need to protect business information from government disclosure. However, despite their differences, there was substantial agreement between the authors on specific recommendations of a procedural nature.[104] Both authors agreed on the following:

There is a need to address business perceptions that the Freedom of Information Act is disclosing proprietary information.

The government ought to design a general reorganization of the information submitted under the Freedom of Information Act, the Sunshine Act, and the Privacy Act.

Congress should not disclose the investigatory files of certain agencies.

Proprietary documents submitted to the government ought to be marked confidential but substantiation of their propriety should be required only upon a third-party request for that information.

A more-homogeneous system should be designed to process information requests among agencies.

The denying and approving of third-party requests should be done at the same administrative level within the agency and by a senior official.

A rule ought to be passed requiring notification of submitters before the release of information marked confidential.

The relationship between the agency and the submitter should be kept informal in deciding if information is confidential.

Submitters should be assured a right to appeal agency decisions concerning disclosure.

The deadlines for responding to requests should be expanded.

Fees should be increased to reflect costs, and liberal waivers should be allowed for nonprofit requesters.

The author's disagreements centered mainly on the following:

The need for amending the standard for confidential information,

Technical venue considerations,

The ability of agencies to make categorical determinations of the propriety of submitted information,

The right to de novo review,

The payment of court costs by businesses losing judicial challenges to information-disclosure requests.

These widely overlapping areas of agreement might lead one to expect similar concurrence on proposed reforms of the Freedom of Information Act. In general, however, Stevenson favors marginal changes in the act.[105] O'Reilly favors substantial revisions in order to secure greater submitter rights to protection.[106]

Between 1981 and 1982, the Administrative Conference met and discussed the findings of three ACUS committees that were reviewing the Freedom of Information Act. While the Stevenson and O'Reilly reports to the Committee on Regulation of Business provided much of the basis for these discussions, additional input was provided by the Committee on Judicial Review and the Committee on Public Access and Information.[107] In its final report, the Administrative Conference recommended that confidential information be withheld by agencies unless some overriding public interest could be shown, that neither submitters of information nor requesters of information be entitled to de novo judicial review, that submitters have a statutory right to notification and the right to submit written objections to agencies deciding on disclosure, and that all acceptance and rejection decisions to FOIA requests be made at the same level within the agency.[108]

When reporting its preliminary findings, the Administrative Conference reinforced that "this availability of FOIA as a tool for low cost commercial information—or, in some cases, industrial espionage—needs to be limited." It went on to report that "agency personnel most likely to be called upon to evaluate claims of exempt status will be program officials or FOIA officers, neither of which is likely to have a fundamental appreciation of the value of private information in the commercial marketplace."[109] These findings are largely consistent with the conclusions we have reached in this book.

The Congressional Forum. Two committees in Congress have had a principal interest in the Freedom of Information Act. In the House of Representatives, oversight responsibilities for the Freedom of Information Act reside with the Government Information and Individual Rights Subcommittee of the Committee on Government Operations. The Senate counterpart to the House committee is called the Subcommittee on the Constitution of the Judiciary Committee.

In 1981, both the House and Senate Subcommittees conducted hearings on the Freedom of Information Act.[110] In the course of their deliberations, testimony was drawn from a wide range of different sources including representatives from academia, federal agencies, businesses, media, trade unions, and public-interest groups.

Following the oversight hearings, the Senate Judiciary Committee favorably reported to the full Congress (20 May 1982) a bill sponsored by Orrin Hatch. Hatch's bill, S. 1730, addressed itself to many of the procedural and substantive problems associated with the Freedom of Information Act.[111] Procedurally, it sought to enact a uniform system of fees that would reflect more closely the cost of handling an FOIA request and a uniform set of procedures for complying with FOIA requests. For all submitted information that was marked confidential, it guaranteed the submitter both the right to notification and the opportunity to object to the release of the information. Moreover, it homogenized the judicial-review process to give submitters the same de novo rights as information requesters.

The bill broadened the coverage of exemption 2 (matters related to internal-agency personnel rules like the disclosure of instruction manuals for inspection and audit reports), exemption 6 (personal information like mailing lists), and exemption 7 (investigatory files for law-enforcement purposes). In addition, the act sought to provide greater protection for information collected by the attorney general on organized crime, technological information covered by the federal export law, and information collected by the Secret Service. In an effort to apply some selectivity to the disclosure requirements, it limited the access of foreigners, felons, and lawyers in their discovery proceedings.

No substantive changes were made in the wording of the trade-secrets exemption to broaden its material coverage or to clarify the meaning of the exemption. However, in the original version of S. 1730, Senator Hatch introduced wording to cover:

> Trade secrets and commercial research, or financial information, or other commercially valuable information obtained from any persons and privileged or confidential where release may impair the legitimate private, competitive, financial, research, or business interests of any person or where release may impair the government's ability to obtain such information in the future.[112]

In the negotiation process, the prodisclosure advocates insisted on a public-welfare override to the exemption. The antidisclosure advocates were willing to accept such an override provision but only for health and safety reasons; they found the public-welfare override unacceptably vague in its wording. As a result of these groups' inability to reach a compromise solution, the trade-secrets exemption was left unchanged and the bill was reported to the Senate in this abridged form.[113]

The Government Operations Committee of the House has, at present, before it two bills, H.R. 3928 (sponsored by Representatives Frank Horton and John N. Erlenborn) and H.R. 2021 (sponsored by Glenn English). These bills have been stalled in committee, and it is unlikely that the House will press for passage of these bills until the Senate votes on S. 1730. Of the two bills, H.R. 3928 is considerably more protective than H.R. 2021 of business submitters' rights to confidentiality. While H.R. 2021 makes no substantive changes in the trade-secrects exemption, H.R. 3928 carries a mandatory withholding provision. Similarly, H.R. 3928 provides for de novo judicial review of submitters' challenges to disclosure; H.R. 2021 does not. Both acts mandate agency notification to submitters of information and provide a statutory basis for reverse-FOIA cases.

The American Bar Association Forum. Two sections of the American Bar Association (ABA) have been interested in the legislative amendments to the Freedom of Information Act in the area of business information—the administrative-law section and the business-law section. Within these committees, participants analyze aspects of the act and recommend changes for the approval of the American Bar Association. The American Bar Association is a lobby group in Congress that brings pressure to bear on certain issues. As one might expect, the procedure for obtaining a committee assignment or for participating in developing section recommendations is "not democratic," and the recommendations are "not the result of scientific sampling."[114] A close look at the members of these sections, in fact, reveals that many of the same participants that have been active in the Administrative Conference and congressional testimony and in helping to draft FOIA legislation are also active on the ABA committees as well.

Recommendations from the American Bar Association are forwarded to the Washington, D.C., office of the American Bar Association, and from there, they are submitted to the appropriate Senate and House subcommittees. The recent ABA recommendations echo many that have been mentioned heretofore. Among its recommendations are the mandatory nondisclosure of trade secrets unless some overriding public interest is at stake, the granting of a statutory basis for reverse-FOIA cases under the Freedom of Information Act, required notice to submitters for all third-party requests, and de novo review of reverse-FOIA cases.[115]

The Combatants

The chief protagonists for either maintaining or strengthening the provisions of the Freedom of Information Act are the media, public-interest groups, and a portion of the academic community. The chief critics of the legislation are certain business representatives, a number of federal agencies, and a small group of academic scholars. The debate also has spawned a number of professional associations that are dedicated to a discussion of the normative and positive aspects of federal disclosure statutes. Prominent among these are the Intellectual Property Owners Inc., and the American Society of Access Professionals.

The Supporters and Their Arguments. In general, the protagonists argue that the Freedom of Information Act is largely responsible for some of the exposés of the turbulent 1970s. They testify about Freedom of Information Act's role in uncovering incidents such as the Watergate break-in, the My Lai massacre, domestic spying by the Central Intelligence Agency, illegal usage of the Internal Revenue Service by the Nixon administration, the corruption in the Federal Indian Program, the COINTELPRO Program to draw certain individuals out of public life, organized-crime connections in the coal industry, Small Business Administration loans to organized-crime figures, and Medicare abuses.[116] The Library of Congress's Congressional Research Service conducted a study that was, by its own admission, "not exhaustive," but that found evidence of 276 stories that were uncovered with the help of the Freedom of Information Act between 1972 and 1980.[117] In addition, the American Civil Liberties Union's Center for National Studies has furnished a list of the FBI and CIA documents that have been uncovered with the aid of the Freedom of Information Act.[118] The Freedom of Information Act has broad support among investigative journalists who emphasize the need for citizen checks on big government in a free society.

The protagonists appear to be particularly sensitive to the criticism made by the supporters of reform that the media and academic community are making a small minority of the FOIA requests. As we shall discuss in chapter 3, the large majority of requests is made by businesses or by third-party intermediaries. Yet, the act was passed, in large part, to provide for government accountability to the people (that is, the press, researchers, and individual citizens.) Is the act being misused? Why do media requests make up such a small percentage of total requests?

FOIA proponents feel that counting the number of formal FOIA requests by the media is a misleading measure of media use. They point to the large number of media requests that are made to agencies by informal phone calls and not by formal FOIA requests. The threat, they posit, of a formal FOIA request is all that is needed to pry this information loose.[119] One media representative cited a multiplication factor as high as twenty in referring to the number of informal information requests relative to formal FOIA requests.[120] On the question of whether other groups, (for example, business) might have a similar multiplier, these commentators were silent. Thus, we have no reason to believe that the present figures distort the proportions of requests by various groups. Moreover, our interviews with agency personnel cast considerable doubt on this multiplication factor, as we see in chapter 3.

Procedurally, the major complaints of the prodisclosure group center on delays in processing requests and the need for changes in the content and number of exemptions. They feel that ever since the *Open America* v. *Watergate Special Prosecution Force* case,[121] agencies have not been compelled to abide by the time limitations set by the 1974 FOIA amendments.[122] Insofar as changes by federal agencies are concerned, their testimony indicates that the media are charged too much and that, regardless of whether the Freedom of Information Act cost $57 million per year to implement in 1980, the cost is worth it.[123]

A rather consistent undercurrent in some of the media's presentation is that the Freedom of Information Act is not crucial to the majority of news journalists. They have their own sources of information, and the story eventually will get out.[124] However, the media share an interest in principle to keep information flows open. Moreover, they point to many state laws that have followed the federal FOIA legislation and thereby have promoted a more-informed citizenry and a more-accountable government.[125] They feel that these externalities associated with the federal Freedom of Information Act are extremely important in its evaluation.

On matters dealing with broadening the trade-secrets exemption to protect confidential business information better or to add a tenth exemption for FBI and CIA files, the prodisclosure group is uniformly against such changes. They rest their case principally upon the paucity of documented horror stories involving agency release of confidential business or FBI/CIA information.[126] This group never mentions any magic number or magnitude of violations required to provide convincing evidence for such a change. They do not deny the existence of good reasons why documented evidence might not be available. In general, they rest their case on objective and measurable examples of exposed harm rather than the process set into motion by the incentives and disincentives of the Freedom of Information Act.

The Critics and Their Arguments. The only executive-agency representative to participate in the 1981 congressional oversight hearings was from the Office of Legal Policy of the Department of Justice. In his testimony, Jonathan Rose cited familiar problems with the act, such as its use by organized crime to discover federal agents and sensitive information, its use by private lawyers for discovery purposes, its high cost, its widespread use by business, and its interference with FBI and CIA investigations.[127] His testimony was intended principally to document the case for a tenth exemption covering FBI and CIA files. As evidence of this need, he noted that the Secret Service informants declined 75 percent because of the Freedom of Information Act.[128]

Business representatives express great concern with the procedural and substantive provisions of the trade-secrets exemption. Among the major business criticisms are the lack of uniformity among agencies with regard to information handling,[129] the integration of confidential business information into various agency reports and the subsequent disclosure of such reports,[130] the disincentives that FOIA disclosure makes to R&D,[131] the asymmetry with respect to submitters' and requesters' rights to de novo judicial review,[132] the speculative nature of the substantial-competitive-harm test of the *National Parks* decision,[133] and the voluntary nature of all FOIA exemptions.[134]

The critics of the current FOIA disclosure rules illustrate the act's misuse by pointing to the very same Congressional Research Service study that documented stories uncovered by the act. They note that during the period from 1974-1978, an average of fifty-one stories were uncovered each year. However, in 1979 this figure dropped to twenty-two, and in 1980 it dropped to nine.[135] At what point, they argue, can we agree that the act is not being used as it was intended and by those for whom it was intended?

A few horror stories of agency disclosure have come to light in spite of industry and agency efforts to minimize the publicity given to these events. Some of these horror stories are summarized in chapters 4, 6, and 7. Among these new cases are the Food and Drug Administration's disclosure of the Procter & Gamble Company's trade-secret masking agent,[136] Dow Corning's unwillingness to apply to the government for drawback funds from its importation of raw materials because the Department of Commerce could not give an assurance to protect Dow Corning's proprietary information,[137] the disclosure of detailed inspection reports of individual meat-processing plants by the Department of Agriculture,[138] and the EPA disclosure of Monsanto's $0.5 billion herbicide formula for Roundup.[139]

The Academic Input

The academic input into the controversy has come from three major sources. On one side are the academic researchers and investigative analysts who have a strong interest in having government files open for investigation.[140] On another side are the applied researchers whose technological discoveries are often patentable or that have unpatentable business applications. This group feels that such information, currently not protected under the trade-secrets exemption, should have such protection.[141] Finally, a group of economic analysts (including the authors of this book), have investigated the implications of the process set into motion by the Freedom of Information Act.[142] Since this testimony and the findings of our research are the basis for this book, the following chapters build our case for the better protection of business information in agency files, not simply because it avoids fundamental harm to business but because such protection is consistent with maintaining a dynamically competitive economy.

Conclusion

This history of information-disclosure legislation serves to show that many of the themes that gave birth to our nation are alive and burning today.

We still are delimiting the power of the executive branch of government both by internal and external checks on its use of discretion. In an effort to accomplish this goal, we all realize the need for sufficient and accurate information on the decisions of executive agencies. The Freedom of Information Act (as amended) is a significant step toward providing this high-quality information; but we live in a world of trade-offs, and therefore, the move toward opening government files has not come without a cost. To the extent that government decisions are based on privately submitted information, disclosure of this information threatens many of our fundamental rights to private property. Significant to the discussion in this book is the release of proprietary business information.

One of the most important factors influencing the high rate of growth in the United States has been its ability to push back the frontiers of human knowledge—to invent new products and processes that provide for the social well-being. However, the production of this information comes at a cost to its producers, and its creation is dependent upon sufficient incentives (that is, expected returns) to make the endeavor worthwhile. Therefore, a paradoxical trade-off emerges. If the government were to distribute this proprietary business information freely to all requesters, the public interest would be served by increasing competition and, thereby, reducing prices. However, this static benefit would be offset by the disincentives to invest in researching and developing new products and processes.

The courts and Congress have made it clear that the Freedom of Information Act is a disclosure statute. While Congress provided for nine categories of information that could be exempted from disclosure, the *Chrysler* decision interpreted these exemptions as voluntary and valid only so long as government agencies endorsed them. Furthermore, the *National Parks* decision put a burdensome objective standard of proof on businesses wishing to qualify for protection under the trade-secrets exemption. The information requester is presumed to have a right to know all information in government files, regardless of the use to which the information will be put. The submitter is the party that is compelled to substantiate his claim of confidentiality, and he must demonstrate that significant harm will result from the information's release.

In the following chapters, we shall show that the disclosure provisions in the Freedom of Information Act have set into motion a process that gives rise to disincentives in the business community. The increased risk of information disclosure and the increased cost of protecting against disclosure result in reduced R&D and/or the movement of these activities to more hospitable shores. In the course of our discussion, we cite various horror stories to illustrate the harm accompanying the release of proprietary information by the government, but our intent is not to dwell on the number of such disclosures or the magnitude of harm accompanying them. Rather, we intend to discuss the market process by which entrepreneurial activities arise and the extent to which the Freedom of Information Act impedes that process.

Notes

1. 112 *Congressional Record* 13,644 (daily ed. 20 June 1966). (King testimony before the House, *Clarifying and Protecting the Right of the Public to Information.* See also U.S., Congress, Senate, Committee on the Judiciary, Subcommittee on Administrative Practice and Procedure, *Freedom of Information Act Source Book: Legislative Materials, Cases, Articles* (hereinafter referred to as *Source Book*), 93d Cong., 2d Sess., 1974, p. 51.

2. Cited in James Russell Wiggins, *Freedom or Secrecy* (New York: Oxford University Press, 1956), p. 9.

3. Letter from James Madison to W.T. Barry, 4 August 1882, in *The Complete Madison*, ed. Saul K. Padover (New York: Harper and Brothers, 1953), p. 337.

4. John Stuart Mill, "On Liberty," in *The English Philosophers from Bacon to Mill*, ed. E.A. Burtt (New York: Modern Library, 1939), pp. 949-1041.

5. Ibid., p. 982.

6. Robert A. Katzmann, "Federal Trade Commission," in *The Politics of Regulation*, ed. James Q. Wilson (New York: Basic Books, 1980), pp. 159-190.

7. See the Symposium, "The Freedom of Information Act a Decade Later," ed. H.C. Relyea, *Public Administration Review* 39 July/August 1979, pp. 310-332.

8. In this study, we use the term *agency* as the standardized reference to both executive departments and agencies.

9. 5 U.S.C. § 22 (Revised Statute 161). The Housekeeping Statute had its origins in 1789 enactments 1 Stat. 28, 49, 65, 68 (1789). See James T. O'Reilly, *Federal Information Disclosure: Procedures, Forms and the Law* (Colorado Springs: Shephard's, 1982), p. 14-3.

10. H.H. Gerth and C. Wright Mills, *From Max Weber Essay's in Sociology* (New York: Oxford University Press, 1946), p. 233.

11. Charles Wolf, Jr., "A Theory of Non-Market Failures," *Public Interest* 55 (Spring 1979):114-133.

12. The classic work on agency behavior in economic terms is William Niskanen, *Bureaucracy and Representative Government* (Chicago: Aldene Co., 1971).

13. 44 U.S.C. § 1500 (1976 ed.) originally created as Act of July 26, 1935, ch. 417, 49 Stat. 500.

14. See Charles H. Koch, Jr., "The Freedom of Information Act: Suggestion for Making Information Available to the Public," *Maryland Law Review* 32 (1972):191; *Source Book*, pp. 374-410; and U.S., Congress, Senate, Committee on the Judiciary, *Administrative Procedure Act: Legislative History*, 79th Cong., 2d Sess., 1946, S. Doc. 248, p. 245.

15. Administrative Procedure Act, Pub. L. No. 404, ch. 324 § 3, 60 Stat. 237 (11 June 1946), 5 U.S.C. § 1002 (1976 ed.).

16. See, especially, ibid. See also U.S., Congress, House, Committee of the Whole House on the State of the Union, *Clarifying and Protecting the Right of the Public to Information*, 89th Cong., 2d Sess., H. Rept. 1497, 1966, p. 24.

17. U.S., Congress, Senate, Committee on the Judiciary, *Administrative Procedure Act*, 79th Cong., 1st Sess., 1945, S. Rept. 752, p. 12.

18. *Administrative Procedure Act*, 5 U.S.C. § 1002 (1976 ed.).

19. Ibid.

20. Ibid.

21. See Charles P. Bennet, "The Freedom of Information Act: Is It a Clear Public Record Law?" *Brooklyn Law Review* 34 (1967):72, 78.

22. House, *Clarifying and Protecting*, p. 6.

23. U.S., Congress, House, Committee on Government Operations, Special Subcommittee on Government Information, *Availability of Information from Federal Departments and Agencies, Part 1, Panel Discussion with Editors et al.*, 84th Cong., 1st Sess., 1955, p. 11 (testimony of Harold L. Cross).

24. See O'Reilly, *Federal Information Disclosure*, pp. 2-12-2-13; and Harold C. Relyea, "The Freedom of Information Act: A Capsule Overview 1966-1980," in U.S., Congress, House, Committee on Government Operations, Government Information and Individual Rights Subcommittee, *Freedom of Information Act Oversight* (hereinafter referred to as *House Hearings 1981*), 97th Cong., 1st Sess., 1981, pp. 945-974.

25. Robert O. Blanchard, "A History of the Federal Records Law," Freedom of Information Center Report no. 189 (Columbia: University of Missouri, Columbia School of Journalism, 1967).

26. Harold L. Cross, *The People's Right to Know* (New York: Columbia University Press, 1953).

27. House, *Availability of Information from Federal Departments and Agencies*, 84th Cong., 1st Sess., p. 1 (letter from William L. Dawson to John E. Moss, committee chariman).

28. House, *Clarifying and Protecting*, pp. 26-27.

29. House, *Availability of Information from Federal Departments and Agencies*, part 1 to part 17.

30. House, *Availability of Information from Federal Departments and Agencies*, part 4, Panel Discussion on Scientific and Technical Information, p. 757 (testimony of Lloyd Berkner). See also "National Security and the Amended Freedom of Information Act," *Yale Law Journal* 85 (1976): 401-407; and Stephen H. Unger, "The Growing Threat of Government Secrecy," *Technology Review*, February/March 1982, pp. 31-39.

31. House, *Availability of Information from Federal Departments and Agencies*, part 4, p. 760 (testimony of Lloyd Berkner).

32. Pub. L. No. 85-619 (12 August 1958), 72 Stat. 547, 5 U.S.C. § 302 (1976 ed.).

33. O'Reilly, *Federal Information Disclosure*; and Blanchard, "History of Federal Records Law."

34. U.S., Congress, House, Committee on Government Operations, *A Citizens Guide on How to Use the Freedom of Information Act in Requesting Government Documents*, 13th Rept. (Washington, D.C.: U.S. Government Printing Office, 2 November 1977), p. 8.

35. S. 1666, 88th Cong., 1st Sess. (1963). S. 1663, 88th Cong., 1st Sess. (1963). S. 1663 was the broader of the two bills covering a wider range of APA changes than S. 1666.

36. U.S., Congress, Senate, Committee on the Judiciary, *Clarifying and Protecting the Right of the Public to Information and for Other Purposes*, 88th Cong., 2d Sess., 1964, S. Rept. 1219, p. 1.

37. See O'Reilly, *Federal Information Disclosure*, p. 14-3.

38. The Broadcasters were concerned with losing trade secrets divulged in the licensing process. See U.S., Congress, Senate, Committee on the Judiciary, Subcommittee on Administrative Practice and Procedure, *Freedom of Information Act*, 88th Cong., 1st Sess., 1963, pp. 88-95 (testimony of Howard H. Bell).

39. Senate, *Clarifying and Protecting*, p. 6 (emphasis added).

40. 110 *Congressional Record* 17,086 (28 July 1964). "Trade Secrets and information obtained from the public in confidence or customarily privileged or confidential" should not be disclosed.

41. 112 *Congressional Record* 13,661 (daily ed. 20 June 1966).

42. Pub. L. No. 89-554 (6 September 1966), 80 Stat. 383, 5 U.S.C. § 552.

43. 5 U.S.C. § 552. Also see 5 U.S.C. § 140 (now codified at 31 U.S.C.A. § 483a (1977 ed.).

44. See Koch, "The Freedom of Information Act," p. 194; *Getman v. NLRB*, 450 F.2d 670, 679 (1974), 404 U.S. 1204 (171), which balanced the individual's right to privacy against the public benefit of disclosure; and *Soucie v. David*, 448 F.2d 1067 (1971).

45. 5 U.S.C. § 552(b)(4).

46. U.S., Department of Justice, *Attorney General's Memorandum on the Public Information Section of the Administrative Procedure Act: A Memorandum for the Executive Departments and Agencies Concerning Section 3 of the Administrative Procedure Act as Revised Effective July 4, 1967*, June 1967.

47. Kenneth Culp Davis, "The Information Act: A Preliminary Analysis," *University of Chicago Law Review* 34 (Summer 1967):802-803. Also in *Source Book*, pp. 281-282. Reprinted with permission.

48. Davis, "The Information Act," p. 285.

49. Ibid.

50. U.S., Congress, House, Committee on Government Operations, *Administration of the Freedom of Information Act*, 92nd Cong., 2d Sess., 1972, H. Rept. 92-1419. The Senate hearing was held in 1973. See U.S., Congress, Senate, Committee on Government Operations, Subcommittee on Intergovernmental Relations, *Executive Privilege, Secrecy in Government: Freedom of Information*. 93rd Cong., 1st Sess. (1973).

51. House, *Administration of the Freedom of Information Act*, p. 7.

52. See Donald A. Giannella, "Implementing the Freedom of Information Act," *Administrative Law Review* 217 (1971):296-349; *Source Book*, pp. 296-349. Also see Ralph Nader, "Freedom from Information: The Act and the Agencies," in *Source Book*, pp. 411-425; and Nader, *Harvard Civil Rights-Civil Liberties Law Review* 5 (1970):1-15.

It should be mentioned that the authors of the survey felt that the statistics were of limited value since only 10 percent of the questionnaires were returned.

53. Ralph Nader, "New Opportunities for Open Government: The 1974 Amendments by the Freedom of Information Act and the Federal Advisory Committee Act," *American University Law Review* 25 (Fall 1975):3.

54. Wiggins, *Freedom or Secrecy*, p. 9.

55. See for example, Robert L. Saloschin, Thomas C. Newkirk, and Donald J. Gavin, "A Short Guide to the Freedom of Information Act" (Manuscripts prepared for the general public, Washington, D.C., Department of Justice, 1979), p. 2.

56. Itzhak Galnoor, "The Politics of Public Information," *Society*, 16 May/June 1979, p. 29.

57. Nader, "Freedom from Information," p. 412.

58. R. Murray, "Twas a Sparkling Fourth for FOIA Crusader," *American Society of Newspaper Editors Bulletin*, August 1966. Also see Blanchard, "A History of the Federal Records Law."

59. Relyea, "The Freedom of Information Act," pp. 945-974.

60. U.S., Congress, Senate, Committee on Government Operations, Subcommittee of the Senate Committee on Judiciary, *Freedom of Information, Executive Privilege, etc.*, 93rd Cong., 1st Sess., 1973, vol. 2, p. 57; and also see *Washington Research Project Inc. v. Dept. of HEW*, 504 F.2d (1974), *cert. denied*, 421 U.S. 963 (1975).

61. Association of the Bar of the City of N.Y., "Amendments to the Freedom of Information Act," Committee on Federal Legislation Rept. 74-1 (1974), p. 25.

62. Ibid.

63. Pub. L. No. 94-409, 90 Stat. 1247, 5 U.S.C. § 522(c) (13 September 1976).

64. In *FAA Administration v. Robertson*, 442 U.S. 255 (1975), the Supreme Court ruled that information could be withheld even though it did not "specifically" fit into exemption (b)(3) so long as nondisclosure was in the public interest.

65. U.S., Department of Justice, *Department of Justice Guidelines on Freedom of Information Act*, 5 March 1972 (letter from Griffin Bell to heads of all federal departments and agencies).

66. 18 U.S.C. § 1905 (1976 ed.).

67. 5 U.S.C. § 552(b)(3).

68. See chapter 3.

69. 18 U.S.C. § 1905 (1976 ed.).

70. *Administrative Procedure Act,* 5 U.S.C. § 1002 (1976 ed.).

71. 5 U.S.C. § 552(b)(3) (1976 ed.).

72. *Chrysler v. Brown*, 441 U.S. § 281 (1979).

73. *General Services Administration v. Benson*, 415 F.2d 878 (9th Cir. 1969).

74. House, *Clarifying and Protecting*, p. 10.

75. For an excellent review of the development of this judicial interpretation, see U.S., Congress, House, Committee on Government Operations, *Freedom of Information Act Requests for Business Data and Reverse-FOIA Lawsuits*, 25th Rept., 20 July 1978, p. 16.

76. House, *Clarifying and Protecting*.

77. House, *Freedom of Information Act Requests*.

78. U.S., Congress, Senate, *Clarifying and Protecting the Right of the Public to Information*, 89th Cong., 1st Sess., S. Rept. 813 (1965), p. 9.

79. See *Sterling Drug Inc. v. FTC* 450 F.2d 689 (1971); *Grumman Aircraft Engineering Corp. v. Renegot Board*, 425 F.2d 578 (1970); *Porter County Chapter of the Isaak Walton League of America, Inc. v. United States Atomic Energy Commission* 380 F. Supp. 630 (1974); *M.A. Shapiro & Co. v. S.E.C.*, 339 F. Supp. 467 (1972); *Ditlow v. Shultz*, 379 F. Supp. (1974); *Rural Housing Alliance v. U.S. Department of Agriculture*, 498 F.2d 73 (1974); and *Ditlow v. Shultz*, 517 F.2d 166 (1975).

80. See *Ditlow v. Shultz*; and *Grumman Aircraft Engineering Corp. v. Renegot Board*, 421 U.S. 168 (1975).

81. Senate, *Clarifying and Protecting*, S. Rept. 813.

82. *National Parks and Conservation Assn. v. Morton*, 498 F.2d 765 (1974); and *National Parks and Conservation Assn. v. Kleppe*, 547 F.2d 673 (1976). O'Reilly argues that the *National Parks* decision was decided after the D.C. Circuit Court had encountered criticism of the conservative interpretation of the disclosure provisions in the Freedom of Information Act. He questions why other courts have not reviewed this unfortunate decision. See James T. O'Reilly, "Regaining a Confidence: Protection of Business Confidential Data through Reform of the Freedom of Information Act," *Administrative Law Review* 34 (1982):263-313.

83. Ibid.

84. See Thomas L. Patten and Kenneth W. Weinstein, "Disclosure of Business Secrets under the Freedom of Information Act: Suggested Limitations," *Administrative Law Review* 29 (1977):195-202.

85. Also see O'Reilly, *Federal Information Disclosure*, pp. 14-20 to 14-49.

86. Ibid.; and House, Subcommittee on Administrative Practice and Procedure. Committee on the Judiciary, *Freedom of Information Act*, 95th Cong., 1st Sess., 1977, pp. 293-308. (testimony of Burt Braverman). Also see Arthur R. Whale, "FOIA—For Our Inquisitive Adversaries" (Presentation at the Spring Meeting of the American Patent Law Association of Rochester, New York, 4 May 1978). Finally, see Patten and Weinstein, "Disclosure of Business Secrets," pp. 195-202.

87. *Worthington Compressors, Inc. v. Costle*, 662 F.2d 45 (1981).

88. See N.D. Campbell, "Reverse Freedom of Information Act Litigation: The Need for Congressional Action," *George Washington Law Review* 67 (October 1976):103-205. The acts are, respectively, 18 U.S.C. § 1905, 5 U.S.C. § 1002 (1946), 5 U.S.C. § 552(b)(3).

89. See *House Hearings 1981* (testimony of Burt Braverman and James O'Reilly).

90. *Administrative Procedure Act* § 10(e)(B)(1).

91. Department of Justice, "Policy Discussion: Business Confidentiality after *Chrysler*," *FOIA Update* 1 (Winter 1980):3-6.

92. U.S., Department of Justice, B.A. Babcock, assistant attorney general, *Memorandum to All Agency General Counsels*, 21 June 1979.

93. Ibid., p. 8.

94. U.S., Department of Justice, William French Smith, attorney general, *Memorandum for Heads of All Federal Departments and Agencies*, 4 May 1981.

95. U.S., Department of Justice, *Memorandum from the Office of Information and Policy Director Robert L. Saloschin to All Federal Departments and Agencies*, 15 June 1979; and Department of Justice, Office of Information and Privacy, "OIP Guidance: Submitters' Rights," *FOIA Update*, 3 (June 1982):3.

96. Department of Justice, "OIP Guidance," p. 4.

97. A survey of the handling procedures at the various agencies was done by the Department of Justice and is reported in Department of Justice, Office of Information and Privacy, *FOIA Update* 3 (June 1982):4.

98. *Administrative Conference of the United States Act*, Pub. L. No. 89-554 (6 September 1966), 80 Stat. 388, 5 U.S.C. §§ 571-576 (1976 ed.).

99. General Services Administration, Office of Federal Register, National Archives and Records Service, *United States Government Manual* (Washington, D.C.: U.S. Government Printing Office, 1980).

100. Ibid.

101. Administrative Conference of the U.S., Contract No. T-15706548-00.923.9.97510.251, 24 September 1979, submitted to ACUS on 15 December 1980.

102. Ibid.

103. Administrative Conference of the U.S., Contract No. T-21174151-00.923.1.97510.251, submitted to ACUS on 22 March 1982.

104. O'Reilly and Stevenson have commented publicly on each other's ACUS reports. These comments along with their written reports furnish the basis for this section.

105. *House Hearing 1981*, pp. 667-680 (testimony of Russel Stevenson).

106. Ibid. (testimony of O'Reilly). See also O'Reilly, "Regaining a Confidence."

107. Administrative Conference of the United States. *Memorandum: Status of Proposed Recommendation in FOIA Exemption (b)(4)*, 1 April 1982.

108. Administrative Conference of the United States. *Letter to Confidential Business Information Mailing List from William C. Bush, Staff Counsel to the Committee on Regulation of Business*, 24 November 1981 and 1 April 1982.

109. 1 C.F.R. § 305.82-1 (1982).

110. U.S., Congress, Senate, Subcommittee of the Committee on the Judiciary, *Freedom of Information Act*, 97th Cong., 1st Sess., 1981 (hereinafter referred to as *Senate Hearings 1981*). Also see *House Hearings 1981*.

111. See U.S., Department of Justice, Office of Information and Privacy, *FOIA Update* 3 (June 1982):3-4. Five bills were under review by the Committee: S. 587 (16 February 1981); S. 1235 (27 April 1981); S. 1247 (27 April 1981); S. 1730 (7 October 1981); and S. 1751 (14 October 1981). Senator Hatch's bill S. 1730 was eventually the one marked up by the committee.

112. S. 1730 § 8(4).

113. See Robert E. Taylor, "Senate Unit Backs Disclosure Safeguards for Sensitive Business Data Given to U.S.," *Wall Street Journal*, 21 May 1982, p. 7.

114. Interview with Thomas Susman, Ropes and Gray and former chairman of the Freedom of Information Committee of the Administrative Law Section of the American Bar Association, 17 September 1982. Reprinted with permission.

115. *House Hearings 1981* (testimony of Robert Evans). Also see *Senate Hearings 1981*, appendix, pp. 379-382 (testimony of the American Bar Association).

116. *House Hearings 1981* (testimony of Jack Anderson, Ed Asner, Harold Fruchtbaum, Ralph Nader, and Paul Perile); and *Senate Hearings 1981* (testimony of Steven Dornfield, Ted Carpenter, James Wieghart, and Paul Fisher).

117. Harold C. Relyea and Suzanne Cavanagh, "Press Notices on Disclosures Made Pursuant to the Federal Freedom of Information Act, 1972-1980: A Compilation," Congressional Research Service of the Library of Congress, prepared at the request of the House Subcommittee on Government Information and Individual Rights, 27 February 1981: *House Hearings 1981* (testimony of Jack Anderson et al.) and *Senate Hearings 1981* (testimony of Steven Dornfield et al.).

118. *House Hearings 1981*, pp. 707-719.

119. Ibid. (testimony of Bob Schieffer, William Cox, and Jack Landau).

120. Ibid. (testimony of William Cox), p. 118.

121. *Open America v. Watergate Special Prosecution Force*, 547 F.2d 605 (D.C. Cir. 1976).

122. *House Hearings 1981* (testimony of Jack Taylor, Bob Schieffer, Jack Landau, and Todd Shields).

123. Ibid. (testimony of Bob Schieffer, William Cox, Jack Landau, Ralph Nader, and Peter Manikas).

124. Ibid. (testimony of Jack Anderson and Jim Polk).

125. Ibid. (especially testimony of Edward Cony).

126. Ibid. (testimony of Edward Cony, Ralph Nader, Todd Shields, Russell Stevenson, John Shattuck, and Joseph Rauh).

127. Ibid. (testimony of Jonathan Rose); and *Senate Hearings 1981*. (testimony of Rose).

128. Ibid.

129. *House Hearings 1981* (testimony of Thomas Houser, James KeFauver, Jack Early, Burt Braverman, and James T. O'Reilly).

130. Ibid. (testimony of Thomas Houser).

131. Ibid. (testimony of Thomas Houser, Burt Braverman, and James T. O'Reilly).

132. Ibid. (testimony of James T. O'Reilly, and Burt Braverman).

133. Ibid. (especially testimony of Burt Braverman).

134. Ibid. See testimony of James O'Reilly for a rather all-encompassing statement of the business community's substantive and procedural criticisms of the act and recommendations for change.

135. Ibid. (cited by Paul Fisher). Fisher disputes the Congressional Research Service's figures and goes on to provide some numbers (that is, documented stories) of his own.

136. Ibid. (testimony of James T. O'Reilly).

137. Ibid. (testimony of Jack Pulley).

138. Ibid. (testimony of James KeFauver).

139. "An EPA Blunder Spurs Move to Seal Data," *Chemical Week*, 19 September 1982, pp. 13-14; and Pete Earley, "EPA Lets Trade Secret Loose in Slip Up, to Firm's Dismay," *Washington Post*, 18 September 1982.

140. *House Hearings 1981* (testimony of Harold Fruchtbaum and Paul Fisher).

141. The *National Parks* standard requires evidence of competitive harm. Therefore, since academic research is noncommercial and, therefore, not vulnerable to such harm, it is not protected. See *House Hearings 1981* (testimony of Stuart Bondurant); and *Senate Hearings 1981* (testimony of Bondurant). See also *Senate Hearings 1981* (letter from R.A. Greenborn, Purdue University, to Orrin Hatch).

142. *Senate Hearings 1981* (testimony of John Marthinsen, William Casey, and Laurence Moss).

3 The Impact of the Freedom of Information Act on Federal Government Agencies

In this chapter, we examine aggregated FOIA data collected from government agencies in order to determine whether and to what extent the Freedom of Information Act is being used by the private sector to acquire submitted business information. Furthermore, we point to certain statistical trends relating to this practice and then describe the cottage industry that has grown up to service information requesters. This chapter focuses on FOIA information flows following the 1974 amendments. In subsequent sections of this chapter, we shall demonstrate that:

The impact of the Freedom of Information Act on particular government agencies has varied widely both in terms of the number of requests received as well as the rate of increase in the number of requests received;

Among all government agencies, those agencies that are concerned primarily with regulating business or acquiring information about business possess the most coveted information and, accordingly, that the rate of growth of FOIA requests from these agencies is typically higher than for the remaining agencies in our study;

The widespread complaint by government agencies that they do not have the manpower available to fulfill the information-take-out service mandated by Congress is reflected to some extent in the reported cost figures for the order-fulfillment activities of the various federal agencies. Those agencies that report falling cost per request are also those in which the rate of growth for information is greatest, suggesting either that, over time, agencies besieged with requests acquire economies of scale in their order-fulfillment functions or else that costs have decreased along the lines suggested by learning-curve analysis.

Our final section of this chapter includes some speculations about future trends in FOIA information flows and the growth of information processing, especially in light of the existence of information-dispensing intermediaries.

The Data

In order to investigate the impact of the Freedom of Information Act on each federal agency, we requested that each agency send us a copy of their annual report (to Congress) for each of the years 1974 through 1981 on the Freedom of Information Act as required by the 1974 amendments discussed in chapter 2 and a total count of FOIA requests received by those agencies for each of those calendar years. We also consulted the Executive Office's *Budget of the U.S. Government* for estimates of the number of individuals employed by each federal agency for each of the years of our study.[1] Ironically, we used the FOIA request procedure to acquire the statistical information about FOIA data that are presented here. All 135 of the agencies we contacted were able to send us a copy of their annual report, but only 64 agencies were able to send us the total number of FOIA requests received for each of the years covered by this report. According to a spokeswoman from the Department of the Interior, the total number of requests is not part of official agency records because there are too many regional offices, none of which sends its tallies to Washington, D.C., in any systematic way.[2] Other agency representatives offered explanations for not having total number of request statistics that echoed the reason offered by the Department of the Interior. More exactly, a spokesman from the Department of Agriculture (in a written reply to our original FOIA request) explained that:

> The reports do not include the number of requests, only the number of denials, appeals, etc., since the law does not require accounting for [the] number of requests. Thousands of requests are handled routinely (such as your request) each year, and it would be an administrative burden to maintain such records.[3]

While we were not successful in securing complete data from all agencies, still 64 agencies did have most of this information on hand, and we have included it in table 3-1.

In the case of seventy-one agencies, our efforts to extract complete information ended in failure. Several of these agencies—for example, the Federal Maritime Administration, the Interstate Commerce Commission, and the Federal Power Commission—are involved deeply in regulating the business sector. Their omission from the analysis that follows is regretable and unfortunate. In other cases we were able to acquire the data only in a more-aggregated form than we would have preferred. Department of Labor, for example, could tabulate total number of requests for the agency but could not break out the figures for the Occupational Safety and Health Administration (OSHA). According to a Department of Labor spokesperson, the administration seldom refuses FOIA requests under the tradesecrets exemption.[4] This may be consistent with certain business-information submitters' complaints that the administration gives out valuable proprietary information. It also is consistent with OSHA's claim that they have no valuable business information to withhold. The Occupational Safety and Health Administration has been the subject of several reverse-FOIA suits, as we shall discuss in chapter 4.

Other agencies that submitted incomplete data, such as Action, the National Credit Union, and the Veterans Administration, are relatively small and probably do not collect or process a significant quantity of business information.

Our sample of sixty-four federal agencies is presented in table 3-1. Under each agency's name we list the following statistics for each of the calendar years 1974 to 1981:

The number of FOIA requests received that year,

The number of FOIA requests initially denied each year in whole or in part by reason of the trade-secrets exemption,

The number of official employees of each agency in the calendar years covered,

The cost per FOIA request.

For each agency, summary statistics are provided that are discussed in subsequent sections of this chapter. Inasmuch as these data will serve as the bases for the statistical calculations that follow, it is important at this point to specify certain interpretive difficulties inherent in the reporting procedures of the agencies.

First, the statistic representing the number of FOIA requests received ostensibly represents the total number of letters that were logged in by that agency and dated within that calendar year. Thus, duplicate requests for the same information but from different requesters or the same party requesting the same information at different times during the year are counted as separate and distinct requests. We did not perceive this to be a serious factor bloating our estimates. Indeed, the Food and Drug Administration keeps computerized records of who has asked for what and simply will refuse to send the same requester duplicate answers to the same request. Informal telephone inquiries to the agency like we employed from time to time (even when the phone inquirer made it clear that, unless this oral request were answered, a formal written request would follow) are not included in the total request figures. Conversation with FOIA officers at a number of agencies suggested that few requests are made by telephone without a subsequent letter. The possibility of the total number of requests being biased seriously in one direction for some agencies and in another direction for other agencies did not seem to be a problem. Thus, we believe this statistic

Table 3-1
Selected Data Based on a Sample of Sixty-four Government Agencies

Agency	1974	1975	1976	1977	1978	1979	1980	1981	Average Number of FOIA Requests 1974-1981	Average Annual Percent Growth Rate of FOIA Requests 1977-1980	1974-1981	D Statistic (percent)
*Agency for International Development										231	[a]	10.12	5.44
F	157	129	186	274	322	270	280	[b]				
DR	0	[b]	[b]	14	23	24	18	9				
E	9,278	6,591	6,154	6,092	6,073	6,180	[b]	[b]				
C/R												
Alcohol, Drug Abuse, and Mental Health Administration (Department of Health and Human Services)										585	3.3	8.82	2.82
F	[b]	[b]	424	580	531	691	639	647				
DR	[b]	[b]	6	45	20[b]	12[b]	3	13				
E	[b]	[b]	[b]	[b]	[b]	[b]	1,927	1,924				
C/R				69	56	84	106					
*Bureau of Alcohol, Tobacco, and Firearms (Department of Treasury)										586	[a]	21.81	3
F	[b]	232	331	547	575	781	739	758				
DR	[b]	5	9	9	33	41	18	4				
E	[b]	3,720	3,993	3,934	3,909	3,804	3,598	3,379				
C/R												
*Bureau of the Census										78	[a]	43.68	20.94
F	[b]	15	49	[b]	73	81	137	132				
DR	[b]	0	1	20	21	26	31	3				
E	[b]	4,015	3,965	3,936	4,028	4,018	3,966	3,805				
C/R												
Bureau of Economic Analysis										18	[a]	34.49	0
F	[b]	[b]	5	13	10	22	15	22				
DR	[b]	0[b]	0[b]	0[b]	0[b]	0[b]	0[b]	0[b]				

	1	2	3	4	5	6	7	8				
Center for Disease Control (Department of Health and Human Services)												
F	b	b	194	334	384	481	539	875	468	17.29	35.16	1.46
DR	b	b	2	2	4	6	16	11				
E	b	b	b	b	b	b	4,084	3,966				
C/R					190	191	125					
Central Intelligence Agency												
F	193	6,609	761	1,252	1,608	1,306	1,212	1,200	1,013	−1	29.83	0.35
DR	b	b	b	3	5	9	10	1				
E	b	b	b	b	b	b	b	b				
C/R				816	850	1,072	1,432					
*Civil Aeronautics Board												
F	b	b	b	190	460	244	185	136	243	20	8.02	3.46
DR	b	b	16	8	9	1	1	7				
E	721	720	753	770	802	727	721	581				
C/R				526	217	410	540					
*Commodity Futures Trading Commission												
F	b	b	b	b	b	400	590	663	551	a	28.74	13.79
DR	b	7	10	27	32	21	71	60				
E	b	249	374	444	453	342	474	469				
C/R												
Community Services Administration												
F	b	b	b	204	211	303	209	b	232	0.8	0.81	1.19
DR	b	b	b	2	2	5	2	b				
E	b	1,006	952	941	947	959	1,014	b				
C/R				5	5	5	6					
Consumer Product Safety Commission												
F	400	3,500	2,100	5,900	7,800	8,900	9,000[c]	9,250	5,856	a	56.63	0.70
DR	4	12	16	15	49	78	69	87				
E	830	884	890	914	897	879	850	752				
C/R												

Table 3-1 *(Continued)*

Agency	1974	1975	1976	1977	1978	1979	1980	1981	Summary Statistic			
									Average Number of FOIA Requests 1974-1981	Average Annual Percent Growth Rate of FOIA Requests 1977-1980	1974-1981	D Statistic (percent)
Controller of the Currency (Department of Treasury)									1,402	a	−11.94	6.13
F	2,400[b]	b	2,134	2,763	1,941	1,063	930	986				
DR	b	20	47	69	59	66	115	226				
E	b	2,546	2,761	2,907	3,003	3,200	3,051	2,934				
C/R												
Copyright Office									11	a	2.50	0
F	b	b	b	b	13	10	6	14				
DR	b	b	b	b	0	0	0	0				
E	b	385	416	482	552	596	593	573				
C/R												
Council on Environmental Quality									15	a	4	0
F	b	b	b	80[c]	80[c]	90[c]	90[c]	b				
DR	b	0	0	0	0	0	0	0				
E	61	51	44	40	32	30	32	16				
C/R												
Defense Communication Agency (Department of Defense)									73	−11	24.18	1.56
F	b	24	57	98	97	81	68	88				
DR	b	0	0	2	4	1	0	1				
E	b	1,669	1,618	1,559	1,540	1,497	1,515	1,614				
C/R			10	11	296	b						
Defense Contract Audit Agency (Department of Defense)									134	2	−13.74	1.49
F	b	335	38	141	58	81	150	138				
DR	b	6	3	3	0	1	0	1				
E	b	3,367	3,334	3,295	3,446	3,511	3,378[b]	3,505				
C/R			500	1,074	681	b						

Agency / Item		1	2	3	4	5	6	7	8	9	10	11
Defense Intelligence Agency (Department of Defense)												
F	b	493	609	838	996	677	841	1,022	782	0.25	12.92	0
DR	b	1	0	0	0	0	0	0				
E	b	2,581	2,543	2,479	2,496	2,487	2,559	2,603				
C/R				178	199	221	187					
Defense Investigative Service (Department of Defense)												
F	b	283	92	62	70	61	105	109	112	19	−41.90	0
DR	b	0	0	0	0	0	0	1				
E	b	1,256	1,113	1,409	1,422	1,500	1,503	2,403				
C/R				38	15	31	b					
Defense Logistics Agency (Department of Defense)												
F	b	5,923	4,238	3,831	4,265	2,890	5,557	4,451		a	−1.27	2.10
DR	b	56	50	40	33	285	97					
E	b	b	46,622	46,174	45,868	44,637	44,557					
C/R												
Defense Mapping Agency (Department of Defense)												
F	b	18	24	29	40	96	154	218	83	75	51.54	1.21
DR	b	0	0	0	0	0	3	4				
E	b	7,517	7,497	7,396	7,621	7,763	8,808	8,206				
C/R				63	37	12	b					
Defense Nuclear Agency (Department of Defense)												
F	b	7	16	29	25	79	94	107	51	49	57.54	3.08
DR	b	0	0	1	0	3	5	2				
E	b	607	632	603	591	581	573	615				
C/R				41	67	48	100					
Department of Army (Department of Defense)												
F	b	9,536	16,017	17,376	19,884	23,912	28,913	31,467	21,015	18.5	22.01	0.61
DR	b	39	70	93	177	135	230	159				
E	b	315,613	307,444	303,278	301,231	294,244	286,321	289,156				
C/R				89	88	78	80					

Table 3-1 *(Continued)*

Agency	1974	1975	1976	1977	1978	1979	1980	1981	Average Number of FOIA Requests 1974-1981	Average Annual Percent Growth Rate of FOIA Requests 1977-1980	1974-1981	D Statistic (percent)
*Department of Energy												
F	b	104	441	2,815	2,185	5,751	7,445	10,170	5,547	84.58	46.88	10.40
DR	b	110	324	287	269	797	932	600				
E	b	b	b	18,078 b	18,863 b	19,005	19,830					
C/R						540	443					
*Department of Labor												
F	b	b	b	5,000 c	6,500 c	7,500 c	10,000 c	15,000 c	8,800	a	31.61	5.75
DR	b	b	b	381	461	458	751	480				
E	14,487	13,434	14,475	15,859	20,129	22,148	22,115	24,293				
C/R												
Department of Navy (Department of Defense)												
F	b	2,790	3,249	4,652	8,218	7,630	7,832	6,141	5,787	19	14.05	1.25
DR	b	15	65	98	56	85	93	93				
E	b	289,484	283,323	296,582	295,689	291,468	289,267	154,638				
C/R				143	115	117	113					
Department of State												
F	b	1,812	2,286	3,504	3,494	2,579	2,742	2,265	2,669	−8	3.79	0.97
DR	b	b	36	36	22	21	51	52				
E	b	22,324	22,634	22,358	22,681	22,118	22,048	22,291				
C/R							730					
*Environmental Protection Agency												
F	b	1,947	4,113	3,847	4,223	5,215	6,814	7,208	4,767	20.97	24.38	4.08
DR	2	79	71	157	133	333	334	254				
E	10,711	9,160	9,481	9,779	10,156	10,153	10,689	10,104				
C/R				37	188	163	161					
*Equal Employment Opportunity Commission												
F	b	184	306	255	293	466	741	1,113	480	a	34.98	0.98
DR	b	0	2	2	0	5	6	18				
E	2,277	2,127	2,328	2,298	2,705	3,516	3,433	3,366				
C/R												

	1	2	3	4	5	6	7	8				
*Export-Import Bank of the United States												
F	b	21	27	20^c	64	74	76	89	82	56	27.21	10.23
DR	3	6	6	4	7	10	15	8				
E	420	444	440	406	406	387	380	361				
C/R				360	442	392	290					
*Farm Credit Administration												
F	b	b	b	16	26	25	24	12^c	21	a	−6.94	10.68
DR	b	3	0	1	1	2	4	0				
E	223	202	214	235	230	244	241	255				
C/R												
*Federal Aviation Administration (Department of Treasury)												
F	b	b	1,157	1,674	2,245	3,558	2,924	18,154^d	2,312	20.43	26.08	2.71
DR	b	b	25	40	50	52	56	90				
E	b	54,905	56,122	55,760	55,227	54,444	53,538	41,259				
C/R				179	132	86	112					
Federal Bureau of Investigation												
F	b	b	2,677	4,641	5,129	6,244	8,729	6,688	5,685	a	20.10	0.17
DR	b	b	16	0	6	9	14	14				
E	b	19,252	19,990	19,200	19,320	18,440	18,150	18,240				
*Federal Communications Commission (Department of Justice)												
F	b	197	126	117	160	231	226	225	187	24.54	4.39	10.97
DR	b	25	19	25	17	27	17	14				
E	2,137	1,968	1,960	2,057	2,068	2,088	2,098	1,977				
C/R				1,570	333	b	b					
*Federal Deposit Insurance Corporation												
F	b	92	237	195	202	236	199	b	193	0.67	16.68	8.79
DR	b	b	b	11	25	18	20	28				
E	3,103	3,164	3,600	3,479	3,585	3,429	3,422	3,553				
C/R				277	282	253	330					

Table 3-1 (Continued)

Agency	1974	1975	1976	1977	1978	1979	1980	1981	Summary Statistics			
									Average Number of FOIA Requests 1974-1981	Average Annual Percent Growth Rate of FOIA Requests		D Statistic (percent)
										1977-1980	1974-1981	
Federal Election Commission									66	[a]	48.50	1.21
F	[b]	[b]	[b]	22	36	81	83	107				
DR	[b]	[b]	[b]	0	1	2	0	1				
E	[b]	62	150	184	215	242	246	230				
C/R												
*Federal Energy Regulatory Commission									81	9	5.95	4.71
F	[b]	[b]	[b]	95[c]	95	100	113	[b]				
DR	[b]	[b]	[b]	0	1	0	15	3				
E	[b]	[b]	[b]	[b]	[b]	[b]	1,605	1,607				
C/R				[b]	1,324	1,487	1,709					
Federal Highway Administration (Department of Treasury)									453	1.9	2.40	3.75
F	[b]	[b]	[b]	442[c]	442	435	459	486				
DR		[b]	[b]	22	22	21	20	[b]				
E	[b]	4,802	4,868	4,649	4,660	4,293	4,076	3,776				
C/R					318	363	333					
*Federal Mediation and Conciliation Service									31	38.67	41.91	6.39
F	[b]	6	13	18	52	33	48	49				
DR		[b]	[b]	0	5	3	0	6				
E	459	490	526	532	533	508	495	465				
C/R					173	45	31					
Federal Prison System (Department of Justice)									1,595	23.77	16.60	0.05
F	[b]	[b]	878	1,175	1,651	1,745	2,228	1,892				
DR	[b]	[b]	1	0	2	0	2	0				
E	[b]	8,098	8,582	8,963	9,156	9,466	10,136	9,476				
C/R				[b]	176	122	96					

	1	2	3	4	5	6	7	8	Total			
*Federal Reserve System												
F	3,969	3,660	3,876	5,405	4,710	5,112	5,274	4,934	4,617	a	3.16	2.19
DR	0	15	34	53	39	257	207	203				
E	1,353	1,456	1,489	1,516	1,516	1,515	1,496	1,570				
C/R												
*Federal Trade Commission												
F	240	529	690	674	1,154	1,732	1,767	1,251	1,005	38	26.60	14.94
DR	12	109	148	159	159	233	187	194				
E	1,626	1,569	1,637	1,648	1,630	1,665	1,573	1,467				
C/R				920	776	705	683					
*Food and Drug Administration (Department of Health and Human Service)												
F	2,600	13,000	21,778	25,100	32,852	31,886	33,589	33,179	24,248	10.2	43.87	0.01
DR	b	82	122	212	378	188	164	208				
E	b	6,441	6,597	7,575	7,718	7,891	7,190	7,756				
C/R				70	60	108	102					
*General Services Administration												
F	b	b	936	1,462	1,861	1,935	1,843	2,115	1,692	8	17.71	4.98
DR	b	b	36	88	96	87	103	96				
E	b	36,400	35,673	34,072	34,320	32,808	32,426	33,755				
C/R				179	202	b	b					
Health Resources Administration (Department of Health and Human Services)												
F	b	b	100	110	149	237	321	196	185	a	14.41	0.36
DR	b	b	1	0	1	0	2	0				
E	b	2,046	2,079	2,099	1,237	1,250	1,208	1,120				
C/R												
Immigration and Naturalization Service (Department of Justice)												
F	b	b	10,625	10,995	10,773	10,894	11,928	10,643	10,976	2.75	0.03	0.01
DR	b	b	1	0	0	2	2	1				
E	b	7,827	8,534	8,785	9,835	9,727	9,948	9,422				
C/R				40	20	23	27					

Table 3-1 *(Continued)*

										Summary Statistic		
									Average Number of FOIA Requests 1974-1981	Average Annual Percent Growth Rate of FOIA Requests		D Statistic (percent)
Agency	*1974*	*1975*	*1976*	*1977*	*1978*	*1979*	*1980*	*1981*		*1977-1980*	*1974-1981*	
Internal Revenue Service												
F	3,936	15,073	9,687	7,913	7,580	9,249	12,651	12,583	9,834	16.93	18.06	0.62
DR	41	76	45	20	13	62	189	40				
E	b	71,710	70,848	70,600	70,926	77,431	71,525	78,425				
C/R				392	435	378	308					
International Communication Agency												
F	b	b	84	130	145	133	133	128	125	a	8.79	2.12
DR	b	b	0	1	3	3	4	5				
E	b	b	b	8,552	8,293	8,020	7,997	7,701				
C/R												
*National Aeronautics and Space Administration												
F	b	709	738	779	956	1,053	1,241	1,269	964	16.8	10.19	14.25
DR	b	115	1	108	159	162	194	222				
E	26,686	24,333	24,039	23,569	23,169	22,633	22,613	21,844				
C/R				132	109	96	133					
*National Highway Traffic Safety Administration (Department of Treasury)												
F	b	b	b	b	b	401	393	458	417	a	6.87	11.34
DR	b	10	3	2	8	40	45	34				
E	b	784	846	818	803	828	805	743				
C/R												
National Institute of Health (Department of Health and Human Services)												
F	b	307	537	782	1,306	1,638	2,795	1,412	1,254	52.89	28.96	0.41
DR	1	2	2	1	4	9	11	6				
E	b	10,708	11,134	11,277	11,554	11,837	11,809	11,859				
C/R				74	129	122	60					

Agency												
National Labor Relations Board												
F	b	1,613	1,677	1,518	1,967	1,953	2,530	3,148	2,058	18.56	11.79	0.32
DR	b	6	4	6	10	7	7	6				
E	2,504	2,349	2,503	2,751	2,849	2,921	2,825	2,786				
C/R				275	225	145	97					
*National Oceanic and Atmospheric Administration												
F	b	39	65	106	120	140	155	172	114	a	28.06	4.39
DR	0	2	1	4	7	2	12	7				
E	b	12,546	12,630	12,835	12,801	12,823	12,725	12,401				
C/R												
*National Science Foundation												
F	b	146	117	107	127	132	105	117	174	1	−3.62	6.06
DR	b	0	9	8	18	17	18	4				
E	1,394	1,226	1,250	1,257	1,298	1,262	1,232	1,210				
C/R				327	370	356	343					
National Security Agency (Department of Defense)												
F	b	402	312	516	704	609	545	490	511	a	3.35	0.56
DR	b	0	3	3	1	2	6	5				
E	b	b	b	b	b	b	b	b				
C/R												
National Security Council												
F	b	506	147	162	154	161	217	363	244	a	−5.39	0.06
DR	b	0	1	0	0	0	0	0				
E	85	72	68	62	39	64	62	60				
C/R												
National Transportation Safety Board												
F	b	b	b	b	100	250	275	295	230	a	43.42	0.33
DR	0	0	0	0	0	0	1	2				
E	b	270	306	377	367	355	354	336				
C/R												

Table 3-1 (Continued)

Agency	1974	1975	1976	1977	1978	1979	1980	1981	Average Number of FOIA Requests 1974-1981	Summary Statistics Average Annual Percent Growth Rate of FOIA Requests 1977-1980	1974-1981	D Statistic (percent)
*Nuclear Regulatory Commission									417	a	37.10	6.96
F	b	78	423	344	349	566	639	518				
DR	b	8	11	69	31	36	28	20				
E	b	2,006	2,289	2,499	2,666	2,691	3,029	3,255				
C/R												
Office of Personnel Management									662	2.5	32.29	1.08
F	59	b	b	718	970	750	b	702				
DR	0	6	1	7	3	7	5	14				
E	7,500	6,632	6,699	6,875	6,539	6,305	6,237	5,745				
C/R				665	202	229	229[c]					
Office of Secretary of Defense									1,137	15	6.28	0.64
F	b	1,165	868	886	898	1,103	1,358	1,679				
DR	b	4	2	5	1	2	11	26				
E	b	336	290	275	263	280	261	271				
C/R				620	658	554	460					
*Securities and Exchange Commission									1,146	6	16.23	6.04
F	b	638	808	1,114	1,252	1,322	1,317	1,573				
DR	b	49	43	72	72	51	96	102				
E	1,889	1,935	1,904	1,930	2,009	2,009	1,972	1,928				
C/R				530	417	375	343					
U.S. Arms Control and Disarmament Agency									1,050	9.45	−24.41	0.08
F	b	1,645	1,743	877	702	1,666	407	307				
DR	b	0	0	1	4	1	0	0				
E	177	167	179	169	185	179	184	155				
C/R				3[c]	3	3	3					

*U.S. Customs Service (Department of Treasury)												
F	[b]	[b]	[b]	2,104	2,806	2,581	3,010	3,991	2,898			
DR	[b]	[b]	[b]	369	288	202	571	650				
E	[b]	14,141	13,602	13,881	15,065	14,583	14,225	13,558				
C/R				760	570	658	229			12.68	17.36	14.35
*U.S. International Trade Commission												
F	[b]	[b]	[b]	58	95	115	123	[b]	98			
DR	[b]	4	5	15	15	20	31	27				
E	384	381	389	348	368	361	399	411				
C/R										[a]	28.48	29.92
U.S. Secret Service (Department of Treasury)												
F	2	641	832	1,294	1,732	1,146	1,002	707	919			
DR	0	1	0	0	2	3	3	0				
E	[b]	3,104	3,534	3,578	3,590	3,561	3,523	3,618				
C/R				137	111	120	196			0.092	1.60	0.12

Source: Survey based on authors' FOIA request to 135 government agencies, 1981 and 1982.

Key: F = Number of FOIA requests
DR = Number of requests denied initially because of trade-secrets exemption
E = Number employed in agency
C/R = Cost per request (dollars)
* = Business-information agency

[a]Noncalculated
[b]Complete data not available
[c]Estimate
[d]Inflated due to Patco strike

is a reasonably good index of what its title suggests—namely, the number of the FOIA requests received by each agency.

The second statistic presented, the number of initial determinations not to comply with a request for records made under the Freedom of Information Act for reasons of the trade-secrets exemption indeed may be reported differently from one agency to the next. Consider a hypothetical FOIA request enumerating 100 items all contained in the agency records. The agency FOIA officer may agree to supply fifty requested items and to deny the remaining fifty. Should this count as fifty determinations not to comply or only one determination not to comply? A spokeswoman for the Small Business Administration, when presented with this hypothetical question, answered that her agency would count this as fifty denials and would record one request.[5] Clearly, other agencies might consider this as only denying parts of one single request and therefore count this as one denial rather than fifty. In telephone interviews with about twenty agency FOIA officers, the general practice seems to be that subrequests within a single letter are not counted separately unless these subrequests are for totally unrelated information. In the absence of evidence to the contrary, our presumption is that variations among the agency reporting practices are not significant enough to distort the interagency comparisons seriously over the entire period under study, 1974-1981. This particular assumption may require modification in future analyses of agency-supplied data.

To decrease the risk of distortion, we pooled the year-to-year values for each of the years in order to construct what we name the *D statistic* (table 3-1). Our D statistic is the ratio of the number of FOIA requests denied totally or partially under the trade-secrets exemption to the total number of requests that were received during the period (that is, $\Sigma DR/\Sigma F$). We shall interpret this statistic to be a rough index of the wealth of confidential business information in the coffers of the various agencies. The greater this index, the greater the wealth in the offices of government agencies.

Finally, we have chosen to use the official statistical manpower count published in the Executive Office's *Budget of the U.S. Government (Appendix)* to get the relative size of each federal agency. Here, we face the familiar objection directed against all manpower measures—they make agencies with highly skilled workers appear to be about the same size as agencies with less-skill-intensive personnel. As J.T. Bennett and M.J. Johnson have argued, higher-paying white-collar employment increased by more than 44 percent, while blue-collar employment by federal agencies declined by approximately 15 percent over their sample of nearly twenty years from 1959 to 1978.[6] It seems likely that these same patterns of relative change apply to our shorter period 1977-1980 that overlaps theirs but that extends somewhat beyond. Thus, our manpower measure underestimates the skill-labor intensity of high-skill agencies.

Also, to the extent that the agencies with more-skill-intensive labor are agencies with greater stocks of valuable business information, the employment measure that we use here will make some agencies seem smaller than they would be if we could measure them directly in terms of the size of their information stocks.

In addition, our employment measure of agency size is not adjusted for the widespread Washington practice of hiring outside consultants to do analysis and research for the agencies. These so-called beltway bandits participate in the design and gathering of confidential business information but are not employed formally by the federal agency. While their participation is measured in the overall agency budgets, labor hours of skill-intensive work effort are omitted completely from our manpower measure. Bennett and Johnson rightly emphasize the importance of outside consultants in making the true extent of government involvement in the economy appear smaller than it is.[7] They point out that, in one extreme case, nearly 90 percent of the Department of Energy's budget is devoted to research done by outside consultants. Clearly, the employment statistic for the Department of Energy seriously underestimates the total number employed by the agency. Despite the defects of our measure, the total employment figure does offer a rough index of comparative agency size for the purpose of the analysis presented here.

Distribution of FOIA Requests

For the sixty-four federal agencies described in table 3-1, the total number of FOIA requests rose from approximately 39,340 in 1974 to over 206,114 in 1981. Measured on an average annual basis, total FOIA requests for all agencies rose at an astounding rate of 26.69 percent per annum.

According to the histogram in figure 3-1, showing the distribution of the number of FOIA requests received by the agencies in 1981 among 13 classes representing numbers of FOIA requests, most of the agencies in our study received fewer than 1,000 requests. Those agencies that received more than 5,000 requests were large-sized agencies as measured by total employment.

The agencies receiving the largest number of requests were the Consumer Product Safety Commission (CPSC) (9,250 requests), Department of Army (31,467), Department of Energy (10,170), Department of Navy (6,141), Environmental Protection Agency (7,208), Federal Aviation Administration (18,154), Federal Bureau of Investigation (6,688), Federal Reserve System (4,934), Food and Drug Administration (33,179), Immigration and Naturalization Service (10,643), and the Internal Revenue Service (12,583).

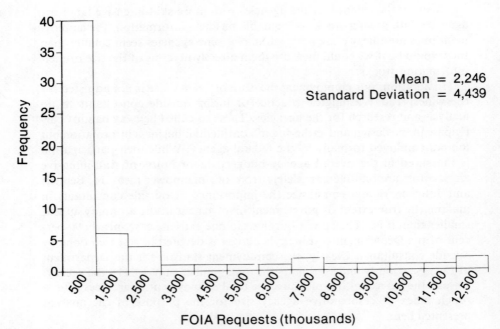

Source: Authors' FOIA request to agencies.

Figure 3-1. Distribution of Average Number of FOIA Requests (1980-1981) among Thirteen Classes

The Consumer Product Safety Commission, the Food and Drug Administration, the Environmental Protection Agency, the Federal Reserve System, and the Department of Energy house a wide variety of business information u.ed for regulatory and research purposes. The remaining agencies, especially the Federal Bureau of Investigation, the Immigration and Naturalization Service, the Department of Labor, the Department of the Army, and the Department of Navy, contain a great deal of information about personnel, immigrant status, military service, and so on. The Federal Aviation Administration appears among the large request-receiving agencies only because of the Patco union strike that produced over 18,000 requests in 1981, a number quite above the more-normal 3,558 total for 1979. Still, the Department of Army as well as the Department of Navy both house a great deal of contract information resulting from military procurement practices, and many of the requests recorded here are for contract information and reviews of contract awards—information that we shall see in later chapters carries with it great financial rewards and is much coveted by the private sector.

In table 3-1, a variety of summary statistics for each of the sixty-four agencies is calculated, reflecting the post-1974 experience with the Freedom of Information Act. One statistic that revealed a great deal about agency experience with the Freedom of Information Act over the duration of our study is the average annual rate of growth of the FOIA requests from 1974 to 1981. For each agency in table 3-1, we pooled the number of FOIA requests received over the period 1974-1981 and listed the average yearly value. Again, the range of agency experience is quite diverse. The mean of the average number of requests for the sixty-four agencies was 2,246 with a standard deviation of 4,439 requests (see figure 3-1).

The distribution of average annual growth rates among sixteen classes is drawn in figure 3-2. We calculated that statistic for each agency and plotted the histogram of these values in figure 3-2. The mean of the average annual rate of growth was 17.15 percent with a standard deviation of 19.56 percent. In this figure, we can see that the great majority of the agencies experienced positive rates of growth in the FOIA requests, ranging from 1 percent to 35 percent. As we can see by visually comparing the two histograms (figures 3-1

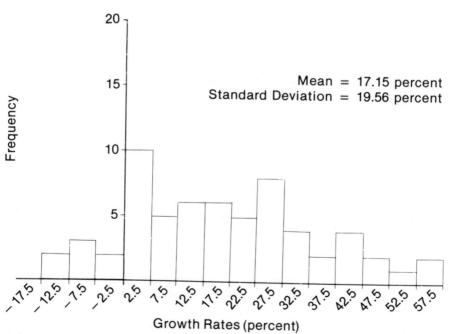

Source: Authors' FOIA request to agencies.

Figure 3-2. Distribution of Growth Rates of Agency FOIA Requests (1974-1981) among Sixteen Classes

and 3-2), the distribution of growth rates is more symmetrical and less dispersed than the distribution of the absolute number of requests. Certain extreme agency growth rates as experienced by the Consumer Product Safety Commission (+56.63 percent), the Defense Investigative Service (−41.90 percent), the Defense Mapping Agency (+51.54 percent), Defense Nuclear Agency (+57.54 percent), Defense Contract Audit Agency (−13.74 percent), and the U.S. Arms Control Agency (−24.41 percent) pull the tail ends of our distribution below 0 percent and above 50 percent, but for the most part, the data laid out in this way support our claim that different agencies have experienced the impact of the Freedom of Information Act differently as measured both by the absolute number of requests and by the average annual growth rate of the requests.

Another generalization we offer is that the great majority of federal agencies has experienced positive rates of growth in the number of FOIA requests, and so this may be taken as evidence that the Freedom of Information Act has become an increasingly popular vehicle by which the U.S. public can gain access to government files. Still, this generalization must be qualified by the fact that a few governmental agencies such as the Civil Aeronautics Board, the Farm Credit Administration, the National Science Foundation, the National Security Council, the Defense Contract Audit Agency, the Controller of the Currency, the Defense Investigative Service, the Defense Logistics Agency, and the U.S. Arms Control Agency experienced negative growth rates in requests over the period under study. With the possible exception of the Civil Aeronautics Board and the Defense Contract Audit Agency, these agencies do not house commercially valuable business information.

Business-Information Agencies

Among our group of sixty-four agencies, there exist a still smaller group of twenty-eight agencies marked with an asterisk in table 3-1. These agencies are involved deeply with regulating the performance of the business sector and/or gathering data about the performance of the private sector. It is reasonable to hypothesize that these agencies contain the bulk of commercially valuable business information among all the agencies listed in the table. The majority of FOIA requests received by these agencies is firm specific and is more concerned with technical and marketing information than with general statistical reporting in an aggregated form or with a non-business matter such as disease control or immigration and naturalization. For example, the FDA inspector files a plant-inspection-tour report with his regional office, and a requester, perhaps an information-requesting middleman asks to see that report. Consider, alternatively, a Commerce Department staff member who has finished a report on the microprocessor industry and a Japanese firm, through its New York legal office, that requests that information. The agencies marked with an asterisk in table 3-1 are most likely to receive requests for what the courts term *commercially valuable* information. This smaller set of twenty-eight agencies has been selected because of our interest in the business-information traffic. We wish to focus our attention on that segment of our sample that is most likely to house the greatest quantity of valuable business information.

In table 3-2, we compare the sample statistics for the selected group of twenty-eight agencies with the remaining group of thirty-six. The mean growth rate of FOIA requests for the group of twenty-eight agencies was 20.77 percent, which is somewhat higher than that of the remaining thirty-six agencies, which was 14.34 percent. The average level of FOIA requests for both groups was also different, with the regulatory group receiving on the average of about 15 percent more requests. One might hypothesize that, since the federal agencies constituting the group of twenty-eight are particularly well stocked with business information, now much coveted by the private sector, both the average annual growth rates of FOIA requests and the average levels consequently would be greater for the regulatory group. These presuppositions are consistent with the data in table 3-2.

In table 3-1, we calculate the D statistic for each government agency. This statistic represents the total number of requests for information for which an initial determination not to comply was made because of the trade-secrets exemption. This rate is important because it represents a first-level decision by an agency that submitted records containing trade secrets or confidential and commercial information. We assume that agencies that make this determination more often than others stock the type of business information eagerly demanded by the private requesters. Comparing the D

Table 3-2
Comparison of Twenty-eight Business-Information Agencies with Thirty-six Non-Business-Information Agencies

Statistic	Business-Information Agencies	Non-Business-Information Agencies	Statistic for Mean Differential
Average growth rate of FOIA requests	.2077 (.1556)	.1434 (.2201)	5.43
Mean of average of FOIA requests, 1980-1981	3286.2000 (6823)	2848.3000 (5724.6)	1.08
Average D statistic	.0852 (.0644)	.0104 (.0129)	24.00

Note: Figures in parentheses are sample standard deviations.
Source: Data based on table 3-1.

statistic for the group of twenty-eight and the group of thirty-six agencies (table 3-2), we find the mean D statistic for the first group is 8.5 percent, which is eight times larger than the mean D statistic for the group of thirty-six agencies, which is slightly higher than 1 percent. The results lead us to conclude that the group of twenty-eight agencies and the group of thirty-six agencies do have significantly different mean D statistics. These results suggest that our D statistic may serve as an index of the level of business information housed in the particular government agencies under study. We shall examine this possibility after we have had something to say about the behavior of the accounting costs each agency experienced when servicing requests for information.

Reported Costs of Order Fulfillment

Table 3-1 displays the average cost of filling FOIA requests for a selected group of thirty-nine federal agencies for which this information was available for the calendar years 1977 through 1980. It is reported by each agency's FOIA officer as part of his annual report to Congress. We calculated the unit-cost value by dividing total cost of order fulfillment by the total number of FOIA requests as reported in table 3-1.

The costs of compliance reported by the various agencies included in this study are the direct accounting costs of compliance as reported by that agency. They are not the economic costs (that is, opportunity costs) of compliance. Such economic costs would include not only the costs of searching for documents and mailing responses to information requesters but also the costs of reviewing the documents for confidentiality determinations and the costs associated with foregone responsibilities of agency employees that result from putting first priority on FOIA requests. We must remember that the law requires that agencies respond to FOIA requests in ten days. This automatically puts FOIA requests at the top of the list of priorities. In this way, the act might very well lead to a misallocation of resources. As an idea of how large these sacrificed alternatives might be, the Internal Revenue Service estimated that approximately $29 million worth of tax returns could not be reviewed because of its need to respond to FOIA requests. Other opportunity costs associated with the Freedom of Information Act are noted—for example, the disincentive to provide accurate information by business and the disincentive for evaluators to state the true risks associated with prospective employees for fear the results might be made available.[8]

Perhaps the most significant and immediately obvious feature of our average dollar-cost figure is the tremendous degree of variation in the numbers from one agency to the next and even for certain years within the same agency. The histogram of the distribution of the 1980 cost-per-request figures for the thirty-nine agencies among fifteen categories of dollar costs is displayed as figure 3-3. The average cost is $354.35. That means that the estimated cost to the taxpayer of the data that we obtained for this chapter was at least $74,340. Particular agencies like the U.S. Arms Control and Disarmament Agency were able to meet all requests in 1980 for an average cost per request of $3, while the reported average cost per request of the federal Energy Regulatory Commission was over $1,700.

Of course, differences in the reporting procedures of the agencies account for observed variations in the cost figures. Assigning dollar-cost totals to particular activities in a complex multiservice agency is essentially an arbitrary exercise. Cost accounting is a notoriously controversial discipline that produces frustrating results for decision makers who are concerned with the marginal rather than the average impact of their decisions.[9] Some agencies include in their reported average cost arbitrary allowances for the fixed overhead costs of the agency operation. Strictly speaking, Congress should be interested in the incremental costs of the activity, as

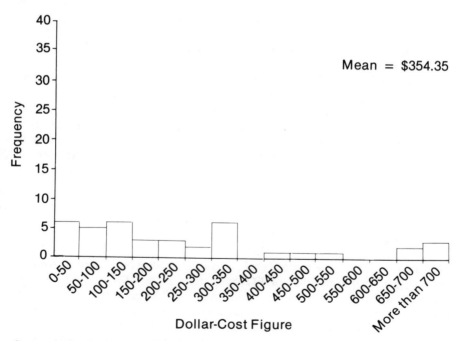

Source: Authors' FOIA request to agencies.

Figure 3-3. Distribution of Accounting Costs per Request among Fifteen Classes

some FOIA officers explicitly state when they send Congress their reports. Therefore, part of the variation observed in the cost-per-request statistic in table 3-1 can be explained by the differences in accounting conventions adopted by the FOIA officers of each agency.

Despite these problems with the consistency of the absolute value of the figures in table 3-1, an interesting pattern emerges among these data that has to do with their changes over time. By restricting our attention to those agencies reporting a decline in the average cost-per-order-fulfillment figures over the 1977-1980 period, we focus on a subset of the group of thirty-nine agencies—namely, the Center for Disease Control, the Defense Investigative Service, the Defense Mapping Agency, the Department of Army, the Department of Energy, the Department of Navy, the Export-Import Bank, the Federal Aviation Administration, the Federal Communications Commission, the Federal Mediation and Conciliation Service, the Federal Prison System, the Federal Trade Commission, the Immigration and Naturalization Service, the Internal Revenue Service, the National Institute of Health, the National Labor Relations Board, the Office of Personnel Management, the Office of Secretary of Defense of the Joint Chiefs of Staff, the Public Health Service, and the U.S. Customs Service. The mean growth rate in FOIA requests for these twenty agencies was 25.58 percent (standard deviation of 22.33), which is much greater than the mean rate of growth for the remaining nineteen agencies that was 7.02 (standard deviation of 13.19).

Can these data be taken to support the hypothesis that agencies with faster-growing FOIA services also tend to develop more-efficient request-processing capabilities so that their reported cost per request falls over time? The evidence, while not overly persuasive, does suggest that the agencies experiencing the most rapid increases in FOIA requests tend to become more efficient in fulfilling these orders. Whether the source of this efficiency is economies of scale or simply lack of diligence in meeting the intentions of the Congress not to give out trade secrets is a question we must return to at other places in this book.

Explaining Variation among Agency Growth Rates

We have seen that the majority of federal agencies experienced a positive growth rate in the number of FOIA requests from 1974 to 1981. Actual growth rates ranged from -41.9 percent to $+57.54$ percent. It is tempting to account for the observed variance among the observed agency growth rates by using the D statistic and employment levels of the agencies as explanatory variables. One may hypothesize that agencies of any given size, filled with commercially valuable business information, may have experienced the most spectacular increase in FOIA requests. Unfortunately, a multiple regression analysis utilizing the data in table 3-1 produced extremely poor results. The regression analysis of the rate of growth of FOIA requests for those business-information agencies indicated by asterisk in table 3-1 produced slightly improved results but not enough to support the hypothesis that the growth rate of requests varies directly with the extent to which that agency is stocked with economically coveted business information.

Our judgment is that future refinement of this statistical framework will produce a strong correlation between measurements of the growth of FOIA requests and measurements of the extent to which agencies house commercially valuable business information. In table 3-3, we list another selected group of executive agencies and their responses to a survey we conducted. In each case the interviewee was the FOIA officer or that person's immediate assistant in charge of servicing FOIA requests. We asked each agency representative to break down the total number of requests according to whether in their judgment (or opinion) the outside requester was a corporation, law firm, FOIA service company, public-interest group, news media, or other. In cases where the agency representatives felt comfortable with only an ordinal ranking of the frequency of requests from each of the aforementioned categories of requesters, we have indicated that ranking in the table rather than to force that person into stating definite percentages. From this table we succeeded in drawing up a cross classification of the ten agencies according to two characteristics: (1) whether that agency experienced a high or low rate of growth in FOIA requests over the period 1974-1981 and (2) whether that agency received requests mostly from business-sector or non-business-sector requesters (see figure 3-4). In order not to bias the results in favor of the thesis we are offering here, we have defined mostly industry requesters as where the combined percentages of corporate and lawyer requesters exceeds 70 percent. Next to each agency classified in this manner we have listed the D statistic in parentheses. The results are consistent with our claim that agencies containing large amounts of business information have experienced the largest growth rates in FOIA requests. The D statistic also tends to be highest for those agencies falling within the cell on the first row, second column of figure 3-4.

The one interesting anomaly is the Food and Drug Administration, for which the D statistic was unusually low in light of our findings in chapter 7. It turns out, however, that the Food and Drug Administration is the only federal agency with a comprehensive set of rules and regulations articulating agency policy on all aspects of information disclosure. These detailed regulations cover all aspects of FDA operations, including the status and treatment of information collected in establishment-inspection reports (EIRs), investigational new drug (INDs), and new-drug applications (NDAs). Accordingly, information requesters have become very sophisticated in knowing

Table 3-3
Percentage of Total FOIA Requests, by Type of Requester

Agency	Corporations	Law Firms	FOIA Service Companies	Public-Interest Groups	Press/Media	Others
Commodities Futures Trading Commission 1981	20	80				
Consumer Product Safety Commission 1981	25	48	1	2	2	22
Environmental Protection Agency						
1980	45	24	6	4	0	21
1979	36	24	6	7	2	25
1978	40	24	11	5	2	16
1977	53	21	7	1	1	17
1976	51	16	8	4	2	19
Export-Import Bank						
1981	22	22		5	0	51
1980	19	27		4	11	39
Federal Aviation Administration 1981		50		50		
Federal Communications Commission 1980	13	45		7	7	28
Federal Trade Commission 1981	25	46		1	7	21
Food and Drug Administration						
1981	31	8	47	1	1	12
1980	38	12	35	2	1	12
1979	36	10	40	2	1	11

Agency					
General Services Administration 1981	75	15			
Securities and Exchange Commission 1981				5	5
*Equal Employment Opportunity Commission 1981		80		20	
*Farm Credit Administration 1981	#2	#1	#4	#5	#3
*Federal Mediation and Conciliation Service 1981		#1	#2		
*National Aeronautics and Space Administration 1981	#1	#3		#4	#2
*Nuclear Regulatory Commission 1981	#2	#3	#1	#5	#4

*Data on percentage distribution not available.

Sources: The Food and Drug Administration keeps detailed log books and calculates the summary statistics. The Environmental Protection Agency does not calculate summary statistics; the data in the table are based on the authors' hand sample. The CPSC data is from a commission memorandum (10 November 1981). The remaining data in the table were gathered in telephone interviews conducted by the authors with FOIA officers and/or their representatives (8-30 November 1982).

Growth rate of FOIA requests / Requesters	Low growth (less than 20 percent)	High growth (20 percent or more)
Mostly industry (70 percent or more)	General Services Administration (4.98 percent)	Commodities Futures Trading Commission (13.79 percent)
		Export-Import Bank (10.23 percent)
	Securities and Exchange Commission (6.04 percent)	Environmental Protection Agency (4.08 percent)
		Food and Drug Administration (0.76 percent)
		Consumer Product Safety Commission (13.79 percent)
		Federal Trade Commission (14.94 percent)
Not mostly industry (less than 70 percent)	Federal Communications Commission (10.97 percent)	Federal Aviation Administration (2.71 percent)

Note: D statistics are in parentheses.

Source: Table 3-3.

Figure 3-4. Cross-Classification of Ten Information-Intensive Agencies, by Growth Rate of Requests and Type of Requesters

what the agency will and will not release. It is not unusual for a requester to ask for everything that is releasable in a particular document. As a result, the agency is required to invoke the trade-secrets exemption very infrequently. Even if some confidential information is requested from a document, the agency can make minor deletions, thereby avoiding a trade-secrets denial.[10] This obviously biases our D statistic downward.

In general, the quantitative and interview data tend to support the claim that guides much of this study—namely, that the Freedom of Information Act, following the 1974 amendments, has been used mostly as a device by the private sector to acquire commercially valuable business information. The economic consequences of this phenomenon are discussed in subsequent chapters of this book after we have taken a closer look at the institutional mechanisms that have grown up in the private sector to facilitate this information transfer.

Composition of Demand for Government-Held Information

This chapter has shown that some federal agencies collect and process significantly more business information than others. It has identified a group of twenty-eight government agencies whose primary activities involve the gathering of economic information. Predictably, the flow of business information into these agencies is greater than in the case of those performing other types of regulatory functions. Their average D statistic was indeed significantly higher than that of the remaining group of government agencies in our study. Of course, business information need not be confidential or sensitive. On the one hand, certain types of information may be released by agencies without producing erosion in the competitive positions of submitting firms. On the other hand, competitive harm may result, in our view, if trade secrets or confidential business information such as contract information, manning tables, and data on marketing strategies are released to the public (see chapter 4).

The aggregated data presented in table 3-1 do not reveal the composition of demand for information collected by any one of these twenty-eight agencies. To determine who is asking for what information requires a disaggregation of these data. Unfortunately, neither federal law nor agency regulations require FOIA officials to gather or report disaggregated statistics of the type needed to conduct such an analysis. However, two of the twenty-eight agencies, the Food and Drug Administration and the Consumer Product Safety Commission, voluntarily calculate a detailed statistical breakdown of FOIA requests by type of record requested, a summary of which appears in tables 3-4 and 3-5.

Data provided by the Food and Drug Administration (table 3-4) reveal that economically valuable information, collected by this agency from private firms, is in demand by information requesters. For example, in 1981, 14 percent of all requests were for records on drugs, 12 percent were for records on medical devices, and 3 percent were for records on foods.

Table 3-4
Analysis of FDA Work Load, by Type of Record Requested, 1979-1981

Type of Record	Percent of Total Requests		
	1979	1980	1981
Third-party requests	37	34	36
Establishment-inspection reports	19	19	20
Drugs	16	17	14
Hearing-clerk/FOIA documents	9	8	10
Medical devices	8	12	12
Foods	4	4	3
Manuals	2	2	2
Other	4	4	3

Source: Food and Drug Administration, FOIA Office, annual data.

Table 3-5
Analysis of CPSC Work Load, by Type of Record Requested, 1981

Type of Record	Percent of Total Requests
Complaints/In-depth investigations	41
Briefing packages/Issue related materials	37
Section 15 files or materials	14
Engineering and health-effects documents	2
Personnel-related materials	2
Contracting documents	1
Miscellaneous	3

Source: U.S. Government memorandum, U.S. Consumer Product Safety Commission, Washington, D.C., 10 November 1981.

As reported by James O'Reilly:

> In carrying out its responsibility to avoid problems in new drugs, new food items, and the growing area of regulated medical device products, the FDA demands and receives formulas, special manufacturing processes, supplies and customer lists and other trade secret information. It also receives a vast quantity of business confidential information, including the business plans of major manufacturing companies for the introduction of new and competitively significant products.[11]

The fact that the level of demand for records on foods, drugs, and medical devices for 1981 was only 29 percent of total demand for FDA information (table 3-4) should not be surprising. This statistic reflects only direct demand and excludes third-party requests that account for 36 percent of total requests in 1981. The game of industrial espionage can be played most effectively under the cloak of anonymity. Therefore, if the intention of an FOIA request is to pirate records on new drugs, foods, or medical devices from an information-submitting rival, then the use of a market intermediary, like FOI Services, Inc., would seem to make good sense. Of course, third-party requests do not necessarily indicate industrial espionage. Clients make use of these market intermediaries for other reasons including the desire on the part of information submitters to monitor the disclosure policies and practices of the Food and Drug Administration by requesting their own records anonymously.

Of the remaining categories of information identified in table 3-4, the most significant would be establishment-inspection reports (20 percent of total information requested in 1981). These detailed reports, generated during the inspections of the facilities of regulated firms, contain a great deal of economically valuable and confidential business information, ranging from blueprints of plant layouts to specific details on innovative production processes.

Finally, two remaining categories are identified in table 3-4 (FDA manuals and hearing-clerk FOIA documents) that seemingly do not involve any confidential business information. Together, however, they account for only 12 percent of total requests in 1981.

A parallel statistical analysis of the composition of demand for information in the files of the Consumer Product Safety Commission (table 3-5) reveals a smaller percentage of requests for trade secrets, narrowly defined. However, there seems to be a very strong demand for types of economically valuable information that extends well beyond the traditional definition of trade secrets.

For example, 14 percent of the sample requests made to the Consumer Product Safety Commission in 1981 were for Section 15 files or materials. Section 15 authorizes the commission to respond to consumer complaints about products by launching extensive investigations, potentially leading to corrective action. It is an enforcement provision, and the law requires that companies cooperate with CPSC investigations by providing detailed information concerning the manufacture and distribution of questionable products. Clearly, some of this information involves trade secrets, narrowly defined. Companies may be required to submit technical documents that reveal, for example, what type of metal is used to produce the particular product in question. However, these investigations also generate information that seemingly falls between the cracks of the trade-secrets exemption of the Freedom of Information Act. In investigating a potentially dangerous product, the Consumer Product Safety Commission obviously is interested in how much of the product was sold, where it was sold, and to whom. As a result, these files collected by the commission contain a wealth of economically valuable information concerning the detailed marketing strategies of companies whose products are under investigation.

The same conclusion can be reached in reference to two other categories of information outlined in table 3-5—namely, engineering and health-effects documents (2 percent of total requests in 1981) and briefing packages/issue related material (37 percent of total requests in 1981). Both trade secrets and other types of economically valuable information are found within these files and documents. The measurement of the health effects of a potentially dangerous product require toxicity tests that may reveal a great deal about the chemical properties of the product. At the same time, however, such a measurement also may involve marketing-strategy data that may be far removed from trade secrets proper. Similarly, when commission staff members put together briefing packages on entire industries, prompted by evidence that new regulations are needed, detailed economic studies of these industries are included. Firm-specific information may be included, ranging once again from technical trade secrets to bits and pieces of information on marketing approaches and strategies.

We take the position (in chapter 5), that the release of personnel-related materials such as manning tables and contracting documents not only can cause competitive harm to a company but also can damage entrepreneurial incentives. Table 3-5 reveals that there is some FOIA demand for personnel-related types of information and contracting documents from the Consumer Product Safety Commission although, admittedly, the levels of demand are relatively low (2 percent and 1 percent respectively of total requests in 1981).

The information category (complaints and in-depth investigations) that attracts the most attention from CPSC information requesters (41 percent of total requests in 1981) has been perhaps the most controversial. The commission takes the position that its complaints files "hardly ever contain trade secrets."[12] The commission's prodisclosure attitude in this regard is colored by its historical self-identification as the "most open and accessible of all the federal agencies."[13] Accordingly, it has regarded its public-protection mission as most achievable with a minimum of information withholding.[14]

Businesses, of course, have legitimate concerns about the negative public-relations and product-image effects of the release of unsubstantiated product complaints that flow into the agency. Such concerns are based on two realities. First, CPSC files contain much information that in no way resembles trade secrets proper; yet, it is evident that the release of this information is capable of producing substantial competitive harm. Second, although the Consumer Product Safety Act, as revised in 1981, does provide businesses some protection against agency disclosure, congressional actions historically have been tempered by the prodisclosure bias of CPSC staff members.[15] O'Reilly argues that the 1981 revision to the act would have succeeded in providing adequate protection against the disclosure of confidential business information from the agency had the CPSC staff not been successful "in obtaining loopholes in the amended Act."[16]

Requesters of Government-Held Information

Certainly, much of the recent debate on the relative social benefits and costs of the Freedom of Information Act has centered on the question of who is taking advantage of the disclosure provisions of the legislation. Proponents of the act argue on the one hand, of course, that the activities of federal agencies now are being monitored by members of the press and public-interest groups in ways not possible before the enabling legislation. On the other hand, opponents argue that press representatives and public-interest spokespersons seldom make FOIA requests. Rather, they point out that the most active requesters of information are corporations or their representatives with motives far removed from those originally envisioned by Congress.

Unfortunately, it is not easy to resolve this debate statistically because federal agencies are not required by Congress to include in their annual reports data on specific information requesters. However, the internal policies or practices of a few agencies do include the disaggregation of such data by information requesters, thereby shedding light on this very important issue. The analysis in this section focuses on the data survey of three important agencies—namely, the Food and Drug Administration, the Environmental Protection Agency, and the Consumer Product Safety Commission.

In the case of the Food and Drug Administration, table 3-3 reveals that from 1979 to 1981, aproximately one-third of all information requests were made by corporations or other private businesses. Of course, this figure understates the extent to which private companies are active in the FOIA market for business information since the use of intermediaries is commonplace. Companies request information indirectly from government agencies through their legal representatives or through so-called FOIA service companies. The latter are significant since their clients are primarily private companies and since they specialize in obtaining information from those agencies that regulate businesses and that are therefore full of business information. These intermediaries are so significant in our estimation that the next section of this chapter is devoted exclusively to an examination of their market activities.

Because of the extensive use of intermediaries by private companies in seeking business information from government agencies, their exclusion from any measure of business demand for FOIA information would distort reality significantly. Given data limitations, we believe that the best measure for estimating the relative importance of private companies as FOIA information requesters is the ratio of requests from corporations, law firms, and FOIA service companies to total requests.

We admit that this measure does tend to overstate the involvement of private businesses as information requesters since not all of the clients of FOIA service companies are businesses and since law firms do request FOIA information for reasons other than the satisfaction of business demand. The ratio is, therefore, more of a barometer or index of business demand than an accurate count. Nevertheless, the ratio is so high in the case of those agencies under consideration that our major conclusions about the dominance of private businesses on the demand side of the market for FOIA information would not be altered if liberal allowances were made for the aforementioned deficiencies of the measure.

For example, in the case of the Food and Drug Administration, 86 percent of total information requests in 1981 emanated from corporations, law firms, and FOIA service companies (table 3-3). This ratio remained remarkably stable from 1979 to 1981 at this very high level (86 percent in 1979, 85 percent in 1980). Table 3-3 also reveals that FOIA service companies alone accounted for nearly one-half of all information requests processed by the Food and Drug Administration in 1981. This did reflect growth in market intermediation, the reasons for which are examined fully in the next section.

Relatively little FDA-held information was requested from 1979 to 1981 by those groups that Congress intended to benefit from the Freedom of Information Act. During this period, only 1 percent of requests per annum emanated from members of the press, and 1 to 2 percent came from public-interest groups.

Although table 3-3 does reveal some minor dissimilarities between the frequency distribution of those requesting information from the Environmental Protection Agency compared to FDA requests, the similarities are more striking. For example, as in the case of the Food and Drug Administration, most requests for EPA information come from private corporations, law firms, and FOIA service companies. The ratio of requests from these sources to total requests averaged 75 percent over the five-year time period from 1976 to 1980. Once again, as in the case of the Food and Drug Administration, this ratio remained quite stable at this high level over this period with the exception of a temporary decline to 66 percent in 1979.

Apparently, public-interest groups seek more EPA than FDA information, relatively speaking, but the difference is not very significant (table 3-3). Members of the news media submit relatively few requests (2 percent of the total or less) to either agency. This statistic is particularly surprising in light of the fact that the press has ranked historically among the most vocal proponents of the prodisclosure aspects of the Freedom of Information Act.

In the case of the Consumer Product Safety Commission, FOIA service companies are inactive (1 percent of total requests in 1981), but corporations and law firms again submit the lion's share of information requests (a combined ratio of 73 percent). In 1981, public-interest groups, and the media together requested only 4 percent of total CPSC information.

Despite these statistics, showing the tremendous participation of corporations and their representatives in the business-information traffic, prodisclosure proponents of the Freedom of Information Act continue to argue that competitive injury is not occurring. For example, Mark Connelly arrives at such a conclusion based on his observation that "not one of the reported reverse FOIA cases concerning affirmative action reports has involved a competitor-requester. All requesters identified in the cases have been either journalists or public interest groups."[17]

The question naturally arises of whether or not the identification of the initial requester is significant. Once that information is released, it is available to others including to competitors and their representatives. The fact remains that the lion's share of information requested from those agencies that regulate businesses is made by corporations or corporate intermediaries. If these requesters are not interested in securing economically valuable

information, the release of which might be harmful to information-submitting firms, then what are they seeking? Chapter 4 sheds some light on this question.

The Cottage Industry

It is likely that the FOIA take-out service of the federal government will remain a growth industry in the 1980s, assuming of course, no significant change in the legislation. Unless the prices charged for an FOIA request is increased substantially (perhaps to reflect the marginal cost of order fulfillment) or the quality of the disclosed information decreases, the ranks of those exercising their congressionally mandated rights will increase steadily. Students will accelerate their use of the federal government to do research for their reports and theses, home-computer owners will order up the data they need for forecasting, and lawyers will continue to use the government to support the discovery phase of their litigations. Finally, businesses will continue to follow the advice of R. Hershey who recommended in the *Harvard Business Review* that every legal means be employed to acquire information about competitors.[18]

Indeed, it is predictable that the level of demand for FOIA information will rise in the 1980s as the result of continued expansion of the marketing activities of FOIA intermediaries, such as FOI Services, Inc., of Rockville, Maryland. FOI Services is the largest member of the cottage industry. Among those served are those who prefer to seek information from federal agencies with anonymity. Located literally within the shadow cast by the U.S. government Health and Human Services complex in Rockville, FOI Services is a market intermediary in the traditional sense of the term. Ample evidence exists that the flow of information between federal agencies, particularly the Food and Drug Administration and information-seeking individuals and organizations, has been spurred by the success of this intermediary in perfecting both market knowledge and mobility.

It is the policy of FOI Services to visit the Food and Drug Administration, the Environmental Protection Agency, and the Federal Trade Commission with regularity (either weekly or daily), the principal purpose being to gather information on data submissions used in the publications of agency logs. These logs, which include detailed subject indexes, are mailed to clients as menus of what is available from the particular agency in question.

Those who defend the Freedom of Information Act and argue against the claim that industrial espionage is rampant usually admit that most FOIA requests emanate from private corporations or their law firms but assert that most requests are merely fishing expeditions. To an extent, this may be true. However, it is hardly descriptive of requests that emanate from clients of FOI Services. Provided with published logs of federal agency information, including detailed subject indexes, these clients know precisely what is available and how to obtain it.

According to FOI Services, the decision to publish the logs of only three federal agencies was market determined.[19] In the case of the Food and Drug Administration, this was a market-sensitive decision by the founders of FOI Services in response to that agency's 1974 announcement that it did not intend to publish its own logs. Also the company's market research determined that the level of demand for information from these agencies was sufficient to justify incurring the cost of log publication; this was simply not the case for other agencies. Requests from clients to obtain information from all other agencies are serviced but without the accompanying logs. Thus, the Consumer Product Safety Commission reported in 1981 that only about 1 percent of its FOIA requests came from FOI Services, while the Food and Drug Administration reported in 1981 that 47 percent of all requests came from this marketing intermediary (table 3-3).

An important distinction seems to emerge here. Insofar as FOI Services has only an informal relationship with federal agencies like the Consumer Product Safety Commission, when information is obtained for clients, the company's services in this regard are clearly demand induced or want satisfying. Clients essentially use the company as a cost-effective and/or confidential way of obtaining information, the nature and location of which they already have identified. However, when clients learn of available information from the publication of the FDA or EPA logs, information not otherwise conveniently available, then these services rendered by the company are demand creating, not demand induced or want satisfying. FOIA requests, in effect, are generated through the effective marketing techniques of publishing information menus.

Although the publications of FOI Services clearly stimulate demand for information submitted to federal agencies, in a sense, the company's activities simplify the tasks of FOIA officials in the three federal agencies referred to earlier. It is easier for agency FOIA officers to deal with an intermediary serving a variety of clients than it would be to deal with each client individually. Since the company understands fully the FOIA procedures and policies in each agency, information requests are processed efficiently with a minimum of delay or confusion. Apparently, agency officials maintain cordial relationships with representatives of FOI Services out of mutual self-interest.

There is a potential administrative problem involved in this practice, however. If a federal agency decides ex post to withdraw or to purge information from documents already released to FOI Services or to any other FOIA intermediary, legally the agency would be on shaky grounds. The company insists that it does not question discretionary decisions made by federal agencies; its policy is to release information that agencies approve for disclosure and not to release what agencies withhold. However, if the company agreed to withhold information in its inventory from further disclosures, this would be a case of voluntary cooperation. Once in the computer inventory of the FOIA intermediary, information is in the private domain and technically open to any third-party request.

The rapid growth of FOIA intermediation is not surprising given the considerable profit potential of such market activity. These companies are able to supply, on a confidential basis, potentially valuable information to clients, obtainable from government agencies at a nominal cost. Since entry barriers are either weak or nonexistent, this cottage industry should grow in the future. Currently, FOI Services visits three agencies on a regular basis. Since we have identified at least twenty-eight agencies that are full of confidential business information, it is likely the FOI Services or a competitor will categorize, catalogue, and market other bodies of government-held information in the future. In turn, the growth of the cottage industry should result in a leveling off of the growth rates of requests experienced by those agencies that specialize in the regulation of businesses since the private service brokers with their information libraries will deflect demand away from the agencies.

Indeed, there is evidence that, in the case of the Food and Drug Administration, this leveling-off process has already occurred. Table 3-1 reveals that the number of information requests made to the administration increased sharply from 2600 in 1974 to 32,852 in 1978, but from 1978 to 1981, requests stabilized at the 32,000-33,000 level. It is not surprising to us that this leveling off of FOIA requests at the Food and Drug Administration happened to coincide with the stepped-up activities of FOI Services in marketing FOIA information from its own computer inventory.

The question arises, of course, why other large FOIA intermediaries seemingly do not exist to compete with FOI Services if, indeed, the business is booming. As indicated, entry barriers in this cottage industry are either weak or nonexistent. Rivals exist, but they do not have office facilities with computer hardware and extensive information inventories.

A company called FACS does provide some competition by servicing clients seeking information held by the Food and Drug Administration. This intermediary specializes in gathering Securities and Exchange Commission (SEC) as well as FDA data. "One of FACS's four staffers . . . spends all of his time at the SEC public-reference room, waiting for instructions by telephone to photocopy documents requested by clients."[20]

The other intermediaries that compete with FOI Services and FACS in the market for government-held information are typically consulting firms that offer clients a wide array of services. For example, some are former FDA employees who know the ropes of the bureaucracy and can advise clients, on how to file new-drug applications and then how to navigate through the maze of agency regulations attempting to expedite the approval procedure in a new-drug application. These consultants will also file FOIA requests for clients, but this is one specialty among many others. We do not predict that these so-called beltway bandits will soon abandon their other services and become FOIA information specialists like FOI Services. However, it is predictable that this side of their business will grow in relative importance unless new legislation strengthens the trade-secrets exemption to the Freedom of Information Act.

The growth of FOIA intermediation is restricted neither, of course, to the seeking of FDA or SEC information nor even to the seeking of business information in general. We seem to have entered an age of paper chasers in which information detectives are available for hire, specializing in tracking down data of any type for clients.[21] In 1980, *Newsweek* reported, for example, that a group of private investigators in Washington, D.C., "wield the Freedom of Information Act the way Mike Hammer uses his fists."[22] This team of detectives, which includes lawyers, journalists, and accountants, has combined the traditional detective skills of being able to locate physically the individuals or companies possessing needed information with the modern skills of being able to "trail paper through the [Washington] bureaucracy," to access data using the Freedom of Information Act, and given the well-publicized information explosion, to find the needle in the proverbial haystack.[23]

It is evident to us that ignorance may be as much a function of too much information as too little. The potential information user may be overwhelmed both by the sheer volume of data available and by the complexities of procedures and regulations on how to access the same. For example, those information seekers who make regular use of the Freedom of Information Act would have to invest considerable research time and effort in keeping track of important developments in legislative, regulatory, and judicial actions relating to the Freedom of Information Act, were it not for another type of market intermediary.

A biweekly newsletter, called *Access Reports*, published in Washington, D.C., is designed to keep readers in tune with current changes and important developments in the Freedom of Information and Privacy Acts. Coverage includes new legislative initiatives, recent judicial actions, and changes in administrative processes and regulations. "Newsworthy developments within every agency of the government and on Capitol Hill are covered completely."[24] These reports are "written and compiled for government officials, corporation executives, attorneys, associations, libraries, news media, law firms and law schools, labor unions, public interest groups, federal courts, publishers, and other organizations or individuals with professional interests in these two vital fields."[25] Included within this list of clientele are those corporations or their representatives who seek business information from federal agencies using the Freedom of Information Act. The benefits are clear. *Access Reports* lowers the transactions costs of securing this information by notifying clients of relevant changes in FOIA procedures and regulations.

The market growth of FOIA intermediaries has been accompanied by the comparable growth of information brokers in the private sector who market research ideas for innovating firms. Historically, U.S. firms invested in R&D for internal use exclusively. However, more and more innovative companies, which tend to generate more new ideas than they can use, have been discovering the external market. Through brokers, they now sell their surplus innovations to other companies.[26]

This type of market activity promotes technological advancement and economic growth since firms that innovate now have this alternate source of revenue. Ideas, not used internally in new-product development, can be sold externally. Either way, revenues needed to cover R&D costs are generated. By way of contrast, when economically valuable ideas are transferred from company to company through FOIA intermediaries, the innovating company receives no compensation. A disincentive to further innovation clearly is created. Chapter 5 addresses this problem in full following a careful examination in chapter 4 of the different types of information that businesses deem to be economically valuable.

Notes

1. Executive Office of the President, Office of Management and Budget, Appendix: *Budget of the United States Government, Fiscal Year 1983* II.1-II.51.

2. Letter of John D. Trezige to Ms. Karen Czapanskiy of the U.S. Department of the Interior, 27 May 1981.

3. Letter of Mr. Stan W. Prochaska to Professor L. Moss, 19 August 1982.

4. Telephone interview, 19 November 1982.

5. Ibid.

6. J.T. Bennett and M.J. Johnson, *The Political Economy of Federal Government Growth* (College Station: Center for Free Enterprise/Texas A&M University, 1981).

7. Ibid.

8. Department of Justice Memo to Robert L. Saloschin from Edward D. Jones III regarding Analysis of the Freedom of Information Act (FOIA) Cost, 17 July 1979.

9. R.S. Edwards, "The Rationale of Cost Accounting," in *L.S.E. Essays on Cost*, eds. J.M. Buchanan and G.F. Thirlby (London: Weidenfeld & Nicolson, 1973).

10. Telephone conversation, Gerald H. Deighton, director FOIA Office, FDA, 12 January 1983.

11. See James T. O'Reilly, *Federal Information Disclosure: Procedures, Forms and the Law*, vol. 1 (Colorado Springs: Shepard's, 1982), pp. 14-52. Also see 21 U.S.C. § 355, § 344 and 21 U.S.C. § 360 (k), § 510(k) of the Food, Drug and Cosmetic Act.

12. Telephone interview with Todd Stevenson, FOIA Officer, U.S. Consumer Product Safety Commission, 18 November 1982.

13. Remarks of General Counsel Andrew Krulwich, Consumer Product Safety Commission, at Product Safety Conference, Washington, D.C. (5 June 1979).

14. See O'Reilly, *Federal Information Disclosure*, pp. 14-67.

15. 15 U.S.C.P. § 2055(b)(1). See revisions, Pub. L. No. 97-35, 95 Stat. 703 (1981).

16. O'Reilly, *Federal Information Disclosure*, pp. 14-69.

17. See M.Q. Connelly, "Secrets and Smokescreens: A Legal and Economic Analysis of Government Disclosures of Business Data," *Wisconsin Law Review* 1981 (1981):269.

18. R. Hershey, "Commercial Intelligence on a Shoestring," *Harvard Business Review* 58, September/October 1980, pp. 22-30.

19. Interviews with FOI Services, Inc., staff members, Rockville, Maryland, 20 August 1980.

20. Lee Smith, "Washington's New Sleuths," *Dun's Review*, October 1976, pp. 70-72.

21. See "The Paper Chasers," *Newsweek*, 21 April 1980, p. 104.

22. Ibid.

23. Ibid.

24. Blanche Schiff, marketing director, *Access Reports: A Bi-Weekly Newsletter on Freedom of Information and Privacy* (Washington, D.C.: Plus Publications, Inc., 1981). Pamphlet.

25. Ibid.

26. See Liz Roman Gallese, "Ideas for Sales: More Firms Buy, Sell the Fruits of the Research to and from Outsiders," *Wall Street Journal*, 18 February 1976; and Gail Bronson, "PRI Serves as Broker for Inventors, Firms Seeking Innovation," *Wall Street Journal*, 7 August 1979.

4

Confidential Business Information: What Information Do Businesses Wish to Keep from Being Disclosed?

In chapter 3, we established that, while the rate of FOIA requests was increasing rapidly among many government agencies over the period, it was increasing most quickly for those regulatory agencies that interact on a regular basis with firms in the economy. In this chapter, we survey the terrain of legal debate about the meaning and significance of disclosure practices under the trade-secrets exemption in order to identify categories of information that business submitters do not wish government to make public.

According to the *Restatement of Torts*, common law takes a broad view of what constitutes trade secrets:

> A trade secret may reside in any formula, pattern, device, or compilation of information which is used in one's business, and which gives him an opportunity to obtain an advantage over competitors who do not know or use it. It may be a formula for a chemical compound, a process of manufacturing, treating or preserving materials, a pattern for a machine or other device, or a list of customers.[1]

While we shall have more to say about the *Restatement* definition in chapter 5, for our purpose here we distinguish among trade secrets narrowly defined, compilations of test data, contract information and supporting materials, manning tables and related equal-employment-opportunity data, and information about marketing strategies. We shall proceed by briefly describing each category of information, and then we sketch some of the legal debates that have surrounded the threatened disclosure of these categories of business information.

Trade Secrets Narrowly Defined

Two government agencies that are likely to acquire a large volume of trade secrets, properly speaking, are the Environmental Protection Agency and the Food and Drug Administration. These agencies are especially privy to technological and chemical reports in which company trade secrets relating to process technologies and chemical formulas are revealed. Competing firms are likely to try to obtain from the government information they cannot get from a detailed examination of the product in the market or from publicly available sources. For example, firm A may learn about the secret catalysts and industrial processes of firm B from perusing the documents submitted to an agency for the purpose of aiding that agency in its regulatory functions. Thus, when the Food and Drug Administration urged that all food ingredients, including those present in miniscule amounts, be posted on any product, Kohnstamm, a food-manufacturing firm, objected. In its segment of the food industry, flavor formulas are principal assets, and Kohnstamm objected to making its carefully guarded assets public knowledge.[2]

The concerns of trade-secret owners regarding agency disclosure of this company's secrets have been articulated forcefully by Shaw Mudge. Mudge and his family own a firm that manufactures deodorizers for medical equipment and cosmetic products. According to Mudge, the Food and Drug Administration has been insensitive to the property rights of trade-secret owners.[3] The disclosure of Mudge's secret formulas or his methods of manufacture to his competitors would lower the market value of his firm significantly, and because of this, he is reluctant to engage in contract work with the government.[4]

As a matter of historical record, the Food and Drug Administration was the first federal agency to have a detailed set of disclosure rules and regulations, articulating agency policy on all aspects of information disclosure.[5] As we shall discuss in chapter 7, new-drug applications, not yet reviewed and approved, are held in strict secrecy by the agency. However, on other matters, this agency is less committed to keeping secrets. Indeed, the agency has acted somewhat arbitrarily in deciding what information was to be kept from disclosure and what information was to enter the public domain. The agency even left to its own judgment the decision as to when an information submitter would be informed of an FOIA disclosure.[6] In 1975, the Pharmaceutical Manufacturers Association tried unsuccessfully to make the Food and Drug Administration more responsive to the needs of the pharmaceutical industry.[7] According to James O'Reilly, after the Food and Drug Administration won this battle, the agency then structured the operation of its disclosure system to speed up request clearance.[8]

The Food and Drug Administration, which as we have seen in chapter 3 is besieged constantly with FOIA requests, does not make a regular practice of notifying information submitters that their files were sent to third parties.[9] This may be the reason why, in 1980, Procter & Gamble lost a valuable trade secret. Under FDA rules for chemical premanufacturing notification, Procter & Gamble submitted a trade-secret formula about an odor-masking agent it had discovered and used in the manufacture of sterilized drape and gown (medical) products. In its submissions to the Division of Surgical and Rehabilitation Devices of the Food and Drug Administration, Procter &

Gamble underscored the fact that what it was submitting constituted a trade secret. It also provided the agency with an abridged copy of the same report for public review, thereby hoping to identify for the Food and Drug Administration exactly what sections of the first report Procter & Gamble considered to be commercially valuable. Shortly thereafter, a mistake was made and both copies of the Procter & Gamble reports were mailed to a competitor.[10]

Is this an isolated incident, or does this agency regularly give out trade secrets in the narrow sense of the term? In the case of food and feed additives, the answer is yes because disclosure is mandated by law.[11] A food processor may retain a secret manufacturing process but cannot produce a food product containing secret ingredients. Recently, the agency has been trying to expand labeling disclosure to include cosmetics as well. Here, the agency has met with stiff opposition from the cosmetic firms, and the courts have shown much sensitivity to the concerns of the cosmetic manufacturers. The debate is still alive.[12]

In general, government agencies are not naive about their role in encouraging the diffusion of trade secrets. At the Environmental Protection Agency, for example, documents pertaining to highly sensitive business information are locked in files in a designated room and must be logged in and out by authorized agency personnel like agency scientists.[13] This agency's concern with protecting the trade secrets of the firms submitting technical information began when Polaroid Corporation refused to provide the Environmental Protection Agency with technical information about the chemicals Polaroid used in its film process. That information was the key to unlocking the secret process by which Polaroid keeps the various self-developing color chemicals separated prior to taking the instant photographs. Polaroid's challenge to the Environmental Protection Agency's authority encouraged the agency to work with the company to set up a top-security procedure that would permit the Environmental Protection Agency to acquire the information it needed while at the same time guarding the exclusivity of Polaroid's intellectual property and preventing that information from being requested by competing firms.[14]

Similarly, this agency receives information about the secret ingredients in pesticides or those proposed for use in new chemical mixtures.[15] While the Environmental Protection Agency currently has one of the most comprehensive sets of regulations among all government agencies and has been given high marks for maintaining the confidential status of secret chemical mixtures and the like, information does leak out of that agency. The release of Monsanto's secret formula Roundup is a case in point.[16]

The Health Industry Manufacturers Association (HIMA) informed Congress of several incidents involving the disclosure of their members' trade secrets. In one case, the firm had a "novel process for detecting and controlling particulate matter."[17] The Food and Drug Administration described this process in an establishment-inspection report, and the agency released it to a competitor in response to an FOIA request. Another case involved a firm whose formulas, manufacturing process, and the names of its vendors were released when a request was made for only a summary of an FDA decision.[18]

In many instances, the federal courts have protected businesses against agency disclosure. In 1978, a case involving the Federal Trade Commission's subpoenae of secret processes and devices from a private firm was resolved in favor of the trade-secret owner. According to O'Reilly, the court displayed "genuine respect for the rights of the trade secret owners."[19] In fact, most of the court cases involving firms trying to determine the status of information in the hands of government agencies have not involved trade secrets in the narrow sense of secret formulas and recipes. Most of the court cases have involved information that is more commercial than trade secret in the language of the trade-secrets exemption of the Freedom of Information Act. While the courts have recognized that the act is a disclosure statute, they have protected marketing, accounting, and profit data for those firms able to bring legal action in federal courts.[20]

Compilations of Test Data

The Environmental Protection Agency, along with several other agencies, makes it a regular practice to inform information submitters when a request has come in under the Freedom of Information Act for test data that they had submitted originally.[21] As a result of this practice, a number of pesticide-chemical makers learned about requests made for their test data on chemical pesticides they manufacture. With regard to test data in the Supreme Court case of *Chevron* v. *Costle*, Chevron argued that the requester was Chevron's competitor and that it was unfair that a competitor should have the "benefit of Chevron's costly and time consuming research at the cost of a postage stamp."[22] In one case involving thirty-five pre-manufacturing notices that DuPont had sent the Environmental Protection Agency, DuPont claimed that all thirty-five contained trade secrets, and DuPont was willing to substantiate this claim in every case.[23]

In 1980, twelve pesticide-chemical makers petitioned the Supreme Court to consider the argument that the disclosure of their trade secrets under the 1978 amendments to the Federal Insecticide, Fungicide, and Rodenticide Act violated the Fifth Amendment to the Constitution.[24] The disclosure of this information would, in the opinion of the pesticide makers, constitute a taking of their property without due process of the law—that is, in violation of their constitutional rights. The agency found itself torn between its commitment to one manufacturer not to disclose information that they considered commercially harmful and the Toxic Substance Control Act that states the public has a right to know the identity of chemical substances in the environment.[25]

A mistake also occurred in the handling of proprietary information submitted by Metropak Company to a plant inspector from the Office of Safety and Health Administration. Metropak was investigated for possible noise-standard violations but refused to allow the plant inspector into the facility because the company's trade secrets might be jeopardized. Plant inspectors often draw sketches and make references to machinery, which could communicate proprietary information to competitors. The judge ordered Metropak to allow the inspector into the plant but required the inspector not to make his report public. As fate would have it, the inspector sent a second copy of this report to his supervisor who did not know about the judge's restrictions. The supervisor showed it to Metropak's competitor in order to get the competitor to install similar equipment as Metropak had done.[26]

Information about applied technology of industrial plants could be termed a trade secret in the narrowest sense of the term and analogous to a chemical formula or mixture of ingredients. This is especially true when the information is a technological procedure consisting of a sequence of operations. A number of cases claim that information submitted to government agencies for seemingly unrelated purposes like a contract bid contains this information about technological procedures. Agency practice regarding the disclosure of contract information varies from one agency to the next. In recent years there has been a concerted effort, especially on the part of the Office of Management and Budget, both to standardize agency contract-disclosure practices and to provide for the protection of proprietary information. A number of outside private-sector organizations like the Intellectual Property Owner's Association (Washington, D.C.) also are advocating reforms in this area.[27]

Test information usually is submitted to government agencies on a regular basis, in a standard format, and subject to well-established reporting requirements. This makes the data extremely valuable to competitors since the otherwise difficult job of comparing and making sense of the measurement categories is standardized largely by government reporting requirements.[28] In a controversial incident, Sikorsky Company withdrew its bid to supply the Coast Guard with S-76 Spirit helicopters.[29] The reason for Sikorsky's volte face was its inability to secure a promise from the Department of Transportation that proprietary data about the S-76 helicopter would not be relinquished to Sikorsky's competitors. The Department of Transportation asserted that it would handle any FOIA requests in the usual way, thereby suggesting that the technical details of the S-76 helicopters would be made available to other bidders. Sikorsky withdrew the contract offer, and a French firm subsequently won the contract.[30] While Russell B. Stevenson, Jr.

does not take Sikorsky's stated reason for withdrawing to be the full story (and attributes Sikorsky's decision to be much more complex than simply a fear of losing information), O'Reilly presented this as a classic example of FOIA disclosure practices' interfering with the ordinary market process.[31]

In our research involving interviews with thirteen high-technology firms from the Boston/Route 128 industrial complex, several firms did cite the fear of losing proprietary technical information as a primary factor in their decisions not to compete for government-contract work.[32] Our research tends to support O'Reilly's interpretation of the Sikorsky episode and suggests that the taxpayer may be paying more for government-procured supplies precisely because the entrepreneurially owned firms cannot be assured of maintaining their proprietary information, especially when it is in the form of compilations of technical information submitted in contract negotiations.

There is no doubt that companies can use the Freedom of Information Act as an easy take-out service for acquiring technical and scientific data produced by other firms. In 1979, we made the acquaintance of a librarian from a major consumer-products company whose main activity was requesting test data submitted by other competing companies to government agencies. It is not known how many companies find it cost effective to retain surveillance personnel now that FOIA intermediaries are willing and able to perform such services for a fee. As indicated in chapter 3, consultant R. Hershey, writing in the influential *Harvard Business Review*, advised his readers to establish a commercial intelligence department "on a shoe string" by using the Freedom of Information Act to acquire information.[33] Is this now established management practice?

Gilson surveyed a number of reverse-FOIA suits in which the disclosure of technical information was at stake.[34] We already have mentioned *Chevron Chemical Co.* v. *Costle* in which the disclosure of information about fungicides and insecticides was the issue.[35] Chevron objected to the distribution of its toxicity studies to other free-riding firms in the industry. In *Westinghouse Electric Corporation* v. *United States Nuclear Regulatory Commission*, Westinghouse wished to set aside an agency rule that jeopardized its proprietary data relating to technical information about its steam-generating systems.[36] While at the time of the suit nobody had requested the information, the Nuclear Regulatory Commission was promoting its availability, and Westinghouse objected.[37]

We may also consider *GTE Sylvania Inc.* v. *Consumer Product Safety Commission* and another case, *Pierce & Stevens Chemical Corporation* v. *Consumer Product Safety Commission*.[38] In the first case, GTE Sylvania tried to stop the Consumer Product Safety Commission from disclosing accident testing data, and in the second case, Pierce & Stevens tried and succeeded in preventing the release of inspector reports that had come in to the

Consumer Product Safety Commission's hands from the Food and Drug Administration. In both cases, the companies complained of a threatened loss of their trade secrets if disclosure occurred.[39] Other court cases involving Firestone Tire and Rubber Co., Bristol Myers & Co., Johnson Products, and Sterling Drug Co., also revolved around the disclosure of test data by certain government agencies.[40]

Finally, consider the testimony of the National Meat Association before the government subcommittee concerning disclosures made by the Department of Agriculture. Meat manufacturers are required to provide weekly reports to the Department of Agriculture that "contain detailed slaughter and production figures."[41] In 1978, an FOIA request was made for this information on a plant-by-plant basis. Without ever contacting the manufacturers in the trade association, a decision was made to release all but the statistics for the most recent twelve months.

Industry reaction was overwhelmingly negative. Eighty letters were sent to the Department of Agriculture explaining the likely competitive harm that would accompany release of inspection reports. One letter expressed disbelief because "we have been repeatedly assured by the USDA in the past that these figures would all be held in the strictest confidence."[42]

How widespread is this fear about the loss of trade secrets and compilations of data once information is in the files of the government agency? Most FOIA scholars agree this fear exists and is deeply ingrained among representatives of the business sector (see chapter 7). Even Stevenson, whose sympathies lie with continued and increased disclosure of nontechnical categories of business information, especially among larger publicly owned corporations, agrees that "the perceptual problem [of the disclosure of business secrets through the operation of the Freedom of Information Act] is real and appears to generate unnecessary friction in the relationship between government and business."[43] During our interviews in the pharmaceutical and chemical industries, we detected the same widespread attitude. Indeed, among some managers, the fear of losing proprietary data was so strong that submitting business information to government was considered analogous to publishing the results.[44]

Consider a recent situation confronting the Dow Corning Company, a company specializing in silicones. Dow imported raw material from foreign nations and was entitled to duty drawback compensation (that is, a subsidy) from the government for tariff duties it paid on these imports. However, the application for the drawback payment required a detailed accounting of the raw materials used. Dow Corning considered this information to be confidential and wanted assurances from the Department of Commerce that its confidentiality would be protected. When such assurances were not given to Dow Corning's satisfaction, no application was made.[45]

While the fear of disclosure exists and is widespread, to what extent is that fear based on a few isolated incidents unrelated to the mass of carefully managed FOIA requests handled each day by the government? We cannot attempt to answer that question fully since statistical estimates of trade secrets disclosed do not exist. Rather, we shall relate a significant incident involving the unintended disclosure of a compilation of information that in its simplicity allows us to arrive at a judgment likely to carry over into other chapters of this book. This incident was reported in the *Wall Street Journal* and involved a blood-valve maker who requested data about another blood-valve maker's use of formaldehyde.[46] The agency decision maker reasoned that, since all the blood-valve manufacturers use formaldehyde, there was no harm in showing one manufacturer the other's report. Apparently, the combinations of different times and temperatures at which the valves are cured as part of the technological process were confidential business information. These combinations cannot be discerned easily by examining the finished product or by analyzing the materials out of which the valves are made. For a nominal sum (the proverbial postage stamp), one firm was able to gain valuable commercial information at the expense of the other.[47]

This incident highlights in what way the administrative procedures followed by the Food and Drug Administration promote the disclosure of proprietary information. For one thing, agency personnel with little knowledge about the industry are in the sensitive position of deciding what falls within the trade-secrets exemption. This is not a wise assignment of responsibility. In many cases, the agency person (as well meaning as he or she might be) has little technical training and certainly no financial stake in avoiding erroneous disclosure. On the one hand, to refuse disclosure when it is warranted carries with it great penalties including dismissal and suspension, and the inevitable turmoil that accompanies a controversial decision against powerful adversaries of the agency in press or public advocacy groups.[48] On the other hand, to disclose confidential information carries with it little or no penalty since such an agency person's behavior would probably not be termed arbitrary and capricious under the Administrative Procedure Act.

Moreover, the likelihood of conviction under the Trade Secrets Act is not great. Indeed it does not seem as if anyone has been prosecuted under this act.[49] The submitter has no clear private right to use this criminal law in a civil law suit challenging an agency's disclosure. The pattern of disclosure practice that emerges from an arrangement with antisecrecy incentives such as is practiced by the Food and Drug Administration (and other agencies as well) provides us with a basis for agreeing with private-sector managers that their firm's confidential information is in jeopardy once it enters the files of government agencies. Our judgment is not based on paranoia or unscholarly extrapolation from a few carefully selected horror stories; rather, we arrive at it by an examination of what we perceive to be the incentives and administrative procedures that exist within large government agencies. Those incentives and procedures promote disclosure: "When in doubt, give it out" was the mantra one government employee recited to the authors of this book when he was queried about the disclosure policies of his agency.[50]

Contract Information and Supporting Documentation

We have mentioned the Sikorsky helicopter case in reference to a situation where contract information was declared by the submitting firm to constitute a trade secret but would not be protected by a government agency. Also, in the previous section we examined compilations of information. According to the *Restatement of Torts* that takes a broad view of trade secrets, compilations of information also come under the heading of trade secrets. In complicated technical contracts, it is not unusual for volumes of compiled information to accompany the contracting process. In *Burroughs Corp.* v. *Schlesinger*, a contract bidder brought suit to prevent disclosure of information in a bid.[51] This reverse-FOIA suit, like many others, involved not only scientific and technical data but also other categories of business information. After the 1979 *Chrysler* decision, it is clear that those seeking to win government contracts cannot count on receiving protection from government agencies. A likely result is that they must increase the price of the project (their offer price) in order to capture the value of the information. The other alternative would be to withdraw from the contract process altogether, as the Mudge family and Sikorsky have done.

The incentives to disclosure set into motion a process that seeks to reduce exposure of confidential information at the lowest cost. Burt Braverman, the lawyer who represented Chrysler in the landmark Supreme Court case, urges his clients, "Do not give confidential business information to the Federal Government agencies if at all possible, and if you do, take precautions to prevent it from being disclosed."[52] The precautions Braverman recommends include the following:

1. Avoid voluntary data submissions to the government and in other cases require a government subpoena for requested information.
2. Furnish inspection information on company premises only, and do not let it leave those premises.
3. Arrange for the immediate return of sensitive information.
4. If all else fails, stop doing business with the government if you cannot be assured of confidential treatment of sensitive information.[53]

Contracts often specify cost breakdowns and reveal original methods of dividing and monitoring work activity. Thus, when a third-party information seeker requested that the Department of Defense send him the audit reports and related memoranda of Lockheed Corporation, revealing what costs were allowed on government contracts and so on, Lockheed objected.[54] Lockheed argued that disclosure would reveal to competitors, among other things, their labor costs and profit rate. It is also possible that disclosure would reveal a cost-accounting scheme that Lockheed pioneered in defense contract work, and Lockheed did not wish to see that scheme copied by others.

In a case decided in 1979, Gulf and Western Industries Inc., protested that its break-even-point calculation was proprietary and not to be disclosed.[55] Break-even analysis determines at what rate of production a plant operation becomes economical. A large number of disclosure cases have involved firms trying to prevent the disclosure of their overhead and operating costs like what is presented in break-even analysis reports. As one analyst from the specialty-chemical industry stated, "There are many pieces of information such as plant capacity, production rates and certain process operating parameters, which are neither patentable nor within the traditional definition of trade secret, but which we consider very confidential."[56] The disclosure of accounting information might also inform competitors about novel methods of metering work performance and monitoring overall industrial performance.

Thus, contract-bidding procedures and procurement practices of government agencies solicit from private-sector firms a blend of financial and commercial information that business firms prefer to keep confidential. A thorough survey of the economic value of information at each step of the way would take us beyond the scope of this book but would constitute an interesting research project in and of itself. We shall return in chapter 5 to the economic effects of the disclosure of contract information in a variety of situations.

Manning Tables and Related Equal-Employment-Opportunity Data

Consider the following list of reverse-FOIA cases[57]:

Chrysler Corp. v. *Schlesinger*

Westinghouse Electric Corporation v. *Schlesinger*

Metropolitan Life Insurance Corp. v. *Usery (National Organization for Women)*

Rubbermaid Inc. v. *Kleppe*

Babcock & Wilcox Co. v. *Rumsfeld*

Hughes Aircraft Co. v. *Dunlop*

General Dynamics v. *Dunlop*

Holiday Inns v. *Kleppe*

In each of these cases, a firm was trying to stop a government agency from mailing out its affirmative-action plans that were submitted in compliance with federal contract requirements. These affirmative-action plans outline the racial and sex distributions of the existing work force by job category and offer projections about how this composition is expected to improve by better reflecting the composition of the work force in the surrounding population.

In many of these cases, the requesting party was a public-interest group, perhaps seeking to expose the unsatisfactory hiring and/or recruiting record of the corporation trying to prevent disclosure. In addition to the negative public-relations image of the firm with a poor equal-opportunity record, disgruntled employees might use this data to support their damage suits. This occurred when the Federal Trade Commission released data on the Ward's Cove Packing Company. This both jeopardized the financial interests of the corporation and encouraged future employees to follow similar legal remedies. It is not surprising, then, that private companies have resisted the dissemination of their manning tables.

What does strain the credulity of a number of Washington attorneys whom we interviewed is the claim by corporations that the revelation of the employment data seriously jeopardizes companies' proprietary information.[58] Are not these businesses simply using the cry of lost proprietary information to conceal their greater concern about the embarrassment that accompanies a poor equal-opportunity record?

It is difficult to prove or disprove claims about a corporation's motives. For one thing, a corporation is a fictitious entity made up of managers, technicians, stockholders, and workers who are not always pursuing the same objectives for precisely the same reasons.[59] Second, corporate attorneys usually are not paid to test legal or economic principles before the Supreme Court. Their role is more practical and results oriented. No doubt the flag of lost trade secrets will be raised by attorneys if that by itself is adequate to prevent the release of any data that might for some other reason jeopardize the financial position of the company. Equal-employment-opportunity data may very well be a case in point.[60]

Is there any merit at all to the argument that manning tables and the rest of equal-opportunity data contain information that might reasonably constitute commercially valuable information? Our answer to this question is yes. Manning tables and the projections of those tables offer competitors essential clues about the future expansion and marketing strategies of the firm in question. If, for example, Sears Roebuck, after investing resources in market research, discovers that a certain suburb around Baltimore is a promising location for a new sales outlet, it obviously would not be to Sears's advantage to have its competitors discover this.

In another case, where a manufacturing plant is either under construction or in the process of expanding, competing firms, by acquiring employment data, can deduce what types of products may be available and what additional capacity the first plant is likely to put into place. It may even be possible for a firm to learn from a comparison of competitors' employment data the production level at which it becomes economical to switch from a labor-intensive technique to a capital-intensive technique. This is one of the issues raised by Chrysler in its effort to prevent the government from releasing its equal-opportunity data.[61]

To keen observers of industry practice, employment data do provide information of value to competing firms in an industry. Thus, it is reasonable to infer that, even in the absence of the current rash of discrimination employment cases, firms would have an economic incentive not to have their employment data disclosed to competitors and probably would sue not to have this information made public. In several instances, the courts have agreed with businesses that detailed employment statistics disclose both plant staffing and the type of equipment that is being used.

Information of this type may not be a trade secret according to the *Restatement of Torts* definition. Information about an ephemeral event like the composition of the workforce is not a trade secret properly speaking.[62] Still, ephermeral or not, it is understandable why one firm would wish to keep another firm from finding out about it. Speed and surprise are often important elements in any successful strategic plan, and a company may be substantially injured by competition if this information is disclosed earlier than it otherwise would have been in the absence of the Freedom of Information Act.

Information about Marketing Opportunities

The *Restatement of Torts* includes customer lists under the heading trade secrets along with trade secrets in the narrow sense of recipes and formulas and in the broader form of test data and other scientific information. Companies will go to great lengths trying to protect the disclosure of their customer lists. Thus, in 1976, Continental Oil sued and succeeded in stopping the Federal Power Commission from disclosing Continental's sales data.[63] More recently, the Chicago Board of Trade, Braintree Electronics, and Audio Technical Services argued against the disclosure of their customer lists by the Commodities Futures Trading Commission, the Department of Energy, and the Department of Army, respectively.[64]

Valuable marketing information can take other forms besides customer lists. Chessie System was able to acquire freight-car purchase and retirement information from the Interstate Commerce Commission. In this way Chessie could infer the competitive capacity and age distribution of the rolling stock of its principal rail competitors.[65] In separate cases, Union Oil and Superior Oil sued the Federal Power Commission and the Federal Energy Regulatory Commission not to disclose their natural-gas-reserve holdings.[66] Again, these companies were concerned that their proprietary information would fall into the hands of rival natural-gas-supplying firms who might calculate more accurately about the future abilities of these firms to meet their customers' requirements.

Several cases have involved firms trying to keep the government from disclosing their pricing schemes. Honeywell Information Systems, for example, insisted the the National Atmospheric and Space Administration not disclose the component-by-component pricing schedules that Honeywell submitted in a contract bid.[67] Pricing data including merchandising patterns and plans were at issue when Thrifty Drug Co. enjoined the Federal Trade Commission from disclosing facts about their company in 1976. Particular financial information like levels of profit on particular business activities was the principal issue in the landmark *National Parks* case where the park concession owners did not want their profits to be made public.[68] In other cases, Parkridge Hospital opposed the disclosure of financial information submitted to Blue Cross, and Sterling Drug opposed the disclosure of profit-and-loss data submitted to the Federal Trade Commission.[69] In chapter 5, we shall examine the economic effects of the disclosure of this sort of information, but here our point is simply that financial information about their particular product lines is information businesses care not to have fall into the hands of their competitors because they recognize that this information will harm them competitively. A number of cases have involved firms trying to prevent disclosure of the prices they pay for contracted goods. Again, information about prices paid, pricing formulas used, and the profit margins recorded on specific business operations are considered to highly confidential business information.[70] Businesses often develop contingency marketing plans that they also wish to keep strictly confidential. That is why, in 1975, National Airlines sued the Civil Aeronautics Board from disclosing National's contingency plans for business operations.[71]

Customer lists and related marketing information were at the heart of the 1977-1980 controversy about the release of commercial information contained in shipper's export declarations. We conclude this chapter with a careful study of that episode because it reveals how, especially in the area of marketing information, the impact of disclosure can extend far beyond the significance of the isolated value of bits and pieces of information whose disclosure is often the focus of the courtroom debates surveyed here. An appreciation of this last category of business information points the way toward a better understanding of the impact disclosure can have on the entrepreneurial nature of the market process.

Shippers' Export Declarations: A Case Study

An excellent example of the value that firms place on commercial information and the reluctance of government to arrive at categorical definitions of proprietary information was illustrated by the controversy leading up to the congressional passage of a "Bill to Protect the Confidentiality of Shippers' Export Declarations, and to Standardize Export Data Submissions and Disclosure Requirements" from 1977 to 1980.[72]

Three export documents formed the basis of this dispute: (1) the outward foreign manifest, (2) the bill of lading, and (3) the shippers' export declaration. U.S. shipping code (46 U.S.C. 91) stipulated that all vessels transporting goods to foreign ports must file an outward foreign manifest with U.S. Customs. This form was general in nature and did not divulge the name and address of the shipper. Similarly, U.S. shipping code (46 U.S.C. 193) required the filing of a bill of lading that listed specific information on transportation, including the name of the shipper and consignee.[73]

Finally, shippers' export-declaration forms were required by the Department of Commerce for exports to all foreign countries, Puerto Rico, and some other territories of the United States for goods valued in excess of $500.00. These documents number 9 million per year and are collected and studied by the Customs Service to enforce the Export Administration Act and as a statistical document for preparing the merchandise trade balance of the United States.[74] While some of the information provided on a shippers' export declaration was identical to that required on the outward foreign manifest and the bill of lading, it was a more-detailed document that truly gave a profile of the product being exported.

The U.S. government has collected information on exported goods and services since 1799. Shippers' export declarations were introduced as a statistical data source in 1915.[75] From the beginning, individual shippers' export declarations were protected from public disclosure (except in a few cases where national interests were involved). Congress realized that the release of detailed information in a shippers' export declaration might result in competitive harm to companies supplying such information. Moreover, such a release could dampen the willingness of the business community to provide such information.[76]

Customs' practice of keeping shippers' export declarations as confidential information was challenged by a trade-journal publisher in 1977.[77]

Following the 1974 amendments to the Freedom of Information Act, Secretary of the Treasury William Simon permitted greater access to export information by "accredited representatives of the U.S. press."[78] Permission was granted to examine outward foreign manifests and to copy from them for publication: the general cargo characteristics, the ship's country of destination, the quantity or value (but not both) of the cargo, the vessel name, and the shipper's (that is, exporter's) name where shown and provided the shipper did not object to his name being published. However, permission was granted neither to inspect shippers' export declarations nor specifically to inspect bills of lading. Problems arose because of the general (but not universal) practice by shippers to attach their bills of lading to the outward foreign manifest. Thus, each of these bills of lading contained the name of the shipper—a bit of information not required in the outward foreign manifest.

In an effort to make its published export and import information more comprehensive and consistent, Twin Coasts Newspaper Company, publisher of the *Journal of Commerce*, petitioned customs to require that all exporters file a bill of lading. Lacking the statutory power to make such a change, the request was refused.[79] With this avenue closed, Twin Coasts Newspaper Company filed suit against both the U.S. Department of Commerce and the U.S. Customs Service to gain access to shippers' export declarations, citing their rights under the Freedom of Information Act. Twin Coasts argued that the Export Administration Act did not provide statutory protection for shippers' export declarations under exemption (b)(3) of the Freedom of Information Act. Moreover, Twin Coasts argued that, since the information it desired was, for the most part already in the public domain, it was not covered by the trade-secrets exemption.[80]

Congress was concerned with the potential competitive harm that the release of shippers' export declarations might produce. On September 26, 1979, Congress passed an amendment to the Export Administration Act that the president signed into law three days later. The act required confidential treatment of shippers' export declarations only until 30 June 1980.[81] Another act of Congress would be required to protect their disclosure beyond that date. This temporarily took away the legal basis for the Twin Coasts suit. In the interim, new legislation, weighing the cost and benefits of disclosure, was to be passed. Should legislation not be passed, this information could be protected only under the trade-secrets exemption of the Freedom of Information Act. As we argued in the section "Compilations of Test Data," there was a strong presumption that much of that information, under these circumstances, would be given out.

In May 1980, Congress passed S. 2419 that provided complete and unequivocal protection for shippers' export declarations and that codified and standardized procedures for export documentation. Essentially, the bill required the shipper's name and address to be added to the outward foreign manifest but carried an opt-out provision that, when renewed biennially, would prevent the disclosure thereof. S. 2419 required that six pieces of information be made publicly available: (1) the name and address of the shipper, (2) the general cargo characteristics, (3) the number of packages and gross weight, (4) the name of the vessel, (5) the port of exit, and (6) the port of destination.

The shippers' export-declaration controversy and its surrounding testimony provided an interesting example of businesses' attempt to protect what they perceived to be proprietary information. The information on a shippers' export declaration was not scientific in nature. It contained no research information or test data. In many cases, it was information already in the public domain. The essential point was that the value of this information could not be determined from the binary consideration of whether any one piece of information or pieces of information were available or not available but in the incremental consideration pertaining to the cost associated with its duplication. Most information is obtainable if one were willing to pay a high enough cost for its compilation.[82]

What appears in a shippers' export declaration are the specific details of an export transaction. This information goes beyond what can be found on an outward foreign manifest. More specifically, a shippers' export declaration contains an exact description of the exported cargo—not in general terms but in terms specific enough to be classified in Schedule B (*The Statistical Classification for Merchandise Exported from the United States*). Horsepower specifications, fiber composition, and chemical inputs are examples of the information furnished by such reporting; in addition, a firm must report the net quantity for each type of good exported. The two types of information combined not only communicate the preferences of the foreign buyers but also offer clues about the strength and composition of their demand. The shippers' export declaration also provides financial information about the f.a.s. (free alongside ship) value of the exported goods. Whereas outward foreign manifests can report any value (for example, insurance and f.o.b.), the shippers' export declaration requires that the stated price include only the cost of the item and transport cost to the port of debarkation. Marketing data also are contained in the shippers' export declaration. The declaration reveals the ultimate consignee and place and country of ultimate destination, while the outward foreign manifest requires that the port of unloading be reported, which may not be the ultimate destination of the exported goods. Finally, the shippers' export declaration states the name of the exporter (that is, the principal seller or licensee), whereas the outward foreign manifest only requires the name of the shipper. As one Department of Commerce representative pointed out, the information on the shippers' export declaration not only is in greater detail and of a better quality than that shown on the manifest but also is the type of information about individual exporters and their transactions that is not available to the public because of its value to competitors, domestic and foreign.[83]

If we desire consistency between what information is disclosable about domestic transactions and what information is disclosable about foreign transactions, then these data should be protected. Indeed, domestic law specifically protects much of the same information contained in a shippers' export declaration. The legal literature is replete with cases where the courts have maintained the confidentiality of similar business information under the Freedom of Information Act.[84]

A survey taken of the export community by the Bureau of the Census revealed that it opposed the release of shippers' export declarations. That survey demonstrated "that a 95% confidence interval would establish a range from 42% to 66% of the exporting community *opposing* disclosure of their shippers' export declarations."[85] The National Foreign Trade Council surveyed 600 exporting companies seeking to identify the most critically important information given in a shippers' export declaration. Those surveyed ranked the sensitivity of the information as follows: (1) the name and address of the consignee, (2) the f.a.s. value of the shipment, (3) the description of the cargo (marks, numbers, Schedule B commodity number), (4) the country of destination, (5) the name and address of the forwarding agency, (6) the name and address of the exporter, and (7) the net quantity.[86] Representatives from industry favored nondisclosure of the entire document. A representative from Caterpillar Tractor Company emphasized that:

> [N]o single piece of information on the [shippers' export declaration], if released alone, would be confidential. What is special about the [shippers' export declaration] is the *detailed picture* it gives of a single transaction.[87]

A trade association pointed to the difficulty in defining which information in the shippers' export declaration is proprietary:

> While information concerning pricing practices probably would be considered sensitive by nearly all exporters, concern would vary from company to company with respect to other items in the [shippers' export declaration]. For example, a company which sells abroad primarily through its foreign subsidiaries would not be concerned about disclosure of the names of those customers but would be concerned about disclosure of other unaffiliated customers. Most companies probably would not be concerned about disclosure of a date of shipment, but others might when, for example, the shipment involved a new product to be introduced in a foreign market.[88]

Finally, O'Reilly pointed to how this information could be used in conjunction with other agency data to undermine the competitive position of U.S. exporters: "For example, information from public sources such as ICC and FMC reports could be linked with this data to seriously undermine the ability of U.S. exporters to compete in foreign markets."[89] Each of these examples illustrates the great difficulty one would have in categorically defining proprietary information.[90] They point to the fruitlessness of trying to divide the information contained within a shippers' export declaration into neat categories of proprietary and nonproprietary.

The overwhelmingly negative response by business to the proposed disclosure of shippers' export declarations gives insight into specific ways companies perceive that they could be harmed by disclosure. A representative of the Procter & Gamble Company, for example, worried that:

> Advance notice of a "test" or introductory market for consumer products provides competitors with lead time to establish a counter strategy, with concentrated advertising, special dealer allowances, "price off" pacts, etc., that can defeat our efforts to enter the new market. . . . By providing public disclosure of information that Procter & Gamble is starting to ship product X, or substantially expanding its shipment to country Y, our competitors in that market could obtain the critical time advantage.[91]

Consider the case of Procter & Gamble and their invention, Pampers, the disposable diaper. Apparently there was an unfounded belief in marketing circles that the Japanese consumer would be reluctant to use disposable diapers since the relative scarcity of paper in Japan might make this product appear to be wasteful and extravagant. But the large-scale interest among Japanese women in returning to the work force was victorious over earlier cultural practices and attitudes, and Procter & Gamble discovered that the Japanese market for paper diapers was much more lucrative than they originally supposed. To gain an early advantage over competing paper diapers, Procter & Gamble was shipping their bulky diapers by 747 jet liners in order not to lose a moment in meeting the demand for their products in the Japanese market.[92]

Imagine the impact of competitors gaining access to the confidential information contained in Procter & Gamble's shippers' export declaration. If, for example, competitors learned that diapers were being shipped by 747 jet liner, that would be a sure sign that Procter & Gamble had found a Japanese market in which their early marketing efforts might establish valuable brand loyalty. Some competitors' jets may have followed Procter & Gamble's, trying to court the Japanese consumer with substitute products. Furthermore, local Japanese diaper manufacturers might have adjusted their marketing strategies based upon the knowledge they acquired about this new import competition. While the Japanese consumer probably would have purchased diapers at a lower price due to the early entry of rival firms, many of the benefits of the pioneering marketing research of Procter & Gamble into the profitable Japanese market would have been transferred to other firms in the industry. One commentator addressed the negative international competitive implications of early disclosure as follows:

> The mere identification that P[rocter] & G[amble] is starting to ship even household paper articles to a country to which we do not now ship them is going to make our competitors or potential competitors in that country or in other countries start looking around and seeing what they can learn about what those products might be specifically and what they need to do to keep us off the beaches when our goods arrive.[93]

Information about the export of chemical ingredients also could tip off competitors about a quality improvement in existing products:

> We might be planning to reformulate one of our foreign detergent brands to improve its quality. This could involve the U.S. export of a key chemical which is also used outside the detergent industry. However, the identity of Procter & Gamble as the exporter could once again tip off our competitors in advance of our strategy.[94]

The importance of timing in marketing strategy was underlined by a representative of the Caterpillar Tractor Company. He also echoed Procter & Gamble's concerns:

> We would not be anxious for foreign competitors to know that a particular shipment originates with Caterpillar Tractor Company, Peoria, Illinois. . . . [T]hat would be, Sir, an early warning signal to foreign competitors with respect to what could be a sizable market opportunity for the particular U.S. industry. . . . [i]t is a matter of timing with respect to market opportunity.[95] [Shippers' export declarations] do reveal information about individual commercial transactions. A market analyst in possession of a number of [shippers' export declarations] filed by a company could learn much about that company's customers, sales, pricing policies, business trends, dealer organization, replacement part sales opportunities, and other information. Other companies with access to such information could use it to significant competitive advantage. They could more carefully target market development efforts, identify potential new customers, adjust production scheduling and inventories, adapt pricing strategies, and make countless other decisions on the basis of hard information—whereas they now must make many such decisions on the basis of estimates or guesses.[96]

Thus, shippers' export declarations contain a variety of marketing information that could, if disclosed, place the information submitters at a competitive disadvantage internationally. Congress recognized this point and mandated nondisclosure of this document. It is vital to note, however, that within the testimony surrounding the debate about shippers' export declarations, we detect a concern not so much with the disclosure of particular pieces of information such as, for example, the syrup formula for Coca Cola or a chemical mixture that we term trade secrets proper but with the disclosure of pockets of marketing information and clusters of facts yielding knowledge about patterns of market behavior.

Conclusion

This chapter offers a useful way of categorizing what businesses consider to be valuable business information. This categorization has its advantages and disadvantages. On the one hand, it helps us to gain a perspective on the legal debates about government disclosure of business information. By way of studying these debates, we learn what types of information disclosure will harm businesses financially. The fact that these firms are willing and able to expend corporate resources to prevent government disclosure suggests they expect disclosure to harm their organizations in one way or another. Here we appeal to the economists' familiar criteria of demonstrated preference as a simple test that disclosure imposes financial harm on business organizations.[97]

The disadvantage of our categorization is that it cannot capture the type of leakage that occurs on another level beyond the disclosure of particular single items of business information. The value of a fact pattern can be larger than the sum of the values of the particular bits and pieces of information that make up that fact pattern, as we have seen in the business testimony surrounding the disclosure of shippers' export declarations. What emerges from this debate is a concern that competitors will learn about a complex marketing plan or strategy by completing an information jigsaw puzzle.

In chapter 5, we shall build on the foundation laid in this chapter and both define circumstantially relevant business information as well as describe it as a species of information often disregarded in legal debates. The untimely disclosure of this information has predictable effects on the market. The elaboration of these remarks requires that we conceptualize the market as a dynamically complex mechanism involving both creative discovery and entrepreneurial activity.

Notes

1. *Restatement of Torts*, chapter 36, paragraph 757, p. 5. Cited in Melvin F. Jager, *1982 Trade Secrets Law Handbook* (New York: Clark Boardman, 1982), p. 28.

2. "Confidentiality: Will Government Give Away Company Secrets?" *Chemical Week*, 127 10 December 1980, p. 32.

3. "Trade Secrets," *Wall Street Journal*, 5 October 1981, p. 31.

4. Also, U.S., Congress, House, Subcommittee of the Committee on Government Operations, *Freedom of Information Act Oversight*, 97th Cong., 1st Sess., 1981, pp. 555-595 (testimony of Burt Braverman).

5. James T. O'Reilly, *Federal Information Disclosure: Procedure, Form and the Law* (Colorado Springs: Shephard's, 1982), chapter 14, p. 53.

6. Ibid.

7. *Pharmaceutical Manufacturers Association v. Weinberger*, 41 F. Supp. 576 (D.C. D.C. 1976).

8. O'Reilly, *Federal Information Disclosure*, p. 55.

9. House, *Freedom of Information Act Oversight*, pp. 596-619 (testimony of James T. O'Reilly).

10. Letter from James T. O'Reilly to Orrin Hatch, 21 August 1981.

11. U.S., Congress, Senate, Subcommittee of the Committee of the Judiciary, *Freedom of Information Act: Appendix*, 97th Cong., 1st Sess., 1981, p. 238.

12. See *Pharmaceutical Manufacturer's Association v. Weinberger* 411 F. Supp. 576 (1975).

13. O'Reilly, *Federal Information Disclosure*, p. 62.

14. "Polaroid Drops Suit," *South Middlesex News*, 9 November 1978, p. 12C.

15. See chapter 6.

16. The release of Dow Chemical Company's hygiene technology by the National Institute of Occupational Health and Safety is similar to the Monsanto episode; telephone interview, James T. O'Reilly, 2 January 1983.

17. Senate, *Freedom of Information Act: Appendix*, p. 458.

18. Ibid., p. 459.

19. O'Reilly, *Federal Information Disclosure*, p. 26.

20. Ibid.

21. Ibid., p. 63.

22. Roger P. Gilson, Jr., "Administrative Disclosure of Private Business Records under the Freedom of Information Act: An Analysis of Alternative Methods of Review," *Syracuse Law Review* 28 (1977):928.

23. "Confidentiality," *Chemical Week*, 10 December 1980, p. 30.

24. Ibid., p. 31. For a critical discussion of this legislation, see George S. Dominguez, *The Business Guide to TOSCA* (New York: Wiley & Sons, 1979).

25. Thomas McGarity and Sidney Shapiro, "The Trade Secret Status of Health and Safety Testing Information: Reforming Agency Disclosure Policies," *Harvard Law Review* 93 (March 1980):837-888.

26. James T. O'Reilly, "Regaining a Confidence: Protection of Business Confidential Data through Reform of the Freedom of Information Act," *Administrative Review* 34 (Spring 1982):263-313.

27. Letter from Leroy J. Haugh (Office of Management and Budget) to Phil Read (General Services Administration), 17 February 1982.

28. Edmund W. Kitch, "The Law and Economics of Rights in Valuable Information," *Journal of Legal Studies* 9 (December 1980):413.

29. "Sikorsky Drops Bid for Copter Design," *The New York Times*, 27 March 1979, p. 4.

30. Ibid.; and for a contrasting evaluation, see Russell B. Stevenson, Jr., "Protecting Business Secrets under the Freedom of Information Act: Managing Exemption 4" (Manuscript for Administrative Conference of the United States, no. T-15706548 00.923.9.97510.251), p. 25. Also see House, *Freedom of Information Act Oversight*, pp. 538-541 (testimony of Jack Pulley).

31. O'Reilly, "Regaining," p. 289.

32. William Casey, John Marthinsen, and Laurence Moss, "Trade Secrecy and Patents: Complements or Substitutes?" (Paper presented at the Atlantic Economic Society Convention, Washington, D.C., 13 October 1978), pp. 19-21.

33. R. Hershey, "Commercial Intelligence on a Shoestring," *Harvard Business Review* 58 (September/October 1980):23-30.

34. Gilson, Jr., "Administrative," p. 926.

35. *Chevron Chemical Co. v. Costle*, 443 F. Supp. 1024 (N.D. Cal. 1978).

36. *Westinghouse Electric Corporation v. United States Nuclear Regulatory Commission*, 555 F.2d 82 (3d Cir. 1977).

37. Gilson, Jr., "Administrative," p. 926.

38. *GTE Sylvania Inc. v. Consumer Product Safety Commission*, 598 F.2d 790 (3d Cir. 1979), *affirmed*, 100 S. Ct 2051 (1980); and *Pierce & Stevens Chemical Corporation v. Consumer Product Safety Commission*, 585 F.2d 1382 (2d Cir. 1978).

39. Ibid.

40. *Firestone Tire and Rubber Co. v. Coleman*, 432 F. Supp. 1359 (N.D. Oh. 1976); *Bristol Myers & Co. v. Kennedy* Cir. no. 77-2122 (D.C. D.C. 1979); and *Johnson v. Department of HEW* 462 F. Supp. 336 (D.C. D.C. 1978).

41. House, *Freedom of Information Act Oversight*, p. 268.

42. Ibid., p. 198.

43. Stevenson, "Protecting Business Secrets," p. 25.

44. Casey, Marthinsen, and Moss, "Trade Secrecy," p. 22.

45. House, *Freedom of Information Act Oversight*, pp. 538-541 (testimony of Jack Pulley).

46. Cited in O'Reilly, "Regaining," p. 270.

47. Ibid., p. 270.

48. As evidence of the strong public enthusiasm for the Freedom of Information Act, see papers and discussions at "FOIA Symposium: The Challenge to Freedom of Information, the Limits of Secrecy and the Limits of Disclosure and the Public's Right to Know in a Democratic Society" (Organized by Professor Sherman Teichman, Emerson College, Boston). Also see 5 U.S.C. § 552(a)(4)(F) and denial authority is limited 21 C.F.R. § 20.47.

49. James T. O'Reilly, "Government Disclosure of Private Secrets under the Freedom of Information Act," *Business Lawyer* 30 (July 1975):1135.

50. Interviewed at Executive Development Training Seminar of Office of Personnel Management, U.S. Federal Government, held at Oakridge, Tennessee, April 1980.

51. *Burroughs Corp. v. Schlesinger (Department of Energy)* 403 F. Supp. 633 (E.D. Va. 1975).

52. House, *Freedom of Information Act Oversight*, p. 555.

53. Ibid.

54. *Military Audit Project v. Kettles*, Civ. no. 75-666 (D.C. D.C. 1976).

55. *Gulf and Western Industries v. US*, 615 F.2d 527 (D.C. Cir. 1979).

56. House, *Freedom of Information Oversight*, p. 540.

57. Gilson, Jr., "Administrative," pp. 925-926. For citations to cases, see bibiography.

58. For a concurring view see Mark Q. Connelly, "Secrets and Smoke-screens: A Legal and Economic Analysis of Government Disclosures of Business Data," *Wisconsin Law Review*, 1981, pp. 107-273.

59. See Oliver E. Williamson, "The Modern Corporation: Origins, Evaluation, Attributes," *Journal of Economic Literature* 19 (December 1981):1537-1570.

60. Connelly, "Secrets and Smokescreens," p. 271.

61. *Chrysler v. Brown*, 441 U.S. 281 (1979).

62. James T. O'Reilly et al., *Federal Regulations of the Chemical Industry* (Colorado Springs: Shephard's, 1982), pp. 15.7-15.8.

63. *Continental Oil v. Federal Power Commission* 519 F.2d 31 (5th Cir. 1975), *cart dem*, 425 U.S. 971 (1976).

64. Ibid.; *Board of Trade of Chicago v. Commodity Futures Trading Commission*, 627 F.2d 392 (D.C. Cir. 1980); *Braintree Electric Light v. DOE*, 494 F. Supp. 287 (D.C. D.C. 1980); and *Audio Tech Services v. Dept. of Army* 487 F. Supp. 479 (D.C. D.C. 1979).

65. "How the Freedom of Information Act Spotlights Many Corporate Secrets," *Management Review* 67 (September 1978):6.

66. *Union Oil of California v. Federal Power Commission*, 542 F.2d 1036 (9th Cir. 1976); and *Superior Oil v. Federal Energy Regulatory Commission* 563 F.2d 191 (5th Cir. 1977).

67. *Honeywell Information Systems v. National Aeronautics and Space Administration* Civ. No. 76-377 (D.C. D.C. 1976).

68. *National Parks and Conservation Assn. v. Kleppe*, 547 F.2d 673 (D.C. Cir. 1976).

69. *Parkridge Hospital v. Blue Cross*, 430 F. Supp. 1093 (E.D. in 1977); and *Sterling Drug Inc. v. FTC* 450 F.2d 698 (D.C. Cir. 1971).

70. O'Reilly, *Federal Information*, 14.13-14.46. See also *Gulf & Western v. U.S.*, 615 F.2d 527 (1979).

71. *National Airlines v. CAB*, Civ. No. 75-613 (D.C. D.C. 1975).

72. S. 2419, 96th Cong., 2d Sess., 12 March 1980.

73. 46 U.S.C. 91 includes the name of the shipper, the ship's nationality, the master's name, the port of loading and unloading, marks and numbers, the number and kind of package, gross weight, and general description of the cargo. 46 U.S.C. 193 includes information on the exporter, the consignee, the party to be notified, the exporting carrier, the port of loading and unloading, the port of discharge, the location of transshipment, marks and numbers, the forwarding agent, domestic routing/export instructions, the number of packages, a general description of the cargo, the gross weight, and measurement.

74. Much of this history is drawn from U.S., Congress, House, Subcommittee on Census and Population of the Committee on Post Office and Civil Service, 96th Cong., 2d Sess., 1980, *Confidentiality of Shippers' Export Declaration*, 26 March 1980, pp. 5-14 (testimony of Shirley Kallek) (hereafter referred to as *House Hearings*, 26 March 1980); and U.S., Congress, Senate, Committee on Government Affairs, *Hearings on Shippers' Export Declarations*, 7 May 1980, pp. 64-85 (hereafter referred to as *Senate Hearings*, 7 May 1980) (testimony of Edward Dear).

75. Ibid.

76. Section 302 of Title 13 of U.S.C. and 7 CC of the *Export Administration Act* prohibits disclosure. This was reaffirmed by Executive Order 12174, "Paperwork," 30 November 1979, and by a study done for the Department of Commerce, "A Framework of Commerce," Office of Federal Statistical Policy and Standards, July 1978.

77. *Twin Coasts Newspaper, Inc. v. United States Department of Commerce*, Civ. No. 78-0975 (D.C. D.C. 1979).

78. 19 CFR 103.11.

79. This was consistent with the rulings in *The American Jewish Congress v. Kreps*, 574 F.2d 624 (1978).

80. It is significant that export information submitted to the government was intended by Congress to be kept as confidential under exemption (b)(4). See U.S., Senate, Committee on the Judiciary, *Clarifying and Protecting the Right of the Public to Information and Other Purposes*, S. Rept. 1219, 88th Cong., 2d Sess., 1964.

81. Export Administration Act of 1979, Pub. L. No. 96-72, 50 U.S.C. App. § 2404(d) (1980 Supp.).

82. See *Worthington Compressors, Inc. v. Costle*, 662 F.2d 45 (1981). The court ruled that disclosure could be barred if the difference between the cost of an FOIA request and private-sector duplication costs are substantial. Thus, information that is not confidential but that would be costly to reproduce can be withheld from disclosure.

83. *House Hearings*, 26 March 1980, p. 9 (testimony of Shirley Kallek).

84. O'Reilly, *Federal Information Disclosure*, pp. 24, 48.

85. Fourth Affidavit of Emanual A. Lipscomb, Civ. Action No. 78-0975, (D.C. D.C. 1979).

86. *House Hearings*, 26 March 1980, pp. 45-48, 91 (testimony of Richard W. Roberts).

87. Caterpillar Tractor Co., "Export Administration Act and the Confidentiality Issue: Summary" (Letter to Congress concerning the release of shippers' export declarations, July 1979), *House Hearings*, 26 March 1980, p. 21. (emphasis added).

88. Machinery and Allied Products Institute, "Confidentiality of Information Related to Exports," *Executive Letter* L-255 (16 November 1979).

89. James T. O'Reilly, Letter to the Bureau of the Census, U.S. Department of Commerce, re. *Twin Coasts Newspaper, Inc. v. United States Department of Commerce*, Civ. Action No. 78-0973 (1979). Reprinted with permission.

90. Rejected at the shippers'-export-declarations level, categorical definitions are still being recommended for the Freedom of Information Act. See Russell B. Stevenson, Jr., "Protecting Business Secrets under the Freedom of Information Act: Managing Exemption 4, A Study for the Administration Conference of the United States," 15 December 1980.

91. *Senate Hearings*, 7 May 1980, p. 35 (testimony of David J. Elliott).

92. Personal telephone conversation with James T. O'Reilly, 14 December 1982. Reprinted with permission.

93. *House Hearings*, 26 March 1980, p. 27 (testimony of David J. Elliott).

94. *Senate Hearings*, 7 May 1980, p. 35 (testimony of David J. Elliott).

95. *Senate Hearings 1981*, p. 39 (testimony of Roger T. Kelley).

96. Caterpillar Tractor Co., "Export Administration Act," p. 8305.

97. I.M.D. Little, *A Critique of Welfare Economics* (London: Oxford University Press, 1957), pp. 38-50.

5

Entrepreneurship and the Case for Protecting Circumstantially Relevant Business Information

In chapter 4, we surveyed the legal debates surrounding the disclosure of business information. We distinguished trade secrets narrowly defined from compilations of data, contract information, manning tables, and marketing information and were able to house specific examples of coveted business information within one or more of these five categories. In addition, we found that in some cases the information content of a whole group of business information was far greater than the sum of the information content of each item of information in the group taken separately. The information contained on shippers' export declaration forms was a case in point. We saw how the mere name of the shipper or even the method used to transport the goods, under appropriate circumstances, might tip off a competitor about a more-complex marketing strategy. Indeed, by the time we came to the last category of business information—marketing information—we had traveled the spectrum from trade secrets in the narrow, specific sense of formula and technical processes to trade secrets in the broad, expansive sense of circumstantially relevant facts. These facts, in the hands of the decision maker, allow him to cipher a complex web of intentions, plans, and expectations of another.

The contrast between information that is relevant to time and place and information that is eternal and capable of being stated by abstract mathematical formulas is a striking one. Both species of information are considered valuable by business decision makers, and decision makers obviously are motivated to take whatever legal measures are appropriate in preventing the disclosure of either type of information. The extent to which business invests in security and legal measures depends upon how detrimental they perceive the disclosure of that information to be to their competitive position. There is nothing about trade secrets in the narrow sense of technical formulas that make them more valuable than marketing information. Indeed, both species of information can be important complementary ingredients in a more-far-reaching business plan.[1] Together, both species of information sometimes can be exploited to great financial advantage in the market.

Yet despite their essential similarity in the realm of business calculations about profit and loss, the two species of information are not held in equal esteem by most legal scholars, economic historians, and government executives. Scientific data are considered to be far more valuable than marketing information. This is not surprising in light of the longstanding Western intellectual tradition favoring abstract thought (that is, the Platonic ideal of knowledge of the forms) to factual knowledge dependent upon a changing world.[2] Marketing information about the particular wants of consumers and the suitability of product characteristics in satisfying these wants hardly fits the Greek ideal of knowledge about the essential nature of earthly phenomena. Even in common law as contained in the *Restatement of Torts*, we are told that trade secrets of continuous use in business are to be distinguished from secret information about "single or ephemeral events."[3]

The older common-law idea is that only information continuously used by the owner and providing a continuing advantage over competitors is worthy of receiving the protection of the law. Certainly, the marketplace knows no such distinction. Knowledge that Jones values property with a lakeside view and is willing to pay as much as $80,000 for it while Harris is willing and able to sell lakeside property for $60,000 offers the possessor of this knowledge an arbitrage opportunity. This opportunity can be quite profitable yet at the same time constitute an opportunity that, once taken, will not repeat itself. If an entrepreneur, Smith, alert to profit opportunities, bought the property from Harris at $61,000 and subsequently sold it to Jones at $79,000, three individuals gain simultaneously. Most economists prefer that individuals have strong incentives to seek out and discover these so-called Pareto-optimal trades, and yet the legal profession is sometimes ambivalent about recognizing the importance of the information on which these trades depend.[4] Fortunately, the modern Uniform Trade Secret Act eliminates the older common-law requirement that the secret be in continuous use and in this way moves trade-secret law in a direction that is consistent with the economist's understanding of market efficiency.[5]

We especially find this older prejudicial attitude about the unimportance of marketing information manifested in debates about disclosure of information under the Freedom of Information Act. Thus, in the case summarized in chapter 4, when a government official made a mistake and sent out both copies of a report containing the trade-secret formula of a medical deodorizer, there was no dispute about the fact that the mistake was unintentional; that is, no one accused the government official of maliciously sending out the formula in order to damage the information submitter. All parties to the incident considered the outcome unfortunate. They might dispute the monetary value of the damages caused by this disclosure and whether or not the incident permitted any recovery at all, but there was no dispute that harm had occurred and a trade secret in the narrow sense had been divulged.

Conversely, when we consider the disclosure of a marketing plan or some information about who is shipping a product to whom and where, then disclosure is not considered to be as unfortunate or damaging as the disclosure of a technical trade secret. This difference in attitude is real and, in our view, at the heart of the debate about reforming the Freedom of Information Act. Unfortunately, the legal terms in which this debate is conducted systematically divert attention from the importance of nonscientific and nontechnical information.

A growing number of FOIA watchers are taking the same position at which the court arrived in *Hughes Aircraft* v. *Schlesinger* that, when the disclosure of equal-opportunity information was at stake, the "submittors are [less] fearful of injuries inflicted by their competitors [than] they are of those flowing from adverse publicity and litigious minority groups."[6] This theme has been developed at length in an article by Connelly who suggests that all this complaining about property rights and the loss of trade secrets is a smoke screen or subterfuge for corporations who do not wish to be publicly embarrassed by the way they treat minorities and other disadvantaged groups.[7] Again, the attitude here is that once the information is found not to be scientific information, then why should the law be concerned with protecting its disclosure?

The main contribution of this chapter is to show how the distinction between static and dynamic efficiency helps us to appreciate the importance of a species of information that includes marketing information and other forms of information that we shall define as circumstantially relevant business information. In the first section, we review the elementary distinction between two notions of economic efficiency. In the second section, we offer some explanations about why the ensuing debate about the trade-secrets exemption of the Freedom of Information Act failed to recognize its importance in promoting dynamic economic efficiency. A final section relates these findings to the concerns about productivity in the United States and establishes the groundwork for the two case studies of the chemical and pharmaceutical industries that follow in chapters 6 and 7 respectively.

Static versus Dynamic Efficiency

Alfred Marshall, the great nineteenth-century architect of neoclassical economics, considered secrecy in business to be a "barbaric relic" of less-civilized times. Secrecy was slated to die out as business life achieved the higher values and became more chivalrous.[8] When modeling markets, economists have favored the civilized assumption of assuming all the actors in the market have perfect information about prices, technologies, and even future states of affairs or at least the probabilities of their occurrence. When George Stigler commented on the sorry state of economic reasoning in which the economics of information is virtually ignored or else housed in "a slum dwelling in the town of economics," he unleashed a reverse movement within the profession that eventually contributed to his receiving the 1982 Nobel Prize.[9] Contemporary economists, spurred on by the Stigler admonition, have made valuable contributions to our understanding of the information-generating processes at work in the economy and how they relate to older ideas of market equilibrium, but there is much more to be done. Unfortunately, traditional textbook treatments of this subject demonstrate a strange reluctance to admit that their tools of analysis, especially those centered about the perfect-information assumption, can be inappropriate for making value judgments about the manner in which markets operate. The often-heard conclusion that, because knowledge is not perfectly and freely available, "most equilibria will not be socially desirable [that is] not be Pareto optimal" amounts to criticizing the world for not being like an abstract mental image of perfect competition.[10] The perfect-competition model is useful for describing the processes at work in the real world. To criticize the real world for not living up to the model's assumptions results in a peculiar form of intellectual idealism that, if allowed to have influence on policymakers, will give birth to public policies that fail to address the imperatives of dynamic efficiency. According to several students of industrial organizations, an ambitious effort to apply the model of perfect competition to antitrust policy has produced grave regulatory errors.[11] At this writing, there is a reaction against the older approach to the regulation of industry founded on the blueprint model of perfect competition.[12]

Many economists would deny strenuously that they are using the model of perfect competition as a framework for evaluating and controlling the market process; yet, it is difficult to describe what appears in economics texts and popular books on economics in any other terms. Rather than taking charge of the tools of the discipline and shaping them in a way that throws light on the processes at work in industry, many economists condemn the industry for not possessing the characteristics of the model. If all actors in the market are assumed to be informed perfectly about the plans and forthcoming actions of the others, then of course, advertising budgets and market research seem to be of little substantive importance to the economic system. Similarly, if technological and scientific information are available to all decision makers like manna from heaven, then all firms possess identical production functions, and the diffusion of innovations is not a subject matter of concern to policymakers.[13] While econometric studies about the relationships among technological information, innovation, and the growth of factor productivity are discussed often in elementary presentations of the subject, the full complexity of the market process and its dependence on a variety of information processes and incentive mechanisms has not yet been fully integrated into the textbook literature. There are, however, several notable exceptions.[14]

Consider Marshall's view of the process of technological entrepreneurship. Marshall's world was one in which innovations occurred in small, incremental steps. The dynamically competitive world that Joseph Schumpeter described in which economic development proceeded in cataclysmic leaps facilitated by the pioneering entrepreneur and his army of me-tooers, was largely alien to Marshall's manner of thinking about social change. Marshall's world was orderly and designed to resemble natural evolutionary processes. At any moment in time, a menu of known inventions was available to businessmen. Each invention could be taken up and adapted when relative prices made one invention appear more profitable than another. If, for example, machine rental prices rose relative to wage rates, then business decision makers would search for inventions that economize on machinery and use more labor. Those businessmen quick to introduce the labor-intensive techniques would make above-normal profits, but the others would quickly follow suit, reducing profits back to the normal level.[15]

Following the pattern set by Marshall, modern neoclassical economics tries to model the case where one firm in competitive industry possesses, perhaps even stumbles across by chance, some information that provides that firm with a competitive advantage over the others. Consider the competitive firm depicted in figure 5-1, producing Q_1 units of output per week at a market price of P_1. Suppose the manager of this firm discovers an innovative process technology that permits him to lower his average total cost curve as shown by the lower U-shaped curve in figure 5-2. Now this firm earns above-normal profits, equal to area P_1TGP_0. Two alternative scenarios may follow to eliminate this condition of disequilibrium. First, the owner of the firm may try to keep the process a secret (on the rare but possible assumption it can be kept secret), but the knowledgeable manager/worker would increase accordingly his salary demands from the firm owner until he captured the (amortized) value of the expected profits as part of his wages. In this case the firm returns to the position shown in figure 5-1 and the above-normal profits are captured by the manager/worker.[16] Second, the process technology may become diffused among the other firms in the industry, and new firms may enter the industry, making use of the new technology and lowering market prices.

In either of these cases, the extra profits will be eliminated by one or the other of these two forms of competition. In the first case, the price the consumer pays remains unchanged, and the profit becomes amortized as part of the rental or hire price of some unique resource like the knowledgeable manager/worker. In the second case, the price will fall, and total industry

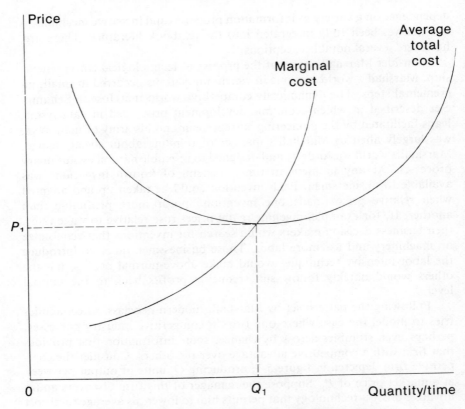

Figure 5-1. Competitive Firm in Long-Run Equilibrium

output will expand to the advantage of the consumer. We could elaborate on this presentation of the neoclassical approach to innovation based on the model of perfect competition, but to do so would take us far beyond what is contained in the standard microeconomic texts. The texts usually are agreed that innovation produces a temporary disequilibrium that competition eventually will "correct." As a rule, the disequilibrium is "corrected" by the quick diffusion of the process technology among the other firms (the second case), ultimately raising consumer welfare in the market as a whole.[17]

If we define an improvement in social welfare to consist of situations in which at least one member of society is made better off without leaving any person worse off (so-called Pareto superiority), then policies that rush resources to where they are most highly valued by consumers improve social welfare.[18] According to the model of perfect competition, the quick

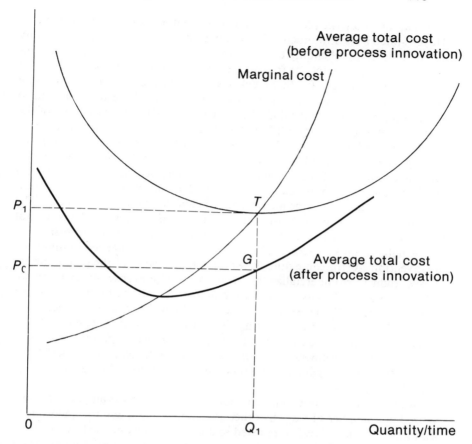

Note: For expository reasons, we have assumed that the process innovation shifts the average total cost downward and to the left. The marginal-cost curve remains unaffected.

Figure 5-2. Competitive Firm with Differential Technological Innovation in Equilibrium

dissemination of information about methods of production is Pareto superior and socially desirable. Even Hayek, whose battle against the notion of perfect competition dates from the 1940s, is in agreement with the broader neoclassical tradition and its emphasis on the dissemination of knowledge and information.[19] According to Hayek, the principal characteristic of the price system is not that it allocates resources efficiently but that it provides a flexible mechanism for inducing individuals to utilize localized bits and pieces of information in ways that produce a prosperous social order. The price system is valuable precisely because individuals do not have perfect information about the plans of others. The "marvel" of the price system, as Hayek stated it, is how much information is utilized at one time without any single mind comprehending even a tiny bit of it. The absence of perfect information is not a defect of free markets but the result of a society made up of many human minds. In Hayek's view, information about changing market conditions becomes disseminated quickly to those in a position to utilize that information through the price system. On the importance of the diffusion of knowledge, both Marshall and Hayek were in agreement.[20]

If Marshall had been told that nearly a half century after his death, the U.S. government would enact a series of disclosure statutes to encourage the dissemination of knowledge about technological innovations, he no doubt would have approved. Secrecy, for Marshall, was the way of tribesmen, cultists, and medicine men. Civilized men shared their knowledge. The sharing of knowledge was, of course, and remains today, a fundamental ideal of a liberal society built on the important value of free expression.

A patent, unlike a secret, discloses much of what is needed to duplicate an invention. At the same time, it confers on the owner of the patent the exclusive right to commercialize the invention or else license others to do so. In figure 5-3, we display a firm with a patent monopoly, pricing its output at P_1 and selling Q_1 per week. If there were the widespread manufacture of that product among any competing firms, the market price would be lower (P_2) and the rate of production larger (Q_2). Consumer surplus (a measure of the net benefit consumers receive by participating in competitive markets) is only ABP_1 with the patent and would be ATP_2 without the patent.[21] Why, then, have patents?

Marshall disapproved of patent monopolies. Innovators already were subsidized in a number of ways by other government laws, and the gains due to lead time that the innovator enjoyed seldom were overwhelmed by the lower production costs of the subsequent group of firms that copied the first firm's invention. While a number of later neoclassical writers shared Marshall's disdain for patent monopolies, many other writers found a legitimate place for an inventor's monopoly in a system bent on maximizing consumer welfare.[22] Those who disagreed with Marshall about the economic effects of patent monopolies point to the important policy goal of creating and nurturing an environment in which inventors will have an incentive to innovate. The prospect of winning profits, as Kirzner explained (in another context), nurtures a fine-tuned perception about how resources can be combined more effectively. Similarly, the confiscation of profits, the taxation of so-called windfalls, or the ominous prospect of these eventualities create in man a chilling effect. The entrepreneurial function does not get performed in the keenest manner if, indeed, anyone bothers to perform it at all.[23] In a centrally planned society, the routine bureaucratization of production results in an environment quite detrimental to the creative energies of the entrepreneur.[24]

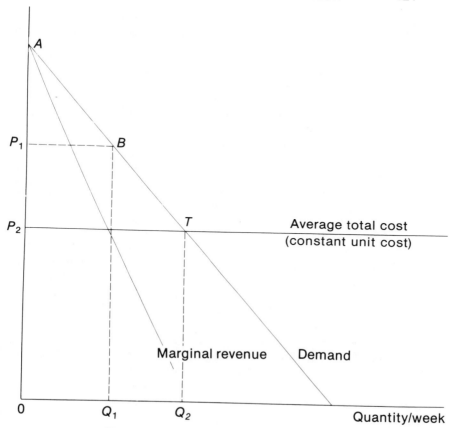

Figure 5-3. Firm with Patent Monopoly

In addition, in industries requiring both heavy commitments of capital equipment and industries dependent on R&D funds, such as the chemical and ethical-drug industries, institutional arrangements may be needed to slow down the diffusion of otherwise profitable inventions. The slowing down provides the innovator with a transition period in which to capture part of the social return on investment.[25]

Patents provide their owners with a legal mechanism to slow down the diffusion of inventions and capture part of the social return. In the simple model of the firm in perfect competition, any such transition period is termed disequilibrium. Realizing this, Schumpeter was one of the earliest to point to a trade-off between competition and the sort of dynamic efficiency we associate with the entrepreneurial process. A dynamically efficient economy requires investment in inventing. If the first inventor's creations can be copied by me-tooers, as in the model of perfect competition that is based on the assumption of perfect knowledge, then the first inventor will have a strong disincentive to invest resources in inventing. Kenneth Arrow stated that free markets will devote a less than socially optimal amount of resources to innovative activities. That is because the quick entrance of me-tooers makes this privately perceived rate of return on investment lower than the social return. By free markets, Arrow meant markets as described by the model of perfect competition.[26]

Marshall's idea is simple and widely accepted in academic circles. It is believed that, once knowledge is created, its dissemination helps to maximize the consumer's welfare. The model of perfect competition makes this point quite clear. The real economic problem, as Schumpeter recognized, is how to provide incentives for this knowledge to be created in the first place.[27] Schumpeter stated that monopoly, or to use the language more recently applied to this problem, concentrated markets, may encourage innovation. Thus, a public policy designed to impose a blueprint of perfect competition on the market processes, in the name of consumer welfare, paradoxically may lower consumer welfare. This insight has come to be known as the Schumpeterian trade-off hypothesis—namely, the static-efficiency losses due to monopoly may be more than offset by the gains from dynamic efficiency.[28]

It is our position that this trade-off exists and is reflected in that large component of U.S. economic growth attributable to knowledge production. Although it is difficult, admittedly, to quantify the precise magnitudes involved in this trade-off, our position is shared by many economists and lawyers who are concerned about technological inventions or well-defined trade secrets like chemical formulas. Typically, a businessman's pleas for nondisclosure of his test data or secret formulas fall on sympathetic ears. Suppose Campbell's Soup has a quality-control procedure that, if disclosed, would place the company at a competitive disadvantage. The taking of this technical information and its widespread dissemination by government would have short-run benefits offset by the chilling effect this disclosure would have on future innovations of this sort.[29] Even Russell Stevenson, a strong supporter of government disclosure of certain categories of corporate information, agrees that this type of technical information constitutes an exception to the rule. All information resources should not be disseminated freely.[30]

By the logic of this argument, policy analysts also should favor safeguards against the forced disclosure of other forms of business information that serve the needs of consumers but that require financial incentives for their continued discovery and application. This apparently is not the case. Information about, say, marketing opportunities is, for many writers, information that should be disseminated quickly. Is this information less important to the market process? Or, perhaps, is this information so simple and so inexpensive to produce that its rapid dissemination is consistent with its continued discovery and application? We believe that a species of business information exists that shares something in common with technical and scientific information—namely, that its discovery and application are necessary to the entrepreneurial process. We shall now turn our attention to the definition of this species of business information.

**Definition of Circumstantially Relevant
Business Information**

Legal scholars and policymakers have overlooked a body of information that is vital to the exercise of entrepreneurship. This knowledge, which we call circumstantially relevant business information, although lacking the luster of pure knowledge of mathematical formulas and technological data, is still equally vital to the functioning of a dynamically efficient market economy. Circumstantially relevant business information is not the sort of information that appears in an engineering text or that constitutes a patentable invention. According to current definitions, it would not come under the heading of trade secrets unless we mean by trade secret simply business information that would not be released customarily to the public.[31]

Circumstantially relevant business information is "knowledge of particular time and place." The existence of this information and its importance to the entrepreneurial process often are overlooked in discussions about government disclosure practices. Our view is that the systematic and continual disclosure of circumstantially relevant business information tends to erode competitive advantage and therefore discourages further entrepreneurial activity.

Circumstantially relevant business information consists of knowledge of where bargains can be found, knowledge of whom to contact in large organizations, knowledge of the cheapest mode of transportation, knowledge of unsatisfied demands and the means of satisfying them, knowledge of the true risks as compared with the perceived risks of an invention. It is knowledge of how to design a laboratory test on a new class of compounds—for example, to use a monkey rather than a laboratory rat.[32] It includes knowledge of where resources are believed to be undervalued and where they are believed to be overvalued. This knowledge, while innocuous and mundane to federal executives and perhaps declared ephemeral knowledge by common law, may be of immense importance to competitors of information submitters. This information may not be the product of human design, and no portion of a firm's R&D budget can be allocated specifically to its production. There are even cases where people stumble upon it much like legendary scientists are supposed to stumble upon research results. Frequently, it is fragmented and its economic value is difficult to assess. The loss of any one piece of this information may not cause significant and statistically quantifiable harm to the firm or even to society. Yet, this information is essential to the impersonal decision-making processes of a free society. It is the means by which a nation can continuously and incrementally devote resources to ventures of varying risks and returns without overcommitting resources to any one venture.

Karl Popper referred to this trial-and-error process that we identify with competitive markets as "piecemeal planning," quite distinct from the blueprint-style planning that often accompanied totalitarian methods of implementation.[33] Hayek has also explained that:

> [The] problem of a rational economic order is determined precisely by the fact that the knowledge of the circumstances of which we must make use never exists in concentrated or integrated form, but solely as the dispersed bits of incomplete and frequently contradictory knowledge which all the separate individuals possess.[34]

Those in possession of circumstantially relevant business information are able to combine the dispersed bits and pieces of knowledge in ways that benefit the plan of various individuals and that produce entrepreneurial profits for themselves.

The dynamics of our economy may be viewed as a multitude of opportunities that are opened and closed with passing events. The key to success is not only the factual availability of opportunities but also the identification and grasping of these opportunities by entrepreneurs. Kirzner has provided the most systematic and thoughtful analyses of entrepreneurial profits and the freshest insights about how entrepreneurs come to perceive profit opportunities. Kirzner emphasized the importance of private ownership of property and free contracting as necessary conditions for the exercise of entrepreneurship in the market. Kirzner's discussion needs to be supplemented by an appreciation of the importance of maintaining a lag between the exploitation of a profitable opportunity by the entrepreneur and the entry into the market by competitors, the so-called me-tooers. If, as we have argued earlier in this chapter, government disclosure practices cut down on this time lag, producing short-term gains to consumers in the form of expanded output and lower prices, they do so by dulling the incentive to engage in entrepreneurial activities.

The Freedom of Information Act may threaten the discovery and exploitation of this knowledge of particular time and place by reducing the time lag between innovation and imitation. It does this by disregarding the importance of circumstantially relevant business information to the entrepreneurial process and encouraging its early and systematic disclosure. What proof can we offer here that this process is contributing to the decline in per capita productivity in the United States?

Unfortunately, dramatic evidence of competitive harm cannot be demonstrated easily. Inasmuch as the loss of entrepreneurial activity always refers to opportunities not taken and decisions not made, objective, hardcore proof of economic loss resulting from disclosure is difficult to obtain.[35] What is discouraged is a process, not a once-and-for-all loss in national product resulting from a misallocation of resources.

As we have explained in the previous sections of this chapter, traditional economic analysis over the last several decades has been concerned almost exclusively with the perfect-competition model of markets. Here, the concern is about the optimal allocation of resources among known ends in existing known markets. The whole issue of how we learn about means and ends and how new markets are erected to economize on transaction costs has been relegated to the appendixes and notes of the textbooks. In our view, these matters lie at the heart of our understanding of dynamic efficiency, and in terms of the process of dynamic competition, we can appreciate the importance of circumstantially relevant business information. It is not enough to state that the economic problem of society is how to allocate resources efficiently among known ends. The problem is how to encourage the discovery of means and ends and the creation of new market institutions to promote these ends.[36]

Many great entrepreneurial success stories identified with technological innovations also involved circumstantially relevant business information. In the 1800s, Gustavus Swift linked the East Coast's demand for fresh meat with the Midwest's supply of meat by means of the refrigerated car. Swift's contribution was not just the refrigerated car but also the realization that meat could be moved from where it was relatively economical to produce to where it was relatively expensive to consume.[37] James Bell merchandised high-grade flour by employing advanced technology, refrigeration, and aggressive marketing techniques.[38] Both Andrew Carnegie and Pierre Dupont developed new markets to make use of their industrial excess capacity. Carnegie was able to redevelop steel manufacturing to accommodate the material requirements of the modern skyscraper at the precise time the railroad expansion had leveled off. Dupont developed artificial fabrics and pryocylin products (that is, photographic film) as government purchases of his explosives (that is, nitrocellulose base products) had diminished.[39] Had these technological entrepreneurs been required to give advance notice of their plans to some centralized agency, it is doubtful whether they could have articulated all of what constituted their vision of future business successes. Even if they could have revealed their visions of where future opportunities appear, the early entry of competitors probably would have made the execution of their plans impossible.

Circumstantially relevant business information is also critically important among marketing entrepreneurs. Berry Gordy, the founder of Motown records, discovered that black recording stars and songwriters were underpaid by New York City agents. Gordy offered them a higher wage and bid their services to Motown. Gordy acted on circumstantially relevant business information, entering into contracts with relatively underpaid singers and songwriters and marketing their talents in a more-valuable way.[40] Would Gordy's meteoric rise have been easier if the large recording studios could have studied his marketing plans by ordering the information he may have been asked to submit to the Federal Communications Commission? Another entrepreneur, Soichiro Honda, acted on the knowledge that the Japanese government had a number of small motors it wished to liquidate at the end of the war. He bought and attached them to bicycles.[41] Would Honda's success have been aided if the Japanese equivalent of the Consumer Product Safety Commission had disclosed a report from Honda about how he intended to use those motors and for what purpose?

The point of these examples is to emphasize how important circumstantially relevant business information is to entrepreneurship. Circumstantially relevant business information tends to exist in abundant amounts mostly during the early stages of product and process development. It is particularly important in the early start-up phase of the product life cycle when knowledge of particular time and place is most valuable to a firm, and it is precisely at this time when government reporting requirements are in some industries most severe and uncompromising.[42] Each government administrator may honestly perceive that no essential information has been given out to information requesters, and yet some innocent phrase or turn of words may be all that a rival firm needs to decipher the first firm's long-range strategy or plan. What we learn from the study of celebrated entrepreneurs is the importance of circumstantially relevant business information to the maintenance and perpetuation of the entrepreneurial process.

Circumstantially Relevant Business Information and the Trade-Secrets Exemption

The fourth exemption to the Freedom of Information Act permits agency officials to withhold "trade secrets and commercial or financial information obtained from a person and privileged or confidential." In earlier chapters we suggested that federal executives are more likely to give out information the more relevant the information seems to be to issues of health and safety, the less dependent that government agency is on the information submitter for future business information, and the more any body of information seems unrelated to scientific knowledge or technical test results.[43]

The first point is illustrated by the statement of McGarity and Shapiro that appeared in the *Harvard Law Review*. They assert, without argument, that market mechanisms "do not adequately protect man and the environment from the risks posed by new products, chemicals and technologies."[44] Executive agencies, therefore, have been charged by Congress to acquire this risk data, and when making rules, these agencies should conclude that "all health and safety test making data are *not* proprietary information and hence should be disclosed."[45]

The second point relates directly to the concern expressed by the Supreme Court in the *National Parks* case. If the disclosure of business information has a chilling effect on businesses' future willingness to disclose information to particular agencies, then these particular agencies may choose not to disclose the information. Nondisclosure is permitted when disclosure might "impair the government's ability to obtain necessary information in the future."[46]

This idea, translated into the economic calculus of the self-interested bureaucrat, suggests that government executives will be more lax in safeguarding information from businessmen whose cooperation is less important to the bureaucrat's job performance. That is perhaps why the slogan in several government agencies is "When in doubt, give it out." A more-appropriate refrain is "When we do not need to rely, requests for information we don't deny." Thus, there is reason to believe there exists a strong bias in government agencies toward disclosing business information, especially the sort of information we term circumstantially relevant business information.

In chapters 6 and 7, we consider the disclosure practices of two large government agencies, the Food and Drug Administration and the Environmental Protection Agency. We argue that, where scientific or technical information is at stake, agency officials are reluctant to disclose information. While horror stories do exist about agency personnel mistakenly mailing out trade secrets in the narrow sense, apparently the practice is much less common than many writers on the subject contend.

Legal scholars such as Stevenson and Connelly do not hesitate to agree with us that certain types of information should not be disclosed too rapidly. They restrict these sorts of information mostly to technological and scientific information that, if rapidly disclosed, may jeopardize future productivity and innovative effort.[47] However, they are reluctant to include marketing information in the same nondisclosure category as knowledge about scientific law and experimental results. Perhaps this is due to the lingering prejudice that the quick-talking marketing man is hardly of the intellectual caliber of corporate research personnel. Neither literature nor the theater has been particularly generous in its appreciation of the marketing function. Consider Arthur Miller's poignant characterization of the salesman Willie Loman and his hypocritical behavior concealed by lies and half-truths.[48] Finally, John K. Galbraith, Vance Packard, and Ralph Nader have produced evidence of the abuses of Madison Avenue, and these works have been read by broad segments of the public.[49] Within some business schools, the marketing major is not held in the highest esteem, and a large number of economists insist that brand loyalty acts as a barrier to entry in markets, thereby preserving monopoly privilege.[50]

The gross ignorance about the importance of marketing information to the entrepreneurial process is the natural, perhaps inevitable, result of using the model of perfect competition as a normative tool for evaluating the market process. After all, if information is perfect, then of what use can the advertising industry be except to lure, seduce, and distort reality? While professional economists increasingly are rejecting this clumsy and misleading view of the role of advertising in a competitive economy, deep-seated prejudice against the marketing function looms beneath discussions of the impact of the Freedom of Information Act. Certainly, Kirzner is correct when he points to the important role advertising plays by informing people about the characteristics of products and the suitability of the products to their needs.[51] This role is extremely important to an economy where the basic economic problem is the coordination of the plans and expectations of separate individual decision makers.

The process that Schumpeter aptly described as "creative destruction," in which new combinations of resources replace old combinations, is one in which entrepreneurs are able to act on a vision of the future.[52] If that vision of the future folds into the course of events, the entrepreneur may make profits; if not, he incurs losses. Often, that vision consists of marketing opportunities that require a decision about whether certain goods or resources are undervalued in their present applications. Ironically, the middleman function that is so important to the functioning of an economic system often is dismissed by those who think of production as consisting of little more than combining inputs in some mechanical way in order to grind out outputs—the image of a sausage machine may be appropriate here. Certainly the model of perfect competition useful for some purposes of analysis is completely inadequate as an aid to understanding the importance of marketing information in the entrepreneurial process. This is the reason why the importance of circumstantially relevant business information is overlooked so frequently.

Contract Information

Many requests for business information housed within government agencies are for contract information. A government agency like the Department of

Army may invite the submission of detailed bids. For example, in 1980, the army requested bids on the "design and installation of an audio-recording system."[53] A losing bidder, Audio Technical Services, wished to view the winning bidder's documents. The government agency decided that the bulk of the information in the bid was proprietary, and the information requester brought the government agency to court. The court found that the army was correct when it decided not to disclose this contract information. A number of FOIA court cases have been of this type, with the courts protecting the rights of the information submitters.[54]

We can distinguish several possible motives as to why a business may wish to look at another business's contract proposals.[55] First, the procuring agency may be dealing with a cartel in which the various cartel members wish to check up on each other to make certain that no member of the cartel chiseled by submitting a lower bid than what was promised. In this case, full disclosure of contract information to competing firms would lower the costs of enforcing cartel agreements to the disadvantage of the overcharged taxpayer who ultimately must pay a monopoly price for the contract proposal. A number of commentators on information-disclosure policy have agreed that in the situation where the government solicits bids from a cartel, nondisclosure may be in the public interest.[56]

In other cases, the disclosure of contract information to firms can result in increased competition rather than in the perpetuation of monopoly. Suppose a group of firms derives its market strength from a specialized body of information that for any one of a number of reasons enters the files of government agencies. The acquisition of this information by others may expand the capability of some firms to compete for contract work. The *Wall Street Journal* reported a case of exactly this type where the National Association of Aircraft and Commercial Suppliers opposed reforming the Freedom of Information Act along the lines recommended by this book. The small aerospace firms claimed that their large competitors wanted secrecy to "preserve the industry's lucrative monopoly in producing spare parts."[57] They argued that small firms needed government disclosure of information about equipment such as tanks, ships, planes, and their replacement parts in order to compete against the large manufacturers for government contracts. Unlike the first case of cartel pricing, here disclosure of contract information presumably would be in the public interest. If, however, the U.S. government initially had negotiated a lower-price contract with the larger firms by promising nondisclosure, then breaking this promise may make future contracts more expensive to the taxpayer. The extent to which this trade-off exists is worthy of future study.[58]

Finally, losing bidders may wish simply to copy the format that the winning bidder used when preparing the contract. There is some evidence to suggest that winning contracts are the ones that contain more than the minimum reporting requirements of government agencies. They maintain creative strategies and innovative approaches that differentiate one particular contract from the others. There is no evidence either way as to whether disclosures of contract information of this type have had an impact on market concentration or competition.[59]

In the recent spate of lawsuits in which companies have sued government agencies to disclose the bid proposals of other companies, the courts have upheld the agency's decision not to give out the contract information.[60] Indeed, contracts do often specify cost breakdowns and reveal original methods of dividing and monitoring work activity. We believe that innovations in accounting practices and financial-management procedures also represent a legitimate asset of the firm, and their continued support and creation is important to the future progress of the economy.[61] Contracts also carry information about customer lists and pricing formulas, both of which are recognized specifically in the *Restatement of Torts* to be trade secrets in the broader sense, but contracts may also contain circumstantially relevant business information, and for that reason nondisclosure of that information will contribute to dynamically competitive market activity. As Alfred Chandler explained, in a related context, innovations about management procedures can be an immense source of competitive advantage to the firm that stumbles upon them first and to the economy as a whole as their ideas and procedures become more widely diffused.[62]

Conclusion

If we elevate the welfare of consumers in the market to the status of a national objective, then the fact that business corporations are injured by disclosure of business information does not by itself necessarily require any remedial action by government. Woe to the firm that tries to slow down the healthy cleansing process of the market that wipes out excessive profits by lowering prices and expanding sales. The firm's loss is the consumer's gain, and the consumer's gain is the object of economic activity in the market. If the Freedom of Information Act has this unintended consequence of greasing the wheels of the market process, then the Freedom of Information Act is much more of a friend to the consumer than Congress originally intended.

In response to this claim that competition dissipates extraordinary profits and that the disclosure of business information hastens the competitive process along, we wish to point out that strategic planning is often profitable only because it amounts to serving new needs of consumers and existing needs more efficiently in the market than hitherto has been the case. In the same way we are concerned with maintaining incentives toward creative and innovative technological research, we also may care to maintain incentives toward strategic planning and the implementation of those plans. To that end, the maintenance of business secrecy may help to increase the returns on this type of activity and to encourage more of it. Government disclosure of circumstantially relevant business information may lower the returns on this type of investment and may discourage it. Business representatives obviously wish to hide their strategic plans so that competitors will not outwit them and so that new market segments will be theirs for longer (more profitable) periods of time. Government policy toward business needs to evaluate not simply the impact of disclosure on one particular company at one moment in its history but the effect the continued practice of disclosure has on the process of strategic planning over time.

To the extent that the disclosure of circumstantially relevant business information is occurring, then government information practices are discouraging the entrepreneurial process. Rushing resources to their most highly valued uses will produce short-term Pareto optimality sometimes at the expense of dynamic creativity and the continued discovery of new opportunities. We judge that this trade-off of long-term dynamic efficiency for static allocative efficiency exists and is contributing to the loss of productivity in the U.S. economy. Our point here goes beyond the claim that government disclosure practices are hurting individual firms by alerting rival firms to their proprietary information. Our point is that government disclosure practices might be dampening a market process of creative discovery and innovation that in turn is linked clearly to gains in material economic behavior. Those participating in the legal debate surrounding the Freedom of Information Act have overlooked this category of business information largely because it does not fit in with any of the existing definitions of trade secrets. Because so much of it appears to be marketing information, its protection has not been considered a major responsibility of government. The ill-suited character of the older legal definition of trade secrets proper is due no doubt to the low regard in which marketing information is held relative to the celebrated abstract mathematical and experimental knowledge. These attitudes are appropriate in the world of perfect competition. They really have a detrimental impact on a decentralized market economy when translated into administrative procedures and attitudes.

Notes

1. See Michael E. Porter, *Competitive Strategy: Techniques for Analyzing Industries and Competitors* (New York: Free Press, 1980), pp. 88-107.

2. Karl R. Popper, *The Open-Society and Its Enemies,* vol. 2 (New York: Harper & Row, 1972), pp. 18-34.

3. Section 757 of the *Restatement* contains the widely cited definition of a trade secret that appears in chapter 4 of this book. The *Second Restatement of Torts* (that appeared in 1978) left Section 757 unrevised. See Melvin Jager, *1982 Trade Secrets Handbook* (New York: Clark Boardman, 1982), pp. 27-38.

4. See Jules L. Coleman, "Efficiency, Utility, and Wealth Maximization," *Hofstra Law Review* 9 (Spring 1980):509-551.

5. Ibid., p. 29.

6. See *Hughes Aircraft v. Schlesinger,* 384 F. Supp. 292 (1974).

7. Mark Q. Connelly, "Secrets and Smokescreens: Legal and Economic Analysis of Government Disclosures of Business Data," *Wisconsin Law Review 1981* (1981):207-273.

8. Alfred Marshall, *Principles of Economics: An Introductory Volume,* 9th ed., vol. 1, ed. C.W. Guilleband (London: Macmillan, 1920), 303-304.

9. Ibid.

10. Kenneth J. Arrow, "Economic Welfare and the Allocation of Resources for Invention," in National Bureau of Economic Research, *The Rate and Direction of Inventive Activity: Economic and Social Factors,* vol. 2 (Princeton, N.J.: Princeton University Press, 1962), p. 616. For a successful critique of Arrow's contention, see Harold Demsetz, "Information and Efficiency: Another Viewpoint," *Journal of Law and Economics* 12 (April 1969):1-22.

11. Stephen C. Littlechild, *The Fallacy of the Mixed Economy: An Austrian Critique of Conventional Economics and Government Policy* (San Francisco: Cato Institute, 1979), pp. 21-33; and Israel M. Kirzner, "The Perils of Regulation: A Market Process Approach, Occasional Paper LEC 4-1/279 (Coral Gables, Florida: Law and Economics Center, 1979).

12. William J. Baumol, "Contestable Markets, Antitrust, and Regulation," *Wharton Magazine* 7 (Fall 1982):23-30.

13. Edwin Burmeister, "Synthesizing the Neo-Austrian and Alternative Approaches to Capital Theory: A Survey," *Journal of Economic Literature* 12 (1974):450.

14. Case Comments, "Accommodating Patent and Antitrust Law: Monopolists' Lawful Patenting Conduct and SCM Corp. v. Xerox Corp." *Boston University Law* (1980):78-114. See also E. Mansfield, *Microeconomics* (New York: Norton, 1970), pp. 460-468.

15. See Laurence Moss, "Biological Theory and Technological Entrepreneurship in Marshall's Writings," *Eastern Economic Journal* 8 (January 1982):3-13.

16. Compare Edmund Kitch, "The Law and Economics of Rights in Valuable Information," *Journal of Legal Studies* 9 (December 1980):684-686.

17. For a sophisticated statement of this argument with qualifications, see J. Hirshleifer, *Price Theory and Applications,* 2nd ed. (Englewood Cliffs, N.J.: Prentice-Hall, 1980), pp. 382-385.

18. See Arrow, "Economic Welfare"; and Coleman, "Efficiency, Utility."

19. Friedrich A. Hayek, "The Use of Knowledge in Society," in *Individualism and Economic Order,* ed. Hayek (London: Routledge & Kegan Paul, 1979), p. 77.

20. See Moss, "Biological Theory," p. 5.

21. On the economic-welfare effects of patents, see U.S., Congress, Senate, Committee on the Judiciary, Subcommittee on Patents, Trademarks and Copyrights, 85th Cong., 2d sess. (testimony of Fritz Machlup).

22. Ibid.

23. For a strong statement of this position, see Ludwig von Mises, *Bureaucracy* (New Haven: Yale University, 1962); and Thomas Sowell, *Knowledge and Decisions* (New York: Basic Books, 1980), pp. 21-44.

24. Burton H. Klein, *Dynamic Economics* (London: Harvard University Press, 1977), pp. 213-223.

25. Case Comments, "Accommodating Patent and Antitrust Law," pp. 89-91.

26. Arrow, "Economic Welfare."

27. Joseph A. Schumpeter, *Capitalism, Socialism and Democracy* (New York: Harper, 1942), pp. 87-106.

28. See Klein, *Dynamic Economics,* pp. 35-67.

29. See Case Comments, "Accommodating Patent and Antitrust Law," pp. 89-91.

30. *Kewanee Oil v. Bicron,* 416 U.S. 470 (1973); see also Russell B. Stevenson, Jr., *Corporations and Information: Secrecy, Access, and Disclosure* (Baltimore: Johns Hopkins University Press, 1980), pp. 27-30.

31. See Jager, *1982 Trade Secrets Handbook,* pp. 27-38.

32. Sometimes the competitor of a pharmaceutical company needs only to know the type of animal on which a particular compound is being tested in order to deduce the type of human malady the research project is trying to remedy. This knowledge triggers quite naturally a great deal of information about future marketing activities.

33. Popper *Open Society,* pp. 259-280.

34. Hayek, "The Use of Knowledge," p. 77.

35. On the difficulty of measuring cost in the form relevant to economics, see James Buchanan, *Cost and Choice* (New York: Markham, 1969), pp. 51-69.

36. On the problem of the encouragement and discovery of new means and ends as at the heart of economic problems, see Israel Kirzner, *Competition and Entrepreneurship* (Chicago: University of Chicago Press, 1973), pp. 1-29.

37. Alfred Chandler, *Strategy and Structure,* (Cambridge, Mass.: MIT Press, 1962), pp. 25-27.

38. Ibid., p. 27.

39. Ibid., pp. 217-219.

40. "Berry Gordy, Jr.," in *Current Biography* (1975), pp. 168-175.

41. J.B. Schnapp, "Soichiro Honda, Japan's Inventive Iconoclast," *Wall Street Journal,* 1 February 1982.

42. James T. Bennett and Manuel H. Johnson, "The Political Economy of Federal Government Paperwork," *Policy Review* 7 (Winter 1979):27-43. This view is a frequently heard complaint by Small Business Administration lobbyists.

43. Thomas O. McGarity and Sidney A. Shapiro call for information disclosure even when technological information is present in order to protect health and safety in "The Trade Secret Status of Health and Safety Testing Information Reforming Agency Disclosure Policies," *Harvard Law Review* 93 (March 1980):837-888. See also Mark Q. Connelley for a supporting view, also quite cynical, about businesses' need for nondisclosure in "Secrets and Smokescreens," pp. 107-173.

44. McGarity and Shapiro, "Trade Secret Status," p. 837.

45. Ibid.

46. *National Parks and Conservation Association v. Morton,* 498 F2d 765, 770 (1974).

47. Connelly, "Secrets and Smokescreens," pp. 265-266; and Stevenson, *Corporations,* pp. 21-25.

48. Arthur Miller, *Death of a Salesman* (New York: Viking Press, 1949).

49. John K. Galbraith, *The Affluent Society* (Boston: Houghton Mifflin Co., 1958), pp. 152-160; and Vance Packard, *The Hidden Persuaders* (New York: Pocket Books, 1958).

50. Nicholas Kaldor, "The Economic Aspects of Advertising," *Review of Economic Studies* 18 (1950):1-27.

51. Kirzner, *Competition* pp. 145-151.

52. The role of vision in the progress of both business and science is a familiar theme in Schumpeter's writings. See his discussion in *History of Economic Analysis* (New York: Oxford University Press, 1963), pp. 41-42.

53. *Audio Technical Services v. Department of the Army,* 487 F. Supp. 779 (1979).

54. See for example, *Wearly v. F.T.C.,* 462 F. Supp. 589 (1978); and *Worthington Compressors v. Costle,* 662 F.2d 45 (1981).

55. Compare Stevenson, *Corporations,* pp. 33-35.

56. Ibid. See also Randolph M. Lyon, "Auctions and Alternative Procedures for Allocating Pollution Rights," *Land Economics* 58 (1982):16-32.

57. Sanford L. Jacobs, "Small Military Suppliers Fight Tightening of Information Act," *Wall Street Journal,* 28 December 1981, p. 11.

58. Compare Richard A. Posner, "Information and Antitrust: Reflections on the *Gypsum* and *Engineers* Decisions," *Georgetown Law Journal* 67 (June 1979):1187-1203.

59. Economists have made a strong start in the direction of work on the question; see Lyon, "Auctions."

60. See, for example, *Gulf and Western Industries v. United States,* 615 F.2d 527 (1979).

61. Ibid.

62. Alfred D. Chandler, Jr., *The Visible Hand: The Managerial Revolution in American Business* (Cambridge: Harvard University Press, 1977).

6 A Case Study: The U.S. Chemical Industry

In chapter 5, we constructed a theoretical framework for the purpose of analyzing the economic effects of information disclosure. We outlined important distinctions between the imperatives of static efficiency and those of dynamic efficiency. Also, we identified a type of information called circumstantially relevant business information, which is of vital importance in a dynamically efficient market economy but which has been ignored by those who have been instrumental in drafting and enacting freedom-of-information legislation.

Debates on the economic costs of the Freedom of Information Act typically focus on those few horror stories of FOIA information disclosure that are well documented in scholarly books and articles on this controversial federal legislation. The next two chapters focus on two industries that have been the center of much of the controversy surrounding the Freedom of Information Act—namely, the chemical industry and the pharmaceutical industry.

These industries were not selected randomly. Because of the public-health and safety issues relating to the production, marketing, consumption and disposal of chemicals and drugs, these industries are regulated highly, with heavy reporting requirements imposed by the federal government. Their mandated disclosures contain much information that would be classified as trade secret by almost any definition. In addition, they contain vital information on employment, marketing, transportation, production, and disposal that fall under the heading of circumstantially relevant business information. This latter category of information is important because it is unlikely that it would be protected as trade-secret information. Yet, it is, in many cases, every bit as important to the success of a new chemical or drug as its molecular formula.

As we demonstrated in chapter 3, the volume of FOIA requests to the Environmental Protection Agency, the primary regulator of the chemical industry, and the Food and Drug Administration, the primary regulator of the pharmaceutical industry, has been large relative to other agencies. In 1981, the Food and Drug Administration ranked first with 33,384 requests, while the Environmental Protection Agency ranked third among those agencies that collect commercially important information with 7,011 requests. As a percentage of total agency requests, those made by industry, third-party intermediaries, and law firms to the Food and Drug Administration and the

Environmental Protection Agency equaled 86 percent and 83 percent respectively in 1981. On the one hand, if we can assume that government agencies are willing and able to protect the clearly obvious and identifiable trade secrets of industry, then the volume and source of requests to these agencies become somewhat of a mystery. On the other hand, if one realizes that some valuable shreds of information usually are not given top trade-secret protection, then the volume of requests becomes more understandable. We posit that circumstantially relevant business information is leaking from federal agencies and that the leakage and threat of leakage is influencing industry behavior.

Chapters 6 and 7 take contrasting approaches to link the Freedom of Information Act to the economic incentives for investment. In this chapter, we take a microeconomic approach. We shall show that the Freedom of Information Act is but one of many layers of regulations imposed on the chemical industry. The Freedom of Information Act is significant because it is a disclosure statute that transcends individual industry and agency boundaries and is superimposed on other laws. We shall show the reader how this layering of regulations has created unintended gaps in confidentiality protection and inconsistencies within and among various laws and, as a result, has led to legitimate concerns among industry representatives about their ability to protect proprietary information.

Chapter 7 views the pharmaceutical industry from a broader, macroeconomic viewpoint. Using industry and agency interviews, as well as documented evidence on the pharmaceutical industry, chapter 7 goes beyond the horror stories to examine new incentives the Freedom of Information Act gives to ethical-drug companies in their investment calculations. It shows that the international location of pharmaceutical facilities may be very much influenced by the regulatory burden imposed on this industry.

An Overview of the Chemical Industry

The chemical industry is not a textbook example of a purely competetive market. In fact, it is not one market at all. Within the category of chemical and allied products, the U.S. Department of Commerce lists twenty-eight separate industries.[1] Of these industries, thirteen have market structures where the top four firms account for at least 50 percent of the total value of shipments.[2] In such an oligopolistic setting, there exists mutual interdependence in the setting of market strategies among firms. One industry analyst, however, has described the short-run relationship among the major chemical firms as "friendly, if not collusive."[3] It is an industry where start-up costs are high and where efficiency often is achieved by increasing the scale of operation.[4] Patents exist and other short-term barriers to entry are common.

In spite of the aforementioned characteristics, the chemical industry, in general, exhibits a high degree of competition. While totally new plants might be expensive to construct and while patents do exist, most of the markets are contestable.[5] Patented products have rival patents surrounding them, creating large cross elasticities of demand among individual firms.[6] R&D expenditures have created inroads into existing markets and have opened new markets for chemical companies.[7] The invention of new products and processes in these industries has turned what are perceived to be friendly relations in the short run into a battle for survival in the long run. Moreover, the competition for skilled technicians has produced above-average returns for industry personnel.[8] In this industry, as in many others, concentration ratios are not a good reflection of the degree of competition. Many competitive products that are excluded from the arbitrary classification system of the government and international inroads that have been made into the U.S. market are ignored by this measure.

Since the 1920s, growth in the chemical industry has been supply oriented or technology based.[9] There has been a stream of pathbreaking inventions and innovations that have changed the patterns of production and consumption.[10] Almost any book written on the important inventions of the twentieth century will be sure to include discoveries such as rayon, nylon, compressed gas, and petrochemical products.[11] In the area of polymerization, it will include synthetic fibers, plastics, and foams. Surface-chemistry inventions such as detergents, hair sprays, and repellants, as well as new solid-chemistry advances, will be mentioned. More recently, it would highlight the advances in biotechnology that have produced vaccines, insulin, and a variety of gene-splicing products that hold the potential for curing many of our most dreaded diseases like cancer.[12]

Because of this combination of static and dynamic competition, Edwin Mansfield was able to report that during the late 1960s the chemical industry provided U.S. citizens with a social return on product innovations that was substantially larger (71 percent versus 9 percent) than the private return to company owners.[13] Similarly, process innovations were found to have social benefits in excess of private benefits (32 percent versus 25 percent).[14] These positive externalities are the by-products of the ingenuity and strength of a highly active industry in which R&D has played a major role.

Over the decade from 1970 to 1980, nominal R&D expenditures in the chemicals-and-allied-products area increased at a 10 percent annual rate, with a 14 percent surge from 1979 to 1980.[15] In 1980, $4.6 billion were spent on R&D—over 10 percent of the total R&D expenditures in the United States.[16] Moreover, sales in 1981 were over $177 billion, and U.S. exports were estimated at over $20 billion, giving the United States a chemical balance-of-trade surplus of nearly $12 billion in 1981.[17]

The growth of the chemical industry has been a mixed blessing. With the increasing sophistication of the technologies used and the potential harm associated with exposure to even small quantities of certain chemicals, a public concern arose that the market system and the legal remedy of tort compensation could not protect health and the environment adequately.[18] Observers realized that the overwhelming majority of chemicals posed no threat to health or safety, but public sentiment for stricter controls was sparked by the publicity surrounding products such as vinyl chloride, polychlorinated biphenyls, flurocarbons, Tris, Kepone, and other proven or suspected carcinogens.[19]

The media have been filled with heart-wrenching stories of families exposed to toxic chemicals.[20] Moreover, scientific studies by the National Cancer Institute have estimated that between 60 and 90 percent of all cancer in the United States was caused by some environmental factor.[21] Inasmuch as cancer is the leading cause of death in the United States, it is not without justification that the public should seek safeguards from the threat of exposure to toxic and/or cancer-causing chemicals.[22]

In 1976, there were an estimated 2 million chemical compounds, and nearly a quarter of a million new chemicals are produced each year.[23] Of these new chemicals, nearly 1,000 of them reach the U.S. marketplace yearly.[24] At present, chemical companies sell over 80,000 chemicals with over 183,000 names.[25] By sheer size alone, no wonder the chemical industry became a target for greater government supervision and regulation.

The Environmental Protection Agency

The Environmental Protection Agency was established in 1970 to regulate air, noise, and water pollution; pesticides; radiation; and solid-waste disposal. In the spirit of the new wave of regulation, the agency was supposed to cut across industry lines and control pollution regardless of its source.[26] Under its jurisdictional umbrella, the Environmental Protection Agency centralized the responsibility for fifteen environmental programs that had been supervised previously by a variety of other agencies. Among the major responsibilities of the Environmental Protection Agency are the enforcement of the Clear Air Act (1976),[27] the Federal Insecticide, Fungicide, and Rodenticide Act (1972),[28] the Food, Drug, and Cosmetics Act (1976),[29] the Marine Protection, Resource, and Sanitation Act (1972),[30] the Noise Pollution Act (1970),[31] the Resource Conservation and Recovery Act (1976),[32] the Safe Drinking Water Act (1976),[33] the Toxic Substances Control Act (1976),[34] and the Federal Water Pollution Control Act (1976).[35]

Each one of these environmental regulations mandates the submission of business information to the Environmental Protection Agency. In many cases, the submitted information is considered to be proprietary by the submitter, and because of the acknowledged sensitivity of some of this information, rights and procedures have been written into each act. Among these acts, confidentiality rules vary, and superimposed over these varying confidentiality rules is the Freedom of Information Act. Inasmuch as the same chemical might have a variety of uses, companies must submit the appropriate information for each one of these uses under each one of these acts. Corporate lawyers and managers, therefore, must be fully aware of the multiplicity of confidentiality rules in each act and with the legal and economic implications of their varying combinations and permutations.

For the purpose of this book, we focus our investigation on the confidentiality aspects of the Toxic Substances Control Act. We have chosen this act because of the apparent degree of concern by business with its information-submitting requirements.[36] In the view of James T. O'Reilly, "the 1976 Toxic Substances Control Act (TSCA) is the single greatest source of chemical industry concern over public disclosure by federal agencies."[37]

An Overview of the Toxic Substances Control Act

The Toxic Substances Control Act (TSCA) was passed by Congress in 1976 to control the manufacture, processing, distribution, use, and disposal of chemicals that are used in the United States and that present or may present an unreasonable risk to society.[38] Congress realized that the complete elimination of chemical risk was impossible and therefore limited the supervisory powers of the Environmental Protection Agency to those products that may present an unreasonable risk or chemicals for which there is a reasonable basis to conclude that they will present an unreasonable risk.[39] However, in those cases where evidence is available to support the Environmental Protection Agency's concern, regulatory decisions also must weigh the potential benefits the chemical will provide.[40] While a strict cost-benefit analysis is usually not possible because of the inadequacy of quantifiable costs and benefits, the hope in Congress was that benefits would influence decision making and that the act would not stifle invention and innovation.[41]

The Toxic Substances Control Act specifically lists products that are not to be regulated by the Environmental Protection Agency.[42] However, a close reading of it shows that Congress gave such an expansive definition to the term *chemical substance* that virtually any product could be brought under the agency's purview.[43] To administer the act, Congress created the Office of Toxic Substances (since 1980 it has been renamed the Office of Pesticides and Toxic Substances). As its first step, the office sought to compile a list of all chemicals (except by-products and impurities) produced in or imported into the United States for commercial purposes since 1975. This inventory would delimit the breadth of the regulatory task and would furnish a guide for all producers to chemicals that were already regulated by the Environmental Protection Agency.

To that end, it initiated a two-phased period over which such an inventory would be compiled.[44] During phase I, an initial inventory was to be prepared and reported by early 1978. After publication of the initial inventory, a 210-day interval would follow that would allow companies to add to the existing list of chemicals. The publication of the initial inventory also would mark the beginning of the 90-day premanufacturing notification program.[45] Notification to the Environmental Protection Agency would be required before any new chemical could be marketed or before a significant new use of an old chemical could be made.[46] Publication of the revised inventory, delayed until 1 June 1979, eventually included 43,278 chemicals.

The premanufacturing notification requirement is the result of a congressional compromise between those who desired to control a chemical before it reached the marketplace and those concerned with protecting its proprietary information.[47] It is an important and sometimes overlooked fact that notification does not imply EPA approval of a chemical. If no action is taken on a product within the ninety-day waiting period, production may begin.[48] Many Americans rest more easily because of the government surveillance of the chemical industry. While a regulatory buffer does exist, the plain fact is that no one knows the long-term risks of a new chemical, and the Environmental Protection Agency has no magic crystal ball or superior analytical talent for evaluating those risks. Moreover, it does not approve or disapprove chemicals for which notification is given; it merely does not disapprove a new chemical.

If an author wanted to write a book entitled *Everything You Ever Wanted to Know about Your Chemical Competitors But Were Afraid to Ask*, he would have to go no further than to report the contents of the revised inventory and the premanufacturing notifications. These two sources of information centralize, classify, and quantify almost all of a company's production, marketing, employment, and disposal information for a chemical.[49] Unrestricted access to these data would provide competitors with information that would take years and thousands of dollars to duplicate or that would be impossible to duplicate. As might be expected, the revised inventory and the premanufacturing notification became the center of the confidentiality dispute over the Toxic Substances Control Act.

The creation of the first document, that is, the revised inventory, was subject to an early industry challenge by the Polaroid Company.[50] Threatened by the potential loss of its valuable trade secrets for twenty film-developing chemicals, Polaroid refused to submit a list of its chemicals to the Environmental Protection Agency. Polaroid claimed that the agency was violating its Fifth Amendment rights to due process.

The Polaroid challenge to the Environmental Protection Agency prompted major changes in the agency's collection and handling of business information.[51] With these improvements, Polaroid dropped its suit without the court ever deciding on the due-process issue. To protect the confidentiality of chemicals on the revised inventory, the Environmental Protection Agency permitted information-submitting firms to use generic names. Moreover, other companies would not be allowed to use the test (that is, health and safety) data of that generic chemical unless by chance they submitted a premanufacturing notification for a chemical with identical characteristics. In that case, the Environmental Protection Agency would be willing to let the second company benefit from the first company's research. Thus, the existence of such a bona fide second producer would permit the Environmental Protection Agency to release health and safety studies that otherwise could not be withheld under the Toxic Substances Control Act.[52] The Environmental Protection Agency published the revised collection and handling procedures in its security manual.[53] The measures were an apparent success. From 1976 to 1980, no major case came to court to challenge the act's reporting requirements.[54]

Like the revised inventory document, the premanufacturing notification was also created by the Toxic Substances Control Act and raised confidentiality concerns. Notification includes information that details the manufacture, processing, use, and disposal of new chemicals or mixtures.[55] This cradle-to-grave report identifies almost every fact about a chemical's life. The only vital pieces of information that are obviously absent from the notification are financial data on price, sales volume, and profit.

Section I of a premanufacturing notification gives general information on the manufacturer's identity, the chemical identity, production and marketing data, methods of transporting the chemicals, risk assessments, and detection methods for identifying the new chemical in the environment. This section lays bare the heart of the chemical's formula and its structural design. The production and marketing information gives estimates of three-year production volumes, the expected markets in which the chemicals could be sold (that is, the categories of use), and the degree to which the firm has lined up buyers of the product. This section goes on to give specific insights into the methods of transportation, the health and environmental risks expected to result from the chemical's manufacture and use, as well as the methods for identifying and quantifying the chemical in the environment.

Section II provides information on human exposure and environmental release. This section is full of important employment data and, indirectly, data on costs, pricing, and profit. It lists the site that will produce the chemical by name, type, hours of operation, and volume of production. A block diagram is provided, showing the major operations, chemical conversions, and reactions; the by-products of the process; and the amount of human exposure at each point that the chemical could be released into the environment. This information is broken down by the number of employees exposed and the duration of that exposure.

Such information gives instant insights into the capital/labor ratios of the chemical process. Combining the estimated production for each facility with its capacity figure can lead to competitive strategies for penetration marketing, pricing policies, capital (location) investments, employment, recruiting, and staffing.

This information can also be helpful in planning strategies for other chemicals as well. In a true sense, the real cost of producing a new chemical is the sacrifice in revenues that could be earned by producing some other product. The employees and plant capacity used in one effort cannot be used simultaneously to produce something else. If a site is producing more of the new product, what product is being curtailed? If no chemicals are being curtailed, where are the new employees and capital resources coming from to support the expansion? What costs are being incurred on the income statement to make such an expansion? These questions find partial answers in the premanufacturing notification. The policy issue is whether or not this information should be protected from public disclosure.

Section III of the notification is a list of attachments including one complete and one sanitized copy of the health and safety studies. While the Toxic Substances Control Act requires that all health and safety studies be released, companies may protect information pertaining to the manufacturing process or the quantities of chemicals used in a mixture.

Full disclosure of a premanufacturing notification would reveal to competitors not only a complete description of the chemical but also a full profile of the markets in which the firm expects to sell, its employment figures, and volume of production. In addition, to the extent a firm has to disclose the contents of a chemical process's waste, valuable insight can be gained about the inputs into that process. There seems to be little doubt that, if the chemical could not be patented and if a company were relying on the lag between innovation and imitation to recoup its investment, disclosure would shorten drastically this time period and profit would be reduced or eliminated. In 1979, George C. Dominguez, an outspoken critic of the act, said that disclosure would amount to "giving them the whole package. You're not only giving them the chemical identity, but you're giving them all the market research information. You're not only telling them what to make, but what to market because you give estimated production volumes. . . . What's left?"[56]

In drafting the Toxic Substances Control Act, Congress tried to balance the rights of the submitter companies to confidentiality and the rights of the public to information that is vital to the market process.[57] To ensure that sufficient consumer information was available, the act mandated the disclosure of all health and safety studies.[58] Such studies must be performed on all chemicals used for commercial, test marketing,[59] or R&D purposes as well as for chemicals on the revised inventory for which the EPA notification is necessary.[60] The tests cover a broad area of human and environmental effects such as epidemiological, occupational exposure, toxicological, clinical, and ecological. However, while release of these studies is mandated, the Environmental Protection Agency is restrained by the act from disclosing the process by which a chemical or mixture is made or the proportions of chemicals used in the mixture.[61]

To receive EPA assurances of protection for confidential information, the submitting company must substantiate its confidentiality claims.[62] EPA regulations require identification and itemization of those parts of the premanufacturing notification that are considered to be confidential, the time period over which confidentiality should last, a list of the measures taken to protect the information from third-party disclosure within the company, the extent to which the information is already disclosed, and estimates of likely harm to future government data gathering.[63]

The Toxic Substances Control Act uses the Freedom of Information Act's trade-secrets exemption as the standard for its confidentiality obligations.[64] Congress relied on the Freedom of Information Act because of its established judicial history.[65] Under the Freedom of Information Act, if information is found to be trade secret or commercial or financial, then the Environmental Protection Agency may not disclose it.[66] This stands in stark contrast to the Freedom of Information Act where the release of information found to be within the trade-secrets exemption is at the discretion of the agency.[67] It should be understood that the Toxic Substances Control Act does not mandate the withholding of any specific information and therefore does not qualify under the third exemption of the Freedom of Information Act— "matters specifically exempted by statute." It requires withholding from disclosure only after a determination is made that the questioned information lies within the trade-secrets exemption of the Freedom of Information Act.

The Toxic Substances Control Act also differs from the Freedom of Information Act in its requirement that notification be given to any company that has submitted information and has marked it as confidential.[68] Notice of thirty days must be given unless an emergency arises that, depending upon its degree, can reduce the time period to fifteen days or twenty-four hours.[69] If the Environmental Protection Agency has not made a predetermination review of the confidentiality status of the information, then it makes no difference whether or not these data are found eventually to warrant protection; notification is required.[70] In most cases where information is submitted to the Environment Protection Agency, a review is not done until an FOIA request is made.[71]

Both EPA rules and the requirements under the Toxic Substances Control Act combine to give information submitters identifiable rights whenever an FOIA request is made. If an FOIA request is received for submitted business information, the Environmental Protection Agency must notify the submitter company and provide it with the opportunity to comment.[72] In cases where the Environmental Protection Agency has predetermined and endorsed the confidentiality status of the information, an immediate rejection of the request is made, and further action awaits an appeal by the requester.[73] In those cases where no predetermination of the confidentiality status has been made, an immediate rejection is sent to the requester, and notice is sent to the submitter company to comment further on its claims of confidentiality. Without this type of substantiation, disclosure is made on the thirty-first day after the information submitter is notified of the third-party request.[74] In this case, a determination of the confidentiality status of the information is made regardless of whether an appeal is made by the third party.[75] When the Environmental Protection Agency decides that information should be disclosed, only a judicial challenge or specific court injunction will prevent its release.[76]

Confidentiality Problems under the Toxic Substances Control Act

In spite of the apparent safeguards that Congress built into the act, many legitimate industry fears exist that confidential information can be disclosed. While part of the concern relates to the disclosure of trade secrets proper, we suspect that there is an equal interest in protecting the generalized bits and pieces of information that we call circumstantially relevant business information. Some of the industry concerns have to do with the wording of the Toxic Substances Control Act and stand apart from the Freedom of Information Act. These concerns about the vagueness in testing requirements and inconsistencies between the sections of the act that mandate the disclosure of health and safety studies and the confidentiality section that permits protection of the chemical's identity are included under this heading. Moreover, industry representatives feel that the disclosures made pursuant to a test-market exemption are such as to nullify many of the benefits it was supposed to provide. Finally, industry has reason to believe the act has caused a decline in chemical innovation.

The interface between the Toxic Substances Control Act and the Freedom of Information Act introduces a panoply of new concerns. First, there is a feeling that the assurances of confidentiality and the requirement of notification under the Toxic Substances Control Act are weakened by the Freedom of Information Act. Second, there are contradictions between the rules of the two acts that have not, as yet, been resolved. Third, there is a major concern not only that domestic harm can result from the disclosure of TSCA-submitted information but also that international trade and investment patterns will be influenced by the acts. Fourth, the cross exchange of information mandated by the Toxic Substances Control Act permits information disclosure to a number of other parties and without notification to the submitter. Industry feels this increases the chance of disclosure as well as the cost of policing the FOIA requests to government.

Finally, industry is concerned that some pieces of information in agency files are practically priceless. Their disclosure would seriously jeopardize the future of the firm and the well-being of its owners. While this information is protected by the full faith and effort of the agency, the disclosure provisions of the Freedom of Information Act along with the possibility of human error make the information vulnerable to disclosure.

Each of these concerns is the focus of the next section of this chapter. It should be apparent that the Toxic Substances Control Act and Freedom of Information Act are legislative realities that chemical manufacturers must consider in their attempts to protect confidential information.[77] Since the Toxic Substances Control Act does not prohibit information release, all information gathered from business by the agency is theoretically subject to disclosure through FOIA requests.[78] While the industry possesses many trade secrets that are valuable in and of themselves, it also possesses those particularized bits and pieces of information that have proprietary value when combined with other types of information or gathered over time.

The fear that such information might cause competitive harm when released in this fragmented form has been articulated by chemical-industry representatives and analysts.[79] Their fears are prompted not only by the volume and the value of the information that businesses knowingly submit to the government but also by the valuable shreds of information that inadvertently find their way into federal records. For instance, O'Reilly, in his book on chemical-industry regulation, advises lawyers to make sure that inspectors do not go beyond the limits of their authority.[80] In many cases, unauthorized questions are asked, pictures are taken, and sketches are drawn that could jeopardize proprietary information seriously. Companies that permit such inspections but that rely on the government inspector to carry out the letter of his job very well could have lost confidential information without knowing it. Moreover, since the Toxic Substances Control Act requires notification only when a company labels the information as confidential, there is no reason for the Environmental Protection Agency to notify the company of the release of the inspection reports.[81]

Problems with the Toxic Substances Control Act

Vague Testing Requirements

When Congress passed the Toxic Substances Control Act, it gave the Environmental Protection Agency broad discretionary powers. As a result, the rules governing premanufacturing regulations are still fluid and have yet to reach final form. For instance, the act requires that firms test products that the EPA administrator finds to present an unreasonable risk.[82] However, the types of tests required were not mandated, and they are largely at the discretion of the administrator. This practice differs from that of the European Economic Community, where the submitter knows beforehand the battery of tests that must be performed. The Act thereby introduces a source of uncertainty into the premanufacturing notification concerning the ultimate cost of the notification and the amount of information that must be produced and disclosed.[83]

The cost of chemical tests varies widely depending upon the type and the duration of the test. The simplest toxicity tests cost about $1,000 per chemical.[84] More-involved tests on a chemical, like animal tests that might last over two years, vary in price between $50,000 and $250,000.[85] Early attempts to quantify the total cost to industry as a result of TSCA compliance brought estimates that varied widely.[86] At one extreme, the Dow Chemical Company estimated the yearly cost at approximately $2 billion, while at the other extreme, the Environmental Protection Agency estimated the cost at close to $80 million.[87] One analysis has shown the results to be closer to the Environmental Protection Agency's projections, but the reader is warned that there are many ways to estimate costs, and accounting textbooks are filled with varying ways to allocate overhead and value resources.[88] Unless one researches the assumptions behind cost studies of this type, no definitive statement can be made about its comparison to other studies.

The act requires test data whenever the administrator finds that a chemical "may present an unreasonable risk of injury to health or the environment."[89] Lacking such a reasonable doubt, the administrator may still order tests if the human or environmental exposure and release will be substantial or if production volume is deemed to be substantial.[90] Should the administrator pass a rule, the judicial standard of review would be conducted under the arbitrary-and-capricious section of the Administrative Procedure Act[91]; the standard for EPA rulings was intended by Congress to be stricter and to require "substantial evidence."[92] However, the courts have been lenient, usually, in reviewing the Environmental Protection Agency's rule-making authority.[93] The future path of judicial decisions is not cast in concrete, but it seems that the agency has been held to the lesser of the standards—namely, the Administrative Procedure Act's arbitrary-and-capricious standard.

Contradictions within the Act

When Congress passed the Toxic Substances Control Act, it wrote a provision into it allowing a company to claim as confidential the chemical identity of the product and to substitute an EPA-approved generic name instead.[94] At the same time, Congress mandated the disclosure of all health and safety studies.[95] Inasmuch as the chemical's identity is revealed in the health and safety studies, a conflict arises. The proponents of the disclosure of the chemical's identity argue that such information is needed to be able to authenticate the validity of the test results.[96] Opponents of disclosure argue that blind tests are done all the time on chemical products, that they are more objective, and moreover, that disclosure would be tantamount to a breach of the confidentiality assurances given to industry when the act was being drafted.[97] In any case, the contradiction results in an act divided upon itself. To the extent the issue is not resolved, it will continue to be a source of industry concern.

Problems with the Test-Market Exemption

Within the Toxic Substances Control Act are provisions for granting test-market exemptions for chemicals that have not been produced as yet for commercial use but that require some market feedback before a company will commit any additional resources to the product.[98] Test-market exemptions are helpful to an innovating firm that is unsure of its market demand and needs time to evaluate the marketability of a product without disclosing information to competitors. The problem with test-market exemptions is that Toxic Substances Control Act requires their immediate reporting in the *Federal Register.*[99] Companies that might apply for such exemptions have expressed the concern that public notice in the *Federal Register* can alert competitors to the production of this product and permit them to offset some of the advantages the innovating firm may have had.[100] Their concern is addressed especially to those products that are either unpatentable or that have close substitutes because these are the products most vulnerable to competitive challenges by other firms.

A second problem with the test-market exemption is that it requires EPA approval of the drug within forty-five days of submission.[101] A premanufacturing notification does not require EPA approval; it only requires a nonaction against the chemical. Moreover, the exemption's review period is half (forty-five days) of the notification review period (ninety days).[102] There is some feeling that as a result of those factors, the Environmental Protection Agency is much stricter in its exemption review than in its notification review. Again, the effect is to reduce the ability of chemical companies to get test-market exemptions.[103]

The Decline in Chemical-Industry Innovation

A recent study done for the Chemical Specialties Manufacturers Association (CSMA) found that the Toxic Substances Control Act had caused a significant decline (26 percent) in innovation among the 198 ingredient suppliers of product manufacturers in the chemical-specialties industry over the 1976-1978 period.[104] It went on to identify small companies of under $100 million in sales as the cause of the overwhelming majority (98 percent) of the decline.[105] Moreover, these small firms had a probability that was fifty times higher than large chemical-specialty firms of rejecting a product due to the cost of TSCA compliance in spite of the fact that the small companies' cost were, on average, 37 percent lower than that of large companies.[106] Finally, the study identified the decline in risky ventures (38 percent) to be over 27 percent higher than the decline in safe ventures (14 percent).[107] In a study of industrial R&D, Edwin Mansfield and his colleagues refuted the Schumpeterian[108] and Galbraithian[109] arguments that R&D is conducted predominantly by the large firms in the industry.[110] They showed significant small-firm and interindustry activity in the innovation and development of chemical products and processes.[111] Their work only serves to reinforce the CSMA-study findings that increases in the costs of innovation, especially for small firms, are likely to cause significant declines in innovative activity.

Problems with the Toxic Substances Control Act and the Freedom of Information Act

Weak Assurances of Confidentiality

In spite of the language that Congress included in the Toxic Substances Control Act to protect business information from disclosure, in fact, the protection is more apparent than real. Information submitters are vulnerable to decision reversals, disagreements over the data's confidentiality status, and court challenges to EPA-protected information. Data marked confidential entitle the submitter to notice before the information is disclosed.[112] Assuming no predetermination review was made, this notice gives the submitter thirty days to convince the agency that the information should not be given out.[113] The burden is on the submitter to demonstrate confidentiality and not on the requester to show that some net social benefit will be gained by the information's release.

Of course, if the agency finds that the information does not warrant confidentiality protection, it will release the information unless the submitter begins a court challenge or gains a restraining order.[114] There is little to criticize here because the companies were not intended to be the sole determiners of the propriety of submitted information under the Toxic Substances Control Act. Yet, if the agency finds that the information does fall within the trade-secrets exemption of the Freedom of Information Act, this bars the agency from disclosing the information discretionally.[115] However, the information is not totally immune from disclosure because the Toxic Substances Control Act is not a withholding statute that would prevent release under exemption (b)(3)—matters specifically exempted by statute—of the Freedom of Information Act. Thus, all submitted information is subject to potential disclosure through an FOIA request. Depending upon the forum (court), the chances of ultimate disclosure can vary substantially.[116]

A related problem occurs when the agency changes its mind about its predetermination review and confidentiality classification.[117] The basis for such a change of heart could be the discovery of new facts, a change in law, or the finding that the previous decision was in error. These are valid bases for such a change in position and would be considered to be one of the risks of being in the chemical business and submitting mandated information. However, when the information was submitted on a voluntary basis, release cannot be considered in the same light.[118] While the Toxic Substances Control Act assures the submitter of notification and a chance to comment before the release, this is little comfort to a company that agreed to submit information only on the grounds that it would be protected.[119]

Contradictions in Law and between the Acts

The Freedom of Information Act is unabashedly a disclosure statute,[120] but the Toxic Substances Control Act has confidentiality protection along with mandatory-disclosure provisions written into it. One of the ways in which these two acts might cause competitive harm is when a company is entering a new area of business or diversifying its product line. In this case, the mere knowledge by competitors of this company's decision might permit them to enact counterstrategies that would offset much of the gain anticipated. Under the Toxic Substances Control Act, the name of a manufacturer may be shielded from disclosure, but at the same time, the Freedom of Information Act requires that a reason be attached to any FOIA denial.[121] If a trade-secrets exemption is given, competitors know, at least, that the Environmental Protection Agency has the company's information to protect.[122]

As an example, suppose that company A heard a rumor that company B had invented a chemical for industrial cleaning. Previously, company B had not been involved in this area, and therefore, company A was able to earn high profit margins by charging premium prices. To check the rumor, company A sends an FOIA request to the Environmental Protection Agency for all the health and safety information on company B's chemical. If the Environmental Protection Agency sends a rejection to company A, claiming that the information is a trade secret, then the rumor is confirmed and company A can begin to plot a counterstrategy.

International Leakages of Information

The United States has enjoyed persistent chemical trade surpluses relative to our international trading partners over the post-World War II period.[123] These exports have earned valuable international exchange that have promoted the two-way flow of goods and services. Moreover, exports have served to draw resources into an area in which the United States has an international comparative advantage and have helped to exploit the economies of scale that exist in the production of chemicals. However, international competition in the chemical industry is vigorous, and the disclosure provisions within the Freedom of Information Act along with the information-submitting obligations under the Toxic Substances Control Act serve to threaten U.S. industry with unfair competition on the one hand and the U.S. consumer with fewer foreign chemicals on the other hand.[124]

Mansfield has shown that foreign development of chemical products is substantial.[125] Disclosure of health and safety studies to these foreign companies could help them to gain licenses in their foreign markets.[126] This is an especially serious problem when the foreign country does not permit patent protection for the U.S. inventor company. Where patent protection is available, the disclosure of information could help foreign rivals to produce goods that are close substitutes to the original product.[127]

Some company representatives have gone so far as to say that the mere identification of a company with even a generically named product might be sufficient to disclose that the company is entering a new line of business and thereby could reduce lead-time advantages.[128] Industry analysts have labeled this provision in the Toxic Substances Control Act as a primary incentive for locating R&D facilities abroad and thereby eliminating some of the risks this provision imposes.[129] Some observers also have suggested that test marketing or the introduction of new chemicals in the marketplace could be done abroad so that problems could be solved prior to huge capital investments and without the threat of disclosure.[130]

To the extent that TSCA requirements are more stringent than foreign countries' standards, the act establishes a nontariff barrier for the importation of chemicals as well.[131] Under its provisions, the Toxic Substances Control Act requires that importers be treated the same as domestic manufacturers.[132] Therefore, a foreign company with a chemical that could not be patented in the United States might be reluctant to submit itself to the disclosure requirements of the Toxic Substances Control Act. While conservative analysts heap considerable blame on both the Food and Drug Administration and the Environmental Protection Agency because of the length of time it takes to approve new drugs, chemicals, and pesticides, we have here a case where desired chemicals may never enter the U.S. approval (or notification) process.[133] The U.S. consumer is the loser. Beneficial products might never reach the U.S. market because of potential confidentiality breaches. We return to this issue in the next chapter to see how similar problems confront the ethical-drug industry.

Cross Exchange of Information

Information collected under Toxic Substances Control Act is extensive, and the Environmental Protection Agency has responded to industry fears by providing a systematic way of dealing with submitted business information that gives companies rights to notification and a hearing. Not all agencies have rules like these. This is a concern to information-submitting companies because the Toxic Substances Control Act permits rather widespread dissemination of this information. Disclosure can be made "to any officer or employee of the United States in connection with [his] official duties . . . or for specific law enforcement purposes"[134]; to contractors such as graduate students, chemical research labs, and college professors if such disclosure is needed for contract performance[135]; to protect public health or the environment from unreasonable risk of injury[136]; and in any proceeding under the Toxic Substances Control Act.[137] The Environmental Protection Agency also may disclose this information to any member of Congress.[138]

Such widespread dissemination of this information multiplies the chances of disclosure, and these chances are magnified further by the fact that the Toxic Substances Control Act places no notification requirements on these aforementioned disclosures.[139] Under the Toxic Substances Control Act, it is possible for information to be distributed to many other agencies and individuals without the submitter company knowing it. This is disconcerting for the company that has hired legal talent or an FOIA intermediary to monitor the FOIA requests submitted to the Environmental Protection Agency for firm-sensitive information. It could very well be that these expenditures are for naught since the surveillance is on the wrong agency.[140]

It becomes difficult for a company to protect its information when the information is collected by one agency for a certain purpose and then is divulged to another agency for an entirely different purpose. In the future, this problem will grow unless it is addressed by Congress. The recently instituted Federal Information Location Service will give each agency an insight into the data collected by other agencies. While this service provides the obvious advantages of saving tax dollars by eliminating duplicative reporting requirements, it also puts at the investigator's fingertip records that might be vital to the information submitter. This service gives greater weight to the argument that a full mosaic of a company's marketing, research, and production profile could be pieced together by accumulating bits and pieces revealed in varying agency reports.[141] As noted by Dominquez, "considering the advanced stage of technology and product imitative capabilities, it may not be necessary to have broad disclosure to result in commercial harm. A small increment may be sufficient."[142]

Human Error and the Risk of Trade-Secrets
Leakages from Agency Files

As in the case of any situation that relies on individuals to carry out the letter of the law, there are bound to be cases of human error. The Environmental Protection Agency has been rather fortunate in that regard. Over the past decade and a half, the Environmental Protection Agency has earned a good reputation in the business community relative to other agencies.[143] Our interviews with a small sample of industrial chemical companies revealed that most of them felt that the Environmental Protection Agency had gone a long way toward protecting their trade secrets.[144] This feeling was reaffirmed by our interviews with EPA personnel.[145] In spite of this, two important points should be made. First, the horror stories that have come to light are significant enough for any company to be chary of submitting trade secrets to the government regardless of how low the probability of disclosure is. Second, the horror stories reported in the media do not begin to reveal the extent to which circumstantially relevant business information is being released. Therefore, the problem is far broader than the number of blatant losses of trade secrets would reveal. To categorize the problem by the number of trade secrets disclosed would be like classifying the public concerns over nuclear power by the number of reactors that have experienced significant radiation releases or meltdowns.

The low probability of EPA disclosure and the persistence of industry fears are not inconsistent. In calculating the anticipated loss associated with disclosure, companies look at the expected value of that loss. This entails weighting the probability that a trade secret will be revealed with the discounted present value of its expected future earnings.[146] In some cases, one or two chemicals provide the lifeblood of a multimillion-dollar company. In positioning its resources, is there any doubt that a company would want to protect these secrets regardless of how small the probability of disclosure was?

Do these accusations reflect the wild and groundless chantings of industry? A preliminary study done for the Chemical Specialties Manufacturing Association found "confidentiality breaks in Environmental Protection Agency's premanufacturing notification files for public inspection . . . in approximately five percent of the files received."[147]

In chapter 4, we cited the example of an unintended release of information from the Food and Drug Administration of an odor-masking agent invented by the Procter & Gamble Company for use in the manufacture of sterilized drape and gown products.[148] Regardless of the fact that Procter & Gamble sent both a complete and a sanitized copy of its reporting form to the Food and Drug Administration, disclosure of the unabridged copy was made and without notification to Procter & Gamble. Is this a normal occurrence at the Food and Drug Administration? No. Will this cause Procter & Gamble plus other information-submitting firms to be more circumspect in their dealings with government agencies? Yes.

In 1972, the Dow Chemical Company was in the process of negotiating a licensing contract with a Japanese firm for an ion-exchange technology. In 1973, these negotiations were broken off abruptly by the Japanese company. Dow later discovered that the Japanese firm had sent an FOIA request to the National Institute of Occupational Safety and Health for the same information and had gotten it for free.[149] As part of its reporting rules, the institute required the submission of this technology.

Consider another disclosure of information that could result in significant losses to the Monsanto Company. On 7 May 1982, the Environmental Protection Agency received an FOIA request from Attorney Clausen Ely for information relating to Monsanto's $0.5-billion herbicide, Roundup.[150] Roundup is sold by Monsanto in 115 countries and contributes 40 percent of Monsanto's earnings.[151] By 1985, it was projected to be one of the first billion-dollar chemicals.[152] Yet, for the cost of a postage stamp, Roundup was rustled.

In reply to media inquiries, John Todhunter, assistant administrator for pesticides and toxic substances at the Environmental Protection Agency, said the following:

> [This] is what happens when you try to comply with the Freedom of Information Act. Let's not kid ourselves. It's a very common vehicle for industrial espionage. There is always a chance information may move (to competitors) inadvertently or inappropriately.[153]

Todhunter goes on to state that this is not the first time trade secrets have leaked out of the Environmental Protection Agency.[154]

If requests like the one Clausen Ely made can turn up such valuable information, is there any doubt that FOIA fishing will become a popular pastime activity? The point is especially striking when you hear a representative of a leading Washington-based research firm advise his audience to submit as many requests to the government as possible and to "rely on the government to screw up."[155] As one analyst stated, this philosophy can give rise to a belief that "whatever is not nailed down is mine, and whatever I can pry loose is not nailed down."[156]

Ultimately, the test of EPA requirements is whether or not they impose costs on the country that exceed the benefits. To the extent that premanufacturing notifications increase industry costs, reduce innovator lead time, and impose other burdens on the investment decision, they will lead to declines in an industry that has been a persistent source of employment opportunities and foreign revenues and that has been the inventor of many useful products. Profits are not assured to those firms that venture into new areas. Many avenues are dead ends and a waste of valuable resources. Perhaps this is why cost-saving discoveries associated with the development of immobilized catalysts have been pursued vigorously by companies such as Monsanto, Amoco, and Dow but have been abandoned by other companies to explore alternative courses.[157]

Conclusion

"Where there is smoke there is usually fire." This chapter has shown that the fears by industry concerning the possible disclosure of its trade secrets proper and, perhaps more important, its circumstantially relevant business information are legitimate. There are conflicts within the Toxic Substances Control Act on confidentiality assurances, conflicts between the Toxic Substances Control Act and the Freedom of Information Act, and in general, gaps large enough to permit considerable seepage of information from government files. If this were an industry that was slow in growth, with few technological advances and little domestic and international competition, would we have written this chapter? Would the repeated analyses by scholars and the complaints by industry representatives have been made? At what point should smoke signals, without knowledge of the extent of the fire, sound the alarm? In our opinion, there is significant enough evidence for the U.S. government to reconsider its treatment of confidential information in the chemical industry and to broaden its view of what constitutes the vital information for industrial competition. In short, government should give significant consideration to the identification and protection of circumstantially relevant business information.

Notes

1. U.S. Department of Commerce, Bureau of the Census, *Census of Manufacturers. Subject Series SR-9 Concentration Ratios in Manufacturing* (Washington, D.C.: U.S. Government Printing Office, 1981).

2. Ibid., p. 7.

3. Alfred E. Kahn, "The Chemical Industry," in *The Structure of American Industry*, ed. Walter Adams (New York: Macmillan, 1961), p. 247.

4. Ibid. Also see Aimison Jonnard, "Chemical Economics and Price Forecasting," in *Chemical Marketing Research*, ed. N.H. Giagosian (New

York: Reinhold Publishing Corp., 1967), pp. 191-224; and Frank Sciancalepore, "Basic Characteristics of the Chemical Industry," in *Chemical Marketing Research*, ed. N.H. Giagosian (New York: Reinhold Publishing Corp., 1967), pp. 1-30.

5. William J. Baumol, J.C. Panzar, and R.D. Willing, *Contestable Markets and the Theory of Industry Structure* (Harcourt, Brace, Jovanovich, 1982); Richard Schmalensee, *The Control of Natural Monopolies*, (Lexington, Mass.: D.C. Heath and Company, 1979). Also see Jules Backman, *Competition in the Chemical Industry* (Washington, D.C.: Manufacturing Chemists' Association, 1964); and Sciancalepore, "Basic Characteristics of the Chemical Industry," pp. 3-17.

6. Backman, *Competition in the Chemical Industry*, pp. 32-42; and Kahn, "The Chemical Industry," pp. 252-258.

7. A review of any edition of *Chemical Week* or *Chemical and Engineering News* will substantiate this claim. For a fascinating discussion of some of the greatest discoveries during the twentieth century, including chemical inventions, see John Jewkes, David Sewers, and Richard Stillman, *The Sources of Invention*, 2nd ed. rev. (New York: W.W. Norton, 1979); and American Chemical Society, *Chemistry in the Economy* (Washington, D.C., 1973).

8. Edwin Mansfield et al., *The Production and Application of New Industrial Technologies* (New York: W.W. Norton, 1979), pp. 44-67.

9. Jules Backman, *The Economics of the Chemical Industry* (Washington, D.C.: Manufacturing Chemists Association, 1970).

10. Ibid; and Jewkes, Sewers, and Stillman, *Sources of Invention;* and Mansfield et al., *Production and Application.*

11. Ibid.

12. "Biotechnology's Drive for New Products," *Chemical Week*, 12 February 1982, pp. 47-52; "Catalysts That Can Slash Costs," *Chemical Week*, 20 October 1982; pp. 44-52; "Now the Generic Drugs Can Be Look-Alikes Too," *Chemical Week,* 30 June 1982, pp. 41-42; "Search for 'Superbugs': Industry Sees a Host of New Products Emerging from Its Growing Research on Gene Transplants," *Wall Street Journal,* 10 May 1979, p. 48; and Julie Ann Mills, "Spliced Genes Get Down to Business," *Science News* 117 (19 March 1980):202-205.

13. Mansfield et al., *Production and Application*, pp. 144-166. Also see Edwin Mansfield, "Contributions of R&D to Economic Growth in the United States," *Science* 175 (4 February 1972):477-486.

14. Mansfield et al., *Production and Application,* p. 157.

15. "R&D: Overview," *Chemical and Engineering News*, 27 July 1981, p. 62; and "Chemical R&D: The Surge Continues," *Chemical Week*, 29 April 1981, p. 40.

16. Ibid.

17. "A Chemical Trade Trend Is Reversed," *Chemical Week*, 3 March 1982, pp. 24-28; and "World Chemical Outlook," *Chemical and Engineering News*, 20 December 1982, p. 50.

18. Thomas O. McGarity and Sidney A. Shapiro, "The Trade Secret Status of Health and Safety Testing Information: Reforming Agency Disclosure Policies," *Harvard Law Review* 93 (March 1980):837-888.

19. Nicholas Wade, "Control of Toxic Substances: An Idea Whose Time has Nearly Come," *Science* 191, 13 February 1976, p. 541. See also U.S., Congress, Senate, Subcommittee of the Committee on Commerce, *Hearings on S. 776*, 94th Cong., 1st Sess., 1975, pp. 171, 178 (statement of Sidney Wolfe, Health Research Group, and Jacqueline M. Warren, Environmental Defense Fund).

20. For a recent example, see "Residents of Missouri Community Are Concerned, Confused by Dioxin," *Boston Sunday Globe*, 2 January 1982, p. 2. Also see U.S., Congress, Senate, Committee on Commerce, *Toxic Substances Control Act: Legislative History, Pub. L. 94-469*, 94th Cong., 1st Sess., S. Rept. 94-698 (hereafter referred to as *Legislative History*).

21. Richard Doll and Richard Peto, "The Causes of Cancer: Quantitative Estimates of Avoidable Risks of Cancer in the United States Today," *Journal of the National Cancer Institute* 66 (June 1981): 1191-1308, and Charles M. Caruso, "Industry Responsibility for Environmentally Caused Cancer under the Toxic Substances Control Act," *Rutgers Journal of Computers and Technology and Law*, 213 (1979):216-217.

22. Caruso, "Industry Responsibility for Environmentally Caused Cancer," p. 216.

23. *Legislative History*.

24. Ibid.

25. Lynne O. Cabot and G. Ronald Fox, "The Work of a Regulatory Agency: The EPA and Toxic Substances," *Harvard Business School Case Services*, 1-380-081, rev. 5181, pp. 1-41. Also see Kevin Gaynor, "The Toxic Substances Control Act: A Regulatory Morass," *Vanderbilt Law Review* 30 (November 1977):1149-1195.

26. Murray L. Weidenbaum, *Business, Government and the Public*, 2nd ed. (Englewood Cliffs, N.J.: Prentice-Hall, 1981); Alfred Marcus, "Environmental Protection Agency," in *The Politics of Regulations*, ed. James Q. Wilson (New York: Basic Books, 1980), pp. 267-303.

27. 42 U.S.C. § 1857-1858a (1976 ed.).

28. 7 U.S.C. § 136-1364 (1976 ed.).

29. 21 U.S.C. § 301-381 (1976 ed.).

30. 33 U.S.C. § 1401-1444 (1976 ed.).

31. 42 U.S.C. § 1858-1858a (1976 ed.).

32. 42 U.S.C. § 6901-6987 (1976 ed.).

33. 42 U.S.C. § 300f-300j (1976 ed.).

34. 15 U.S.C. § 2601-2629 (1976 ed.).

35. 33 U.S.C. § 1251-1376 (1976 ed.).

36. "Confidentiality: Will Government Give Away Company Secrets?" *Chemical Week*, 10 December 1980, pp. 28-33. Reprinted from the 10 December 1980 issue of *Chemical Week* by special permission. Copyright 1983 McGraw-Hill, Inc., New York, New York; Chris Murray, "Chemical Companies Wary over Toxic Substances Law," *Chemical and Engineering News*, 3 January 1977, p. 16. Reprinted with permission; and George S. Dominguez, *The Business Guide to TOSCA* (New York: Wiley & Sons, 1979).

37. James T. O'Reilly et al., *Federal Regulation of the Chemical Industry* (Colorado Springs: Shepard's, 1982), pp. 15-17.

38. *Toxic Substances Control Act*, 15 U.S.C. § 2601(a)(2).

39. *Toxic Substances Control Act*, 15 U.S. C. § § 2603(a), 2604(e).

40. *Legislative History*, p. 4492. *Toxic Substance Control Act*, § 2603(c)(1).

41. *Toxic Substances Control Act*, § 2(b)(3) (1976 ed.).

42. *Toxic Substances Control Act*, § 3(B).

43. *Toxic Substances Control Act*, § 3(a)(2).

44. A fascinating history of the eventual inventory reporting requirements and the disclosure versus nondisclosure controversy can be found in Cabot and Fox, "The Work of a Regulatory Agency"; and Gaynor, "The Toxic Substances Control Act."

45. *Toxic Substances Control Act*, § 5; 15 U.S.C. § 2604.

46. Office of Toxic Substances, *Toxic Substances Control Act, Public Law 94-469, Reporting for the Chemical Substance Inventory; Instructions for Reporting for the Revised Inventory*, (Washington, D.C.: U.S. Government Printing Office, June 1979). Pub. L. No. 94-469, § 5(a)(b)(2), and 15 U.S.C. § 2604 (1976 ed.).

47. *Legislative History*.

48. Pub. L. No. 94-469, § 8; 15 U.S.C. § 2607 (1976 ed.).

49. Pub. L. No. 94-469, § 5(d); 15 U.S.C. § 2604(d) (1976 ed.).

50. *Polaroid v. Costle*, No. 78.1133-S (D. Mass filed 23 May 1978); *Polaroid v. Costle* Envir Rep CAS (BNA) 2134 (D. Ma 1978).

51. Office of Toxic Substances, *TSCA Confidential Business Information Security Manual*, (Washington, D.C.: U.S. Government Printing Office, July 1977). Also see 40 C.F.R. § 2.201-2.308.

52. Pub. L. No. 94-469, § 5(h); 15 U.S.C. § 2604(h) (1976 ed.).

53. Office of Toxic Substances, *TSCA Confidential Business Information Security Manual*.

54. Patrick Phillips, "Are Trade Secrets Dead? The Effect of the Toxic Substances Control Act on Trade Secrets," *Journal of the Patent Office Society* 62 (November 1980):663.

55. Pub. L. No. 94-469, § 8; 15 U.S.C. § 2607 (1976).

56. Murray, "Chemical Companies Wary," p. 16 (see the statement of George Dominguez of Ciba Geigy).

57. *Legislative History.*

58. Pub. L. No. 94-469, § 14(b); 15 U.S.C. § 2613(b) (1976 ed.).

59. The Environmental Protection Agency can grant a test-market exemption for some chemicals. Pub. L. No. 94-469, § 5(h)(1); 15 U.S.C. § 2604(h)(1).

60. 40 C.F.R. § 2.306(3). The courts have ruled that companies must submit premanufacturing notifications on R&D chemicals but that the Environmental Protection Agency has the right to waive this requirement. See *Dow Chemical v. EPA,* 605 E.2d 673 (3d Cir. 1979).

61. Pub. L. No. 94-469, § 4(b)(B); 14 U.S.C. § 2613(b)(B) (1976 ed.); C.F.R. § 2.306(ii).

62. The Environmental Protection Agency has the authority to classify broad groups of data as confidential, but it has not, as yet, done so and prefers case-by-case substantiation. 15 U.S.C. § 2613(b) and (c)(2); 40 C.F.R. § 2.207. Also see 40 C.F.R. § 2.204(e)(4)(i) to (ix); *Revised Interim Policy* 45 F.R. 74,378, 74, 380; and James T. O'Reilly, *Federal Information Disclosure: Procedures, Forms and the Law* (Colorado Springs: Shephard's, 1982), chapter 14.

63. Ibid.

64. Pub. L. No. 94-469, § 14(a); 15 U.S.C. § 2613(a) (1976 ed.).

65. *Legislative History.*

66. Pub. L. No. 94-469, § 14(a); 15 U.S.C. § 2613(a) (1976 ed.).

67. *Chrysler Corp. v. Brown,* 99 U.S. Sup. Ct. 1705 (1979).

68. Pub. L. No. 94-469, § 14(c); 15 U.S.C. § 2613(c) (1976 ed.); also see 40 C.F.R. § 2.203.

69. Ibid.

70. Ibid.

71. Interview with Mr. James Nelson, lawyer at the Environmental Protection Agency, 10 June 1980.

72. Pub. L. No. 94-469, §§ 6(c)(2), 14(c)(2)(A); 15 U.S.C. §§ 2605(c)(2), 2613(c)(2)(A) (1976); 40 C.F.R. §§ 2.204(e), 2.205(f)(2), 2.306(3), 2.113(a)(6). If the request is denied, the Environmental Protection Agency still may notify the information submitter but is under no obligation to do so. See 40 C.F.R. § 2.204(c)(2). If the information was not marked initially as confidential, the agency is under no obligation to notify the submitter. See 40 C.F.R. § 2.203(a)(2) and (c).

73. 40 C.F.R § 2.205(a)(2)(i) and (A)(2)(ii).

74. Pub. L. No. 94-469, § 14(c); 15 U.S.C. § 2613(c) (1976); 40 C.F.R. §§ 2.205(f), 2.306(B). In emergency situations, information can be released in fifteen days; in cases of imminent risk, twenty-four hours is given.

75. 40 C.F.R. § 2.205(a)(2)(ii).

76. 40 C.F.R. § 2.205(f)(2).

77. For a contrasting point of view, see McGarity and Shapiro, "Trade Secret Status," pp. 837-888.

78. A good example of a company losing such information is the Monsanto Company. See "Reporting for the Toxic Substances Control Act: Can EPA Keep Data Secret?" *Chemical Week,* 1 February 1978, p. 41.

79. "Confidentiality: Will Government Give away Company Secrets?," pp. 28-33. Also see Dominguez, *Business Guide to Toxic Substances Control Act.*

80. O'Reilly et al., *Federal Regulation of the Chemical Industry.*

81. 40 C.F.R. § 2.203(a)(2) and (c).

82. Pub. L. No. 94-469, § 4(a); 15 U.S.C. § 2603(a) (1976 ed.).

83. Charles R. Wunsch, "Trade Secret Confidentiality and Toxic Substances Regulation: A Non-Tariff Trade Barrier in the Chemical Trade," *Cornell International Law Journal* 14 (Winter 1981):173-193.

84. Committee for the Working Conference on Principles of Protocols for Evaluating Chemicals in the Environment, *A Report of the Committee,* Environmental Studies Board, National Academy of Sciences, National Academy of Engineering, and Committee on Toxicology, National Research Council, pp. 139-154 (1975); and Murray, "Chemical Firms Wary," p. 16.

85. Ibid.

86. A review of these studies can be found in Dominguez, *Business Guide to Toxic Substances Control Act,* pp. 55-58.

87. Ibid.

88. See for example, A. Thompson Montgomery, *Managerial Accounting Information: An Introduction to Its Content and Usefulness* (Reading, Mass.: Addison-Wesley, 1980).

89. Pub. L. No. 94-469, § 4; 15 U.S.C. § 2603 (1976 ed.).

90. Ibid.

91. 5 U.S.C. § 706(2)(A) (1977 ed.).

92. Pub. L. No. 94-469, § 19(c); 15 U.S.C. § 2618(c) (1976 ed.).

93. *Abbott Laboratories v. Gardner,* 387 U.S. 136 (1967); *Citizens to Preserve Overton Park v. Volpe,* 401 U.S. 402 (1971); *Industrial Union Department AFL-CIO v. Hodgson,* 499 F.2d 467 (1974); *Amoco Oil Co. v. EPA,* 541 F.2d 722 (1979); *Ethyl Corp. v. EPA,* 541 F.2d 1 (1971); and Caruso, "Industry Responsibility For Environmentally Caused Cancer," pp. 222-223, 230-238.

94. Pub. L. No. 94-469, § 5 (d); 15 U.S.C. § 2604(d) (1976 ed.).

95. Pub. L. No. 94-469, § 14(b); 15 U.S.C. § 2613(b) (1976 ed.).

96. McGarity and Shapiro, "Trade Secret Status," pp. 840-841.

97. U.S., Congress, House, Committee on Interstate and Foreign Com-

merce; Subcommittee on Consumer Protection and Finance, *Toxic Substances Control Act: Hearings on H. Rept. 7229 and H. Rept. 7664,* 94th Cong.,1st Sess.,1975, pp. 352-355, 479 (testimony of J.P. St. Clair of Shell Oil Company).

98. Pub. L. No. 94-469, § 4(c); 15 U.S.C. § 2603(c) (1976 ed.).

99. Pub. L. No. 94-469, § 5(b); 15 U.S.C. § 2604(h) (1976 ed.).

100. O'Reilly et al., *Federal Regulation of the Chemical Industry.*

101. Pub. L. No. 94-469, § 5; 15 U.S.C. § 2604 (1976 ed).

102. Ibid.

103. O'Reilly et al., *Federal Regulation of the Chemical Industry,* pp. 3-11-3-13.

104. Chemical Specialties Manufacturers Association, *Impact of the Toxic Substances Control Act on Innovation in the Chemical Specialties Manufacturing Industry* (Washington, D.C.; Chemical Specialties Manufacturers Association, Inc., January 1982).

105. Ibid.

106. Ibid.

107. Ibid.

108. Joseph Schumpeter, *Capitalism, Socialism and Democracy,* 3d ed. (New York: Harper and Row, 1942), pp. 131-139.

109. John K. Galbraith, *The New Industrial State,* 2d ed. (New York: Mentor, 1971).

110. Mansfield, et al., *Production and Application,* pp. 44-67.

111. Ibid.

112. Pub. L. No. 94-469, § 14(c); 15 U.S.C. 2613(c) (1976 ed.). Also see 40 C.F.R. § 2.203.

113. Ibid.

114. 40 C.F.R. § 2.205(F).

115. Pub. L. No. 94-469, § 14(a); 15 U.S.C. § 2613(a) (1976 ed.).

116. See O'Reilly, *Federal Information Disclosure.*

117. 40 C.F.R. § 2.205(h).

118. If disclosure would threaten this source of information in the future, the *National Parks* test for confidentiality would permit its classification under the trade-secrets exemption. *National Parks and Conservation Assn. v. Morton,* 498 F.2d 765 (1974); *National Parks and Conservation Assn. v. Kleppe,* 547 F.2d 673 (1976); Pub. L. No. 94-469, § 14(a); 15 U.S.C. § 2613(a) (1976 ed.).

119. Pub. L. No. 94-469, § 14(c); 15 U.S.C. § 2613(c); see also 40 C.F.R. § 2.204.

120. *Chrysler v. Brown,* 441 U.S. 281 (1979).

121. 5 U.S.C. § 522a(6)(A)(i).

122. 40 C.F.R. § 2.113 does make a provision for such cases.

123. "A Chemical Trade Trend Is Reversed," pp. 24-28.

124. Wunsch, "Trade Secret Confidentiality and Toxic Substances Regulation," pp. 173-193; Murray, "Chemical Companies Wary," p. 16 (statement of Marvin E. Winguist); and "Innovative Japanese Drugs Move into the U.S.," *Business Week,* 10 May 1982, pp. 150-151.

125. Mansfield, *Production and Application;* Jewkes, Sewers, and Stillman, *Sources of Invention,* pp. 169-193.

126. McGarity and Shapiro, "Trade Secret Status," p. 849.

127. Ibid.; "Confidentiality: Will Government Give Away Company Secrets?," p. 32; and *Hearings on H. Rept. 7229 and H. Rept. 7664* (statement of Donald D. McCollister, Dow Chemical Company).

128. *TSCA Hearings (1975).*

129. Wunsch, "Trade Secrets, Confidentiality and Toxic Substances Regulation," pp. 173-193; and "Confidentiality: Will Government Give Away Company Secrets?," p. 32.

130. Ibid.

131. Ibid.

132. Pub. L. No. 94-469, § 2(7); 15 U.S.C. § 2601(7) (1976 ed.).

133. McGarity and Shapiro, "Trade Secret Status," pp. 837-888.

134. Pub. L. No. 94-469, § 14(a)(1); 15 U.S.C. § 2613(a)(i) (1976 ed.).

135. Pub. L. No. 94-469, § 14(a)(2); 15 U.S.C. § 2613(a)(2) (1976 ed.). See also Paula R. Latovick, "Protection for Trade Secrets under the Toxic Substances Control Act of 1976," *University of Michigan Journal of Law Reform* 13 (Fall 1979):329-365.

136. Pub. L. No. 94-469, § 14(a)(3); 15 U.S.C. § 2613(a)(3) (1976 ed.).

137. Pub. L. No. 94-469, § 14 (a) (4); 15 U.S.C. § 2613(a)(4) (1976 ed.).

138. Pub. L. No. 94-469, § 14(e); 15 U.S.C. § 2613(e) (1976 ed.). *Exxon Corp. v. FTC* resolved that disclosure to Congress did not require notification since it was not public disclosure. Also see *Eastland v. United States Servicemen's Fund,* 421 U.S. 491 (1975) for justification for congressional disclosure of confidential information. Finally, disclosure to Congress ensures confidentiality by means of the House Rules. According to Paula R. Latovick, these confidentiality assurances are rather weak. See Latovick, "Protection for Trade Secrets," pp. 329-365.

139. Pub. L. No. 94-469, § 14(a); 15 U.S.C. § 2613(a) (1976 ed.). However, EPA rules governing disclosure provide for notification. Therefore, there is an inconsistency between the rules. Notice under the EPA rule is limited to ten days and may be in the form of a *Federal Register* notification. 40 C.F.R. § 2.209.

140. "Your Business, Your Trade Secrets and Your Government: A Seminar on Protecting and Obtaining Commercial Information from the Government" (Sponsored by the American Bar Association, Washington, D.C., 11 May 1981) (statement of Ronald L. Plesser, attorney for Blum and Nash).

141. Ibid. "Confidentiality: Will Government Give Away Company Secrets?," p. 32 (statement of Laurence R. Lee of Eli Lilly).

142. Dominguez, *Business Guide to TOSCA,* p. 143.

143. Personal interviews with a sample of five chemical companies (whose names have been withheld).

144. Ibid.

145. Interview with James Nelson, lawyer at the Environmental Protection Agency, 10 June 1980.

146. See Barbara Bund Jackson, *The Value of Information: Course Module* (Cambridge, Mass.: Harvard University Press, 1979).

147. Chemical Specialty Manufacturers Association, Inc., *Toxic Substances Newsletter,* 1981. Also see "Reporting for the Toxic Substances Control Act: Can EPA Keep Data Secret?," *Chemical Week,* 3 February 1978, p. 41 (see the statement of Paul Krizov of the Monsanto Company on his discovery of firm-confidential information he found in the EPA reading room).

148. U.S., Congress, Senate, Committee on the Judiciary, *Freedom of Information Act,* 97th Cong., 1st Sess., 1981, pp. 260-274 (testimony of James T. O'Reilly).

149. U.S., Congress, House, Committee on Government Operations, *Business Record Exemption of the Freedom of Information Act,* 95th Cong., 1st Sess., 1977 (letter from James H. Hanes, vice president and general counsel, Dow Chemical Co., 1 November 1977).

150. "An EPA Blunder Spurs Move to Seal Data," *Chemical Week,* 18 September 1982, pp. 13-14. Reprinted with permission; and Pete Earley, "EPA Lets Trade Secret Loose in Slip Up, to Firm's Dismay," *Washington Post,* 12 September 1982. This release was made under the *Federal Insecticide Fungicide and Rodenticide Act* and not the *Toxic Substances Control Act,* but the confidentiality portions are almost identical between the two acts. 40 C.F.R. §§ 2.306 and 2.307; or Pub. L. No. 94-469, § 14 (1976) and Pub. L. No. 95-396, § 136(h) (1978).

151. "An EPA Blunder Spurs Move to Seal Data," p. 14.

152. Ibid.

153. Ibid.

154. Ibid.

155. "Washington Information Seminar" (Washington, D.C., 21 September 1981) (statement of a representative of the Washington Researchers Co.). Also see Robert Hershey, "Commercial Intelligence on a Shoestring," *Harvard Business Review,* September/October 1980; pp. 21-30.

156. "Your Business, Your Trade Secrets and Your Government" (statement of Harold Relyea, Library of Congress).

157. "Catalysts that Can Slash Costs," *Chemical Week,* 20 October 1982, pp. 44-52. Also see "Costlier Efforts to Fend off Copycats," *Chemical Week, 2 November 1982, p. 15.*

7

A Case Study: The U.S. Pharmaceutical Industry

In chapter 6, the impact of the Freedom of Information Act on the U.S. chemical industry was assessed essentially through a detailed examination of the federal government's regulatory relationship with the industry through the Toxic Substances Control Act. In examining this relationship, the analysis was conducted primarily at the microeconomic level. The focus of this chapter is on the U.S. pharmaceutical industry. We address international issues for the purpose of developing a more-global view of how the Freedom of Information Act has affected innovation and attitudes about innovation within the industry and measure and evaluate effects of the act on the level, direction, and location of pharmaceutical production and R&D activities.

The U.S. pharmaceutical industry clearly ranks among the most highly regulated industries in the country. Government involvement in the nation's health-care system has increased steadily over the years, particularly since the mid-1960s. Although the industry interacts with a number of federal agencies and offices, the closest relationship and certainly the one most relevant to this book exists with the Food and Drug Administration.[1]

Government concern about the safety and efficacy of new drugs entering the U.S. market has translated historically into very stringent testing and reporting requirements that, in turn, have produced over time substantial outflows of test data and other company-specific information from the industry to the Food and Drug Administration.[2] Much of these data and information contain trade secrets or confidential business information, the release of which would compromise the competitive market position of supplying firms. Because of the nature and extent of the reporting requirements, U.S. pharmaceutical firms are particularly vulnerable to leakages of proprietary or privileged information from the government. Few industries, if any, submit as much information to government as the pharmaceutical industry, and few submit information that is as sensitive, particularly in the R&D area.[3]

The Risks of Damaging Information Disclosures: Industry Perceptions and Realities

The industry and company-specific data that comprise the empirical base of this chapter were gathered from a variety of secondary sources as well as

165

through interviews with representatives from the Pharmaceutical Manufacturers Association and with representatives from a sample of medium-
sized and large-sized U.S. pharmaceutical firms. Extensive interviewing was
conducted with five firms with net annual sales ranging from $1.3 billion to
$2.7 billion (1979-1980). Anonymity was requested by two firms as condi-
tions for their cooperation and participation in the study; therefore, the
decision was made to extend anonymity to all.

Our interviews revealed that some U.S. pharmaceutical firms are re-
sentful of the fact that the Freedom of Information Act has threatened what
Bert Braverman has described as the nation's "long-standing and well
founded practices of business secrecy."[4] There is general opposition on
philosophical grounds to current provisions with the Freedom of Information
Act permitting the release of business data. Even though the data released by
government agencies may not be trade secrets, as narrowly defined in the
Restatement of Torts, industry opposition apparently rests on the conviction that government has no right to release proprietary information that
business considers proprietary unless, of course, there are clearly demon-
strable and significant social benefits involved. Disclosure should be the exception rather than the rule.

Beyond this philosophical concern, interviewees with whom we spoke
were not convinced that government agencies are protecting from disclosure
either trade secrets or confidential information of a commercial and financial nature with any degree of consistency. Despite this clearly articulated
position, participants were unable to support it by citing new horror stories.
Once again, the horror stories heard were those few that have been documented already in congressional hearings and in scholarly works in the field.[5]

Respondents normally took the position that the absence of a large
number of documented horror stories does not prove in any way that industrial espionage through the Freedom of Information Act is a myth. They
mentioned that it is simply too easy for perpetrators of these acts to cover
their tracks, particularly if information requests are channeled through
third-party intermediaries. It is not easy for an innovating firm to trace the
development of a me-too drug by a rival back to an FDA disclosure. Firms
commonly suffer market-share erosion without being able to identify the
source.

Furthermore, those who have lost their trade secrets are not likely to run
to court and sue. A comparison of FOIA horror stories with reported rape
cases is appropriate. Police authorities use a large coefficient to multiply the
number of reported rapes in order to estimate the number of rapes that really
have taken place. Not only do the rapists have an obvious and strong incentive not to reveal their violent acts, but the victims do as well for reasons
ranging from embarrassment and shame to a strong desire to avoid legal
uncertainties and complexities and shattered reputations.[6] A firm that loses

trade secrets or confidential information through FOIA disclosure channels may indeed be embarrassed if that fact becomes known publicly. Also, two possessors of a trade secret are still preferable to three, four, or five; hence, there exists a bias against reporting a loss that has occurred.

In the case of a corporation, large or small, professional managers are held responsible for the protection of the firm's proprietary knowledge. Any unauthorized disclosures, regardless of the source, reflect badly on managerial competence and resourcefulness. Furthermore, the legal difficulties and complexities to block disclosure or to seek damages after disclosure in the courts are such as to discourage these efforts. Those who pursue their cases to the Supreme Court have made the search for justice a cause célèbre because the economic payoff here is likely to be very small in relation to the legal expenses incurred. For these reasons, documented instances of the loss of trade secrets and other confidential information are going to be hard to find.

If a large volume of disclosures of trade secrets and confidential business information goes unreported, it is reasonable to suppose that unreported disclosures of circumstantially relevant business information are taking place on a much broader scale, since at least trade secrets and confidential business information are recognized by legal scholars and manifest some tangible form such as technical formulas or blueprints.

Insights into the specific risks of information disclosure can be gained from another look at the statistical breakdown of total FOIA requests made to the Food and Drug Administration by the type of information requested (see table 3-4). The specific categories that contain privileged or confidential information and that particularly concern pharmaceutical firms are establishment-inspection reports (20 percent of total requests in 1981), drug data (14 percent of the total), and medical-devices data (12 percent of the total). Sensitive data also may be involved in the largest category, FOIA log requests (36 percent of the total), in which third parties seek data by citing file numbers from the FDA log book. This would not involve requests for confidential information, of course, if such requests emanate from companies checking on the release of their own information.

Concerns about damaging information disclosure by federal agencies seem to be most pronounced in the cases of facilities data contained with establishment-inspection reports and safety and efficacy data contained in investigational new-drug applications (INDs) and new-drug applications (NDAs).

The Food, Drug, and Cosmetic Act of 1938 (under Section 704) authorizes the Food and Drug Administration to require the preparation of establishment-inspection reports. These are prepared by investigators to report the findings of inspections of food, drug, and cosmetics facilities. Since 1938, drugs may not be marketed in the United States unless a manufacturer files a new-drug application and receives FDA approval. In

1963, the added requirement for companies to file investigational new-drug applications was passed into law. The IND requirement is designed to control the clinical investigations of new drugs. IND filings are preceded by pharmacological and animal testing and, if successful, are followed by a new-drug application by the manufacturer to the Food and Drug Administration for final approval.

The question arises, of course, about the economic value of safety and effectiveness data contained in the new-drug or investigational new-drug applications. In the words of former FDA Commissioner Alexander M. Schmidt, the costs implications are considerable:

> Such information costs hundreds of thousands, and in some instances, millions of dollars to obtain. Release of such information would allow a competitor to obtain approval from the Food and Drug Administration for marketing the identical product at a mere fraction of the cost. . . . If a manufacturer's safety and effectiveness data are to be released upon request, thus permitting "me-too" drugs to be marketed immediately, it is entirely possible that the incentive for private pharmaceutical research will be adversely affected. . . . The issue of trade secrets protection for preclinical data on the safety and effectiveness of therapeutic substances is exceedingly complex and warrants a sober and extensive inquiry. The risks to the public, if research and innovation are inadequately rewarded, are immense.[7]

It is revealing that our interviewees, representing some of the more-innovative members of the U.S. pharmaceutical industry, expressed deep concern about, or disagreement with, current FDA policy relating to the following:

The release of safety and efficacy data in abandoned or withdrawn investigational new-drug applications,

The release of safety and efficacy data relating to existing drugs,

The release of summary data in active investigational new-drug applications or new-drug applications,

The release of protocols [plans of action] for tests or studies,

The release of information voluntarily submitted to the Food and Drug Administration, as defined by the agency.[8]

In the early 1970s, the Pharmaceutical Manufacturers Association took a strong stand against the release of these types of information by the Food and Drug Administration. The association's president, C. Joseph Stetler, argued that such information disclosure would have a damaging effect on the industry by discouraging investment in research and new-product development.[9] A decade later, the existence of a significant drug lag in the industry, a subject of subsequent discussion in this chapter, seems to lend some support to this prognostication.

Concern about the possibility of damaging information leakages among U.S. firms apparently extends well beyond the category of trade secrets proper. In an interview published in *Chemical Week*, Laurence R. Lee, general counsel for Abbott Laboratories, stated "that the problem with FOIA is not that it permits theft of trade secrets, per se, but that it gives competitors the chance to get general information about company operations that would not otherwise be available to them."[10] Establishment-inspection reports, for example, may contain drawings on plant layouts that may seem to be innocuous at first glance but that in fact may reveal a great deal about the inspected company's manufacturing processes and procedures. According to Gerald H. Deighton, director of the FOIA staff of the Food and Drug Administration, "Companies don't like [establishment-inspection reports] of their own to be public, but they love getting them for other companies."[11] Deighton indicated that in 1980, one pharmaceutical company requested 100 establishment-inspection reports on its competitors.[12]

Given the complexities of R&D in the pharmaceutical industry, it is difficult to determine which technical information, if released, will compromise competitive advantage and which will not. Simply the name of the animal upon which the clinical testing is being carried out can reveal a precious entrepreneurial discovery about how to design a test to identify the characteristics of a particular chemical group.[13] This information may be more valuable than the numerical results of the test. Or consider how investments in R&D for today's generation of drugs establish a foundation for generations of drugs in the future. The release of data on existing drugs or on withdrawn investigational new-drug applications may provide rivals with a clearer picture of the R&D strategy of the firm that supplied the data. Clearly, no demonstration of competitive harm can be made since the decision not to market this particular drug precludes such evidence. Yet, in terms of having a more-far-reaching distant marketing plan, competitive harm has taken place.[14] The upstream direction of R&D planning has been revealed prematurely to competitors.

In the view of our participating companies, it is impossible for FDA officials, no matter how bright or conscientious, to determine what types of information may or may not be valuable objects to industrial competitors. Individually, the bits and pieces of information—the circumstantially relevant business information—may be meaningless. Over time, however, they may fit together, as in a completed puzzle, revealing a great deal about the R&D programs, processes, and strategies of information-supplying firms. If an innovating firm is fearful that the information puzzle will be completed ultimately by a rival, then the disincentive to innovate in the United States clearly exists.

One respondent argued that the complexity of FOIA regulations guarantees some inconsistency in implementation. The discretionary nature of disclosures is another factor that leads our participating firms to conclude that inconsistency in data release must be a fact of life in the Food and Drug Administration and in other agencies as well. Finally, implementation problems were assumed by at least two of our respondents to be a function of decentralized FOIA authority, particularly among the Food and Drug Administration's regional offices. It is possible, if not likely in their view, that FOIA officers in Boston and Chicago, for example, may share neither the same interpretation of appropriate FDA regulations nor the same philosophical commitment to the protection of information that is confidential and privileged. An information requester writing to both regional officials and the Washington office may acquire three different censored versions of the same report and therefore piece much of it together.[15]

There is little evidence that federal-agency administrators would be alert to these subtleties of information no matter how conscientious, sensitive, and probusiness their sentiments might be. A significant industry criticism is that the Food and Drug Administration is far too arbitrary in determining what is releasable and what is not. It is really not that easy to draw a line of demarkation between those pieces of information that are economically valuable and those that are not. Information that is not economically valuable today may be in the future.

Based on interviews with FDA officials, it would appear as though, to some extent, the perceptions of firms in the industry overstate the degree of decentralization in FOIA decision making in the agency and understate the degree of consistency in such decisions. With reference to FOIA disclosures, there seems to be a divergence between industry perceptions and agency practices. To an extent, these industry perceptions tend to be distorted because of misunderstandings. For example, one of our respondents was convinced that the Food and Drug Administration released all data automatically on withdrawn investigational new-drug applications. In reality, agency policy disallows release until assurances are received from the appropriate firm that no application renewal in the future is likely.[16]

Of course, firms, in their decision-making activities, act on perceptions of reality, not necessarily on reality itself. Without question, the pharmaceutical firms in our sample, in varying degrees, perceived the Freedom of Information Act to be a threat to the successful and profitable maintenance of trade secrets and protection of proprietary information over time.

The argument has been made, of course, that the trade-secrets exemption to the Freedom of Information Act should not be altered merely to allay the fears of information-submitting firms—particularly if those fears are based on false perceptions. If such is the case, public-interest groups believe that the solution to this corporate anxiety is simple. Perceptions should be adjusted to reflect reality.[17] Many economists would agree, adding perhaps that the adjustment would occur automatically as producers adapt their expectations to reality.

If it were possible for a corporation to measure and reduce risk, for example, by having an army of lawyers to track each document, then we could apply expected-value analysis to the problem. Essentially, the problem would be one of project selection. Unfortunately, industry interviewees expressed the concern that risk was not measurable. Even if lawyers could be hired to protect against conscious disclosure, the possibility of human error or poor judgment remains. Moreover, the ultimate settlements of FOIA court cases seem to be dependent, in part, upon the specific courts in which such cases are heard.[18] The determination of venue is not based on the preferences of information-submitting firms.

There is another explanation for the observed gap between industry perceptions and agency policies and practices. The problem is in part definitional. Officials at the Food and Drug Administration predictably adhere to the strict definition of trade secrets, according to the *Restatement of Torts*. Spokespersons from our participating firms define trade secrets more broadly. They expressed concern about the possible leakage of various types of economically valuable information, including the type we have labeled circumstantially relevant business information. The guaranteed nondisclosure of trade secrets, narrowly defined, and of confidential information of a commercial or financial nature would be a necessary, but not a sufficient, condition to allay the fears and apprehensions of those pharmaceutical firms in our sample.

The Economic Costs of Stringent FDA Regulations

The negative impact of the Freedom of Information Act on R&D incentives in the U.S. pharmaceutical industry must be examined within a broader context. There is an enormous literature documenting the negative impact of the 1962 amendments of the Federal Drug Act on innovation in the industry. The act requires the submission of both safety and efficacy data in support of applications to market new drugs. Cost increases since 1962 can be traced to the expanded safety and efficacy data that companies must submit, seeking new-drug approvals, and to the increase in time that now lapses between the earliest R&D effort and final FDA approval of the new product.[19] Despite recent efforts made by the Food and Drug Administration to reduce the testing and reporting burdens on pharmaceutical companies, without trading off public health and safety, regulations remain burdensome and will likely remain so in the future.[20]

The cost and time commitments that U.S. firms now must make to bring new products onto the market are staggering. R. Hansen, in a 1976 study, estimated that each new chemical entity that reached the U.S. market during that particular year represented a total investment of approximately $54 million.[21] A substantial portion of this cost is attributable to government reporting requirements. The Pharmaceutical Manufacturers Association reported that in 1978, a single new-drug application submitted by a U.S. pharmaceutical firm "consisted of 125 volumes and 40,242 pages. This compares with 11 volumes and 4,642 pages for a similar submission to meet new drug approval requirements in the United Kingdom."[22] Former U.S. Health and Human Services Secretary R. Schweiker estimates that for 1982, full new-drug applications in the United States will average 100,000 pages.[23]

The 1962 amendments not only have increased the real cost of drug innovation but also have served to reduce expected returns. Specifically, because of the time required to gain the approval of the Food and Drug Administration on new-drug applications, the effective average life of patents in the industry has been shortened.[24] According to the estimates of W. Wardell, a successful new chemical entity requires approximately three years of testing at the IND stage and two years for the NDA review.[25] Prior to that, firms conduct preclinical pharmacological and toxicological tests in house that take two to three years on average to complete. Some observers have estimated that this seven-to-eight-year time lag between product innovation and NDA approval reduces the effective life of a patent to between nine and ten years on average.[26] Therefore, for post-1962 patentable products, U.S. pharmaceutical firms are faced with a shorter period of time over which it is possible to capture returns on innovations for the purpose of covering sharply rising research and testing costs.

This raises a time-honored social-welfare issue, relating to what one may view as an overriding public good. It may be argued that, because of the public-health effects and implications of new-drug development, government has an obligation to protect the public by imposing stringent regulatory requirements on pharmaceutical companies regardless of the effects of such regulation on expected returns and profits in the industry. However, in the case of the Food and Drug Administration, approvals of new drugs seem to be delayed unnecessarily. A 1980 study by M. Eisman and W. Wardell concluded that, for a sample of multinational pharmaceutical companies in the 1970s, FDA approval of new drugs introduced in the United States lagged by an average of fourteen months overseas approvals of these same drugs by foreign governments with relatively stringent testing requirements.[27]

Given the recent history of U.S. federal regulations relating to new-drug development, it is surprising neither that the number of new single-entity drugs introduced to the U.S. market since the early 1960s has declined nor that new-drug filings have declined as well (tables 7-1 and 7-2). A significant effect on drug patenting in the United States is also evident. Since the early 1960s the number of new U.S. patents overseas has risen in relation to those originating in the United States (table 7-3).

Of course, it may be argued that firms have a viable option to the seeking of patent protection in the form of trade secrecy. The substitutable relationship between the two has been discussed in the literature.[28] Indeed, there is some evidence that U.S. chemical and pharmaceutical firms are depending more on trade secrecy, particularly in exciting new areas of recombinant-DNA technology. Reporting in *Science News*, J.A. Miller concluded that the adequacy of patent protection may not be crucial in this fledgling industry:

> Many of the entrepreneurs favor the protective cloak of secrecy over patent protection. For example, the bacteria that now are used to make antibiotics are not patented; they are kept under lock and key instead. Some industrial scientists working on recombinant DNA say they would never apply for a patent because in the process they would have to reveal too many trade secrets.[29]

If it were true, in general, that trade secrecy in the pharmaceutical industry is a close substitute for patent protection, then it is predictable that, with the aforementioned decrease in the effective average life of patents on new drugs, there will be a substitution effect in favor of trade secrets. Furthermore, if firms are successful in maintaining trade secrets over the extended R&D period, then the possibility of capturing sufficient returns on innovations to cover rising R&D costs will be promoted.

At this point, the Freedom of Information Act should become a concern to those firms that must submit information to federal agencies and

Table 7-1

New Single-Entity Drug Introductions to U.S. Market, 1940-1978
(Five-year averages)

Period	Average Number of Entities
1940-1944	13
1945-1949	25
1950-1954	41
1955-1959	50
1960-1964	30
1965-1969	17
1970-1974	15
1975-1978	17

Source: Data from Pharmaceutical Manufacturers Association, *Prescription Drug Industry Fact Book: 1980* (Washington D.C., 1980), p. 30.

Table 7-2
New-Drug Filings with the Food and Drug Administration, 1963-1978

Year	Original Investigational New-Drug Applications Submitted	Investigational New-Drug Applications Discontinued by Sponsor	Original New-Drug Applications Submitted	New-Drug Applications Approved	New Molecular Entities
1963	1,066	6	192	71	16
1964	875	215	160	70	20
1965	761	306	221	50	13
1966	715	580	216	50	17
1967	671	627	128	74	16
1968	859	564	108	56	11
1969	956	482	60	39	11
1970	1,127	n.a.	87	53	18
1971	923	1,167	256	68	14
1972	902	452	272	42	10
1973	822	311	149	77	14
1974	802	399	129	95	23
1975	876	472	137	68	15
1976	855	524	127	101	23
1977	925	802	124	63	21
1978	925	588	121	86	22

Source: Pharmaceutical Manufacturers Association, *Prescription Drug Industry Fact Book: 1980* (Washington, D.C., 1980), p. 40. Reprinted with permission.

Table 7-3
Number of New U.S. Patents on Drugs and Medicines, 1963-1977

Year	Total Patents	Patents Originating in the United States	Patents Originating Elsewhere
1963	1,532	1,034	498
1964	1,802	1,180	622
1965	1,865	1,182	683
1966	2,532	1,703	849
1967	2,438	1,637	801
1968	1,664	1,164	500
1969	2,630	1,654	976
1970	2,537	1,596	941
1971	2,417	1,509	908
1972	3,843	2,292	1,551
1973	3,166	1,817	1,349
1974	3,705	2,059	1,736
1975	4,395	2,476	1,959
1976	4,720	2,448	2,272
1977	4,168	2,235	1,933

Source: Pharmaceutical Manufacturers Association, *Prescription Drug Industry Fact Book: 1980* (Washington D.C., 1980), p. 41. Reprinted with permission.

that are exposed therefore to the risk of information leakages. There is always the possibility, of course, that trade secrets or confidential business information will leak out of the innovative firm directly for reasons ranging from employee carelessness to traditional industrial espionage. However, if the expected payoff from drug innovations like interferon is sufficiently high, firms will be motivated to incur the costs of a tighter system of industrial security. To some extent, the innovating firm can control its own destiny in this regard.

Conversely, if the leakage of trade secrets or confidential business information is from a government agency involving information released through the disclosure provisions of the Freedom of Information Act, then the position of the company is quite different. The company cannot protect its market position by investing in bolts and locks. There is a greater vulnerability to external conditions, which are beyond the control of the company's policies. If the company is not guaranteed through political lobbying pressure or legal action that government agencies will protect its confidential information, then a disincentive to innovate will be created. Indeed, the public may lose a generation of potentially valuable drugs as resources are diverted into other areas, like the development of oil-tank cleaners, where federal regulations are less stringent.

In deciding whether or not to invest in a new-product concept, the extent to which the company believes that resulting trade secrets or confidential information are protectable would seem to be of crucial importance. To reiterate an earlier point, if the company is required to submit information to the government, what is important to the decision is not only whether or not government is conscientious in protecting secrets entrusted to it but also whether or not the company believes that government is conscientious in this regard. The issue of perceptions is like the issue of commercial reputations. If government is weak or is perceived to be weak, its reputation suffers just as any market trader suffers when it is assumed that he or she cannot be trusted. In effect, federal agencies have psyches, reputational capital, at risk when they make disclosure decisions.

Government agencies must avoid even the appearance of indiscretion. In implementing FOIA policy, federal agencies have been neither discrete nor consistent in the past, at least in the view of some members of the pharmaceutical industry. As indicated earlier, the pharmaceutical firms in our sample do lack confidence in the willingness and ability of government agencies to protect trade secrets and confidential commercial information. In isolation, concerns about the Freedom of Information Act may not be significant as investment disincentives. However, when considered as a part of a total package of other ill-conceived government policies and regulations, it is easy to see how industry attitudes about the act might tip the scales in the decision not to innovate.

Of course, if government policies and regulations significantly increase the real cost of innovation and/or significantly decrease the expected return on investment, firms may opt to invest overseas where regulations are less stringent or nonexistent rather than not to invest at all. There is evidence that U.S. pharmaceutical companies have been exercising this option to a considerable extent. In the area of ethical pharmaceuticals, the foreign R&D expenditures of U.S. companies as a percentage of total expenditures increased from 7 percent in 1963 to 18.1 percent in 1979 (table 7-4). As reported by the Pharmaceutical Manufacturers Association, the shares of U.S.-company-funded R&D conducted overseas more than doubled in the ten years ending in 1978.[30]

Various studies of the rate and location of pharmaceutical R&D during the 1960s and 1970s reveal two basic trends—namely, the increasing percentage of R&D being performed overseas by U.S. pharmaceutical manufacturers and the faster overall rate of growth of pharmaceutical R&D performed in foreign countries compared to the United States.[31] Historically, pharmaceutical companies were quite nationalistic in their approval of new-product development, centralizing R&D activity in the home country. The current trend is clearly toward the decentralization of innovative activities, and U.S. companies are leading the way.[32]

Table 7-4
U.S. R&D Expenditures for Ethical Pharmaceuticals, 1963-1979

Year	Domestic Expenditures as Percent of Total Expenditures	Foreign Expenditures as Percent of Total Expenditures
1963	93	7
1964	92.4	7.6
1965	92.5	7.5
1966	91.9	8.1
1967	91.6	8.4
1968	91.3	8.7
1969	91.8	8.2
1970	91.7	8.3
1971	91.7	8.3
1972	90.1	9.9
1973	85.6	14.4
1974	84.6	15.4
1975	85.1	14.9
1976	84.6	15.4
1977	83.3	16.7
1978	83.1	16.9
1979	81.9	18.1

Source: Pharmaceutical Manufacturers Association, *Annual Survey,* various issues; and Pharmaceutical Manufacturers Association, *Prescription Drug Industry Fact Book: 1980* (Washington D.C., 1980), p. 23.

U.S. pharmaceutical firms that are multinational in operation have more flexibility than competitors that cater to local markets by being able to relocate R&D, production, and distribution channels.[33]

> First, they can introduce new products in foreign markets (where regulatory conditions are less stringent) prior to (or in lieu of) introduction in the United States. This allows them to gain knowledge and realize sales revenue while a new drug compound remains under regulatory review and development in this country. . . . In addition, multinational firms also can perform R&D activities in foreign countries in order to reduce time delays and the overall costs of developing a new product.[34]

An additional incentive to concentrate R&D activities overseas, of course, could be the total absence of the stringent American Freedom of Information Act.[35] In conducting R&D overseas, firms very well may be in a superior position to capture returns on innovations by escaping the jurisdiction of the federal government. Could the changing nature of the product life cycle that now characterizes the pharmaceutical industry be, in part, an industry adjustment or reaction to the Freedom of Information Act?

The Freedom of Information Act and the International Product Life Cycle for Pharmaceutical Products

A number of commentators have questioned the descriptive accuracy of the *product life cycle* when applied to large multinational corporations in the 1970s. In the past, U.S. multinationals typically would develop a new product in the United States and then would export the product to foreign countries. However, according to recent findings, there is a "tendency for non-standardized products to be produced abroad, and for products to be carefully differentiated to suit the local market."[36]

According to the traditional, product-life-cycle analyses of R. Vernon and L.T. Wells, innovating firms launch new cycles by successful R&D ventures, the fruits of which are new products.[37] Since R&D activities of this type are both costly and time consuming, investments will not be made unless sufficient entry barriers exist in the market to permit the capturing of returns on innovations. Innovators will be unable to extract the necessary revenues from the sale of new products if the specialized knowledge and insight gained in the innovational process are disseminated or divulged immediately to competitors. As discussed earlier, innovative firms attempt to guard against such disseminations by gaining patent protection and/or by maintaining trade secrets. If successful, of course, a firm gains market dominance, initially at home, but when foreign demand arises at some point in the cycle, an export advantage is created as well.

Assuming that it is a U.S. firm that innovates, the United States initially would gain an export advantage. However, that export position would erode ultimately, according to theory, as the product becomes more standardized in world markets. The predicted shift in the trade position of the innovating country is presented schematically in figure 7-1.

In phase I, entry barriers are sufficiently high to exclude foreign competitors despite rising world demand for the product. However, as the dissemination and diffusion of technology through trade ultimately dissolve these barriers (phase II), foreign producers are tempted to enter the market. As the technology gap diminishes, production and distribution cost differentials become more significant. The location of the most competitive plants now shifts from the United States to other industrialized countries (phase III). Producers in these latter countries now begin to take larger shares of local markets away from U.S. producers because of lower distribution costs, trade barriers, and other advantages on the supply side like the opportunity created through technology transfers for foreign producers to ride down their learning curves.[38]

Whereas in phase II the United States gradually loses its trade advantage in relation to other industrialized countries and exports mostly to lesser-developed countries, in phase III European and/or Japanese exports, for example, to the Third World become increasingly more competitive, ultimately eliminating this last vestige of U.S. comparative advantage overseas.[39]

Two key questions arise at this point. To what extent is the traditional, product-life-cycle model capable of explaining recent developments in the U.S. international-trade position in pharmaceuticals? To what extent, if any, has U.S. government policy, relating to the development, production, and marketing of pharmaceuticals by U.S. companies, altered the international life cycle of these products?

Clearly, U.S. exports of pharmaceutical products have grown at a steady rate over the past decade and one-half. Furthermore, throughout this period, U.S. exports have exceeded U.S. imports consistently in value by ratios that have ranged between 2:1 and 3:1.[40] The aggregate figures seem to indicate a continuing, indeed a widening, comparative advantage in the U.S. manufacture and sale of pharmaceuticals in world markets.

Closer inspection, however, reveals that a significant change has occurred in the composition of U.S. exports. "In large part, U.S. exports of pharmaceutical products consist of ingredients and intermediate products sent abroad to be processed and packaged."[41] The United States has experienced some erosion in its comparative advantage in the exportation of finished pharmaceutical products. World demand is being satisfied increasingly by the production of subsidiaries of U.S. firms operating overseas and by that of foreign firms. Table 7-5 reflects the extent to which U.S. pharmaceutical sales from overseas manufacturing grew significantly to exceed direct exports

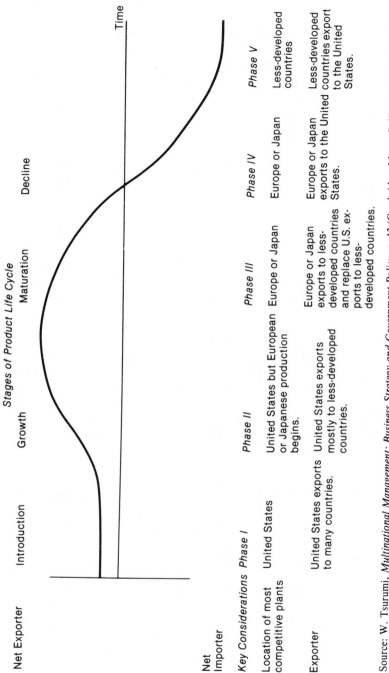

Source: W. Tsurumi, *Multinational Management: Business Strategy and Government Policy*, p. 13 (Cambridge, Mass.: Ballinger, 1977). Copyright 1976, Ballinger Publishing Company. Reprinted with permission.

Figure 7-1. The Product-Life-Cycle Model of International Trade: The U.S. (Innovator) Trade Position in the Product-Life-Cycle Model

Table 7-5
Foreign Sales of Ethical Pharmaceuticals Produced by U.S. Firms, 1965-1978

Years	Exports	Subsidiary Sales	Exports as Percent of Total Foreign Sales	Subsidiary Sales as Percent of Total Foreign Sales
	(Millions of Dollars)			
1965	180	917.7	16.4	83.6
1966	201	1,074.6	15.8	84.2
1967	216.5	1,281.5	14.4	85.6
1968	225.9	1,424.8	13.7	86.3
1969	297.3	1,559.5	16	84
1970	344.1	1,807.7	16	84
1971	382.4	2,005.5	16	84
1972	377.9	2,428.4	13.5	86.5
1973	565.6	2,712.4	17.2	82.8
1974	734	3,206.2	18.6	81.4
1975	753.7	4,042.6	15.7	84.3
1976	894.8	4,398.9	16.9	83.1
1977	947.6	4,862.9	16.3	83.7
1978	1,064.7	6,026.3	15	85

Source: Data from Pharmaceutical Manufacturers Association, *Prescription Drug Industry Fact Book: 1980* (Washington, D.C., 1980), p. 65.

from the United States during the 1960s and 1970s. Overseas production of pharmaceutical products by U.S. and other companies was concentrated largely in Western Europe during the past two decades, but in the 1980s, Japan is expected to increase its relative share. The large U.S. market seems to be the prime target of current Japanese efforts. Although Japan's trade deficits with the United States in pharmaceuticals remain sizable, the gap is diminishing as the result of a steady inflow of significant new drugs from Japan that have entered the U.S. market.[42]

Of course, what may be disadvantageous from the standpoint of immediate U.S. balance-of-trade interests is not necessarily disadvantageous from the standpoint of the profitability of U.S. pharmaceutical companies. Through the operations of overseas-based subsidiaries and the formation of joint ventures with foreign firms, U.S. pharmaceutical companies have been reacting rationally and profitably to both market incentives and regulatory disincentives.

Ample evidence exists that the foreign-trade position of the United States in pharmaceuticals has been altered significantly by the federal government's regulatory policy, particularly over the past two decades. U.S. government policy not only has accelerated the swing in the composition of U.S. exports from finished to intermediate products but also has curtailed artificially the importation of finished pharmaceuticals. It is acknowledged that U.S. policy on new-drug testing is the most stringent in the world, and

U.S. companies are precluded by law from exporting for sale any new drug (finished product) that has not yet been approved by the Food and Drug Administration, even though it may be acceptable to regulatory authorities in other countries.[43] Furthermore, restrictive U.S. drug regulations also serve as an effective nontariff barrier on the import side. There are numerous examples of drugs used successfully overseas but that cannot be used at all in the United States or that cannot be used in certain therapies.

It may be true also that these changes in the international trading pattern of U.S. pharmaceutical products have been spurred by the Freedom of Information Act. Typically, a product developed and marketed overseas cannot be imported into the United States unless additional testing data are generated to satisfy FDA requirements: "Historically the FDA has been unwilling to accept data from foreign clinical trials or patent experiences."[44] As a result of recent regulatory changes, foreign testing data are accepted by the Food and Drug Administration but not usually in sole support of new-drug applications; further testing is required.[45] Additional testing means, of course, additional data submitted to the agency, which in turn, promotes the possibility of unauthorized leakages of proprietary information through FOIA disclosures. The same risk exists on the export side since finished pharmaceutical products may not be exported from the United States unless FDA testing and data requirements are satisfied fully.

A number of studies confirm that significant changes in the product development and marketing strategies of pharmaceutical companies have taken place over the past two decades. H. Grabowski and J. Vernon traced the marketing stages of new drugs discovered in the United States during the early 1960s and the early 1970s.[46] The study revealed that a substantial majority of the U.S.-discovered drugs introduced into the United Kingdom during the early 1960s became available there only after they were marketed first in the United States. Conversely, during the early 1970s nearly two-thirds of the new drugs discovered in the United States and introduced into the United Kingdom were introduced later into the United States than into England or not at all.[47] This phenomenon has come to be known as the "drug lag."

A multicountry analysis by E. Reis Arndt and D. Elvers, also focusing on the 1960s and early 1970s, lends strong support to the conclusion that during this period, increasingly higher percentages of new chemical entities for human consumption, discovered by the U.S. pharmaceutical companies, were introduced abroad first.[48] The lagged entry of these drugs into the U.S. market clearly was linked to regulatory differences between the United States and other countries.[49]

It seems that stringent U.S. government testing and other requirements have produced a significant shift in the location of clinical testing by U.S. firms. Citing a study by L. Lasagna and W. Wardell of fifteen large U.S.

pharmaceutical firms over the period 1960-1974, H. Grabowski and J. Vernon agree that a significant shift has occurred:

> There results an increasing tendency for U.S. firms to perform clinical testing of new drug compounds first in foreign locations. Specifically, [Lasagna and Wardell] found that in 1974 these firms clinically tested approximately one-half of all their new drug compounds abroad first, whereas before 1966 they performed virtually all of their clinical testing in the U.S.[50]

According to Dr. Marion J. Finkel, director of the FDA's Office of Orphan Products Development, 51 percent of new chemical entities for human consumption introduced in 1979-1980 relied significantly on non-U.S. clinical studies.[51] Clearly, there is strong evidence that U.S. pharmaceutical companies are testing and marketing new drugs overseas to an increasing extent before doing so (or in lieu of doing so) in the United States.

For finished pharmaceutical products, therefore, the traditional product-life-cycle pattern would seem to be inappropriate. Figure 7-2 suggests a revision of the traditional model. With reference to a hypothetical pharmaceutical product, it traces the U.S. trade position over the course of the cycle under a set of specific assumptions—namely, that the United States (the innovating country) has superior technological resources, that these resources are transferable, that U.S. government policies create more disincentives to innovate than government policies elsewhere, and that the product in question is finished, not intermediate or primary.

In phase I, the United States neither produces nor imports the new drug because of prohibitive market and trade barriers arising from government policy. During this stage, the innovating company opts to test, develop, and market the product abroad in order to avoid the high costs of stringent regulations in the United States, as well as to avoid the possibility that trade secrets or confidential business information may leak from those federal agencies to which test information must be submitted. Production would take place initially in other industrialized countries, specifically those that host the subsidiaries of the innovating company. Traditional factors relative to research efficiency, production efficiency, and market size would determine exactly where the product would be developed and marketed first.

At some point, however, after the product has been developed and market tested fully, it will be cleared for importation into the United States (phase II). The innovating firm is now willing to incur the higher costs and to assume the higher risk of satisfying U.S. governmental requirements for two reasons. First, expected returns, inflated by successful marketing ventures abroad, are now sufficient to justify the expensive additional testing that the Food and Drug Administration requires. Second, the company has a significant market lead over potential rivals at this point so that the

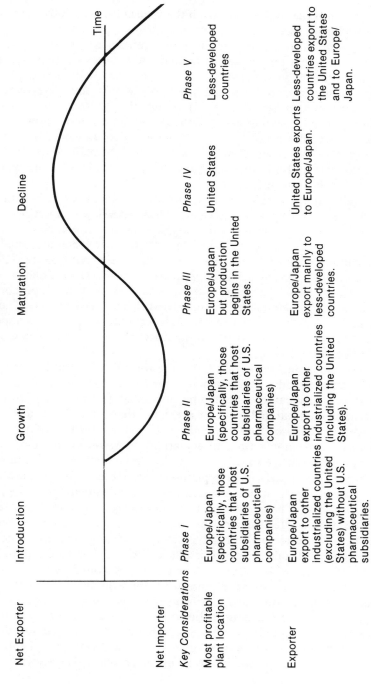

Source: Reproduced from W. Casey, J. Marthinsen, and L. Moss, "Productivity, Research and the Freedom of Information Act" (Paper presented at the Eastern Economic Association Convention, Philadelphia, 10 April 1981).

Figure 7-2. The Revised Product-Life-Cycle Model of International Trade

possibility of information leakages from the agency (through FOIA disclosures) are no longer threatening.

The importation of the product into the United States will be accompanied by technology transfer, and at some point, the combination of U.S. market size, production efficiency, and technological superiority (technology that is imported, refined, and improved) will attract a reverse flow of foreign direct investment (phase III). Production begins in the United States, thereby displacing imports, and then U.S. exportation follows. The United States becomes a net exporter of the product, and the export advantage expands through phase IV, during which U.S. plant locations become the most profitable in the world and during which U.S. trade advantage extends throughout the world.

Ultimately, unless a new product life cycle is launched, the United States will lose its trade advantage vis-à-vis lesser-developed countries. As the traditional model predicts, less-developed countries ultimately will gain an upper hand in world export markets because of their eventual assimilation of technology transfers combined with their relatively low resource costs. In reference to pharmaceutical production, of course, one may question the relevance of this last stage in the model. Drug making is not labor-intensive and source materials are sophisticated chemical byproducts. There are natural barriers to the transfer of high technology to less-developed countries—for example, the absence of qualified engineers—that would not exist in industrialized countries.

This new model indicates, of course, the ways in which differences in government policies and regulatory environments can alter the level and location of pharmaceutical research and production as well as the pattern and composition of international trade. It is evident that these effects are particularly adverse in phase I for those countries—notably, the United States—with the most stringent government regulations on new-drug development.

The argument that the social benefits of such regulations (safer, more-effective drugs) likely offset the economic costs (erosion in comparative trade advantage, employment losses, lost lives, and human suffering) is suspect in our view. The delayed entry of new drugs, developed overseas and proven safe and effective overseas, into the U.S. market is not without cost. Furthermore, attempts to resolve this issue through the use of cost-benefit analysis predictably produce results biased in the direction of maintaining stringent regulations. A part of the bias arises from the impossibility of accurately measuring foregone innovative opportunities in the cases of those pharmaceutical firms totally turned off by regulatory disincentives.

We believe that the Freedom of Information Act has contributed to a regulatory environment in the United States that has discouraged new-drug innovation and that also may have contributed to an alteration in the international product life cycle for pharmaceutical products in ways that are detrimental to U.S. interests. U.S. government policy has created significant disincentives to the profitable and socially beneficial development, production, and marketing of pharmaceutical products domestically. The concerns expressed by those representatives of U.S. companies whom we interviewed are based on fact, not fiction. These concerns extend well beyond the negative effects that federal legislation has had on the economic performance of the industry. Indeed, the central issue that has emerged from the debate over FOIA legislation is one of property rights. Our position on this vital issue is summarized in the final chapter.

Notes

1. Paul J. Quirk, "Food and Drug Administration," in *The Politics of Regulation*, ed. James Q. Wilson (New York: Basic Books, 1980), pp. 191-235.

2. Ibid.

3. Pracon, Incorporated, "Study to Assess Impacts of Releasing Safety and Effectiveness Data on the Pharmaceutical Industry's Incentives to Invest in and Conduct Research and Development Programs," Contract 223-77-8052. Vienna, Va., 1978. Also see James T. O'Reilly, *Federal Information Disclosure: Procedures, Forms and the Law* (Colorado Springs: Shepard's, 1982), pp. 14.51.-14.56.

4. U.S., Congress, Senate, Committee on the Judiciary, *Oversight of the Freedom of Information Act*, 95th Cong., 1st Sess., 1977, p. 307.

5. See U.S., Congress, Senate, Committee on the Judiciary, *Freedom of Information Act*, 97th Cong., 1st Sess., 1981, pp. 458-461, 616.

6. See Mary B. Deming and Ali Eppy, "The Sociology of Rape," *Sociology and Social Review* 65 (July 1981):357-382.

7. Ronald W. Hansen, "Comments on the Proposed Change in FDA's Trade Secrets Policy," *Journal of Pharmacy* 159 (September/October 1978):135-136. Reprinted with permission. For an opposing prodisclosure point of view and analysis, see Thomas O. McGarity and Sidney A. Shapiro, "The Trade Secret Status of Health and Safety Testing Information: Reforming Agency Disclosure Policies," *Harvard Law Review* 93 (March 1980):837-888.

8. For a summary of FDA regulations in this regard, see *Federal Register* 42 (daily ed. 14 January 1977), pp. 3094-3109.

9. "Drug Disclosures Proposals Rapped Again by PMA," *Chemical Marketing Reporter* 202 (17 July 1972):1.

10. "Confidentiality: Will Government Give Away Company Secrets?," reprinted from the 10 December 1980 issue of *Chemical Week* by special permission. Copyright 1983 by McGraw-Hill, Inc., New York, p. 30.

11. Ibid., p. 31. Reprinted with permission.

12. Ibid.

13. This example was obtained from an interview with a chemical-company physician.

14. Patrick Phillips, "Are Trade Secrets Dead? The Effect of the Toxic Substances Control Act and the Freedom of Information Act on Trade Secrets," *Journal of the Patent Office Society* 62 (November 1980):653n.

15. Interview with a senior government executive (GS-15), U.S. Food and Drug Administration official, Oak Ridge, Tenn., April 1980.

16. Interview with Gerald H. Deighton, director, Freedom of Information Staff, U.S. Food and Drug Administration, August 1980.

17. Senate, *Freedom of Information Act*, pp. 336-357 (testimony of Nancy Duff Campbell).

18. For a discussion of venue procedures under the Freedom of Information Act, see Russell B. Stevenson, "Protecting Business Secrets under the Freedom of Information Act, Managing Exemption 4" (Paper presented at "Your Business, Your Trade Secrets, and Your Government," Seminar on Protecting and Obtaining Commercial Information from the Government, American Bar Association, Washington, D.C., 11 May 1981), pp. 102-106.

19. See the Pharmaceutical Manufacturers Association, *Prescription Drug Industry Fact Book: 1980* (Washington, D.C., 1980), pp. 29-39; W. Reekie and M. Weber, *Profits, Politics and Drugs* (New York: Holmes and Meier Publishers, 1979), pp. 54-57; and H.G. Grabowski, *Drug Regulation and Innovation: Empirical Evidence and Policy Options* (Washington, D.C.: American Enterprise Institute, 1976), pp. 17-37.

20. *Federal Register* 47 (Daily ed. 19 October 1982):46622-46666.

21. R.W. Hansen, "The Pharmaceutical Development Process: Estimates of Development Costs and Times, and the Effects of Proposed Regulatory Changes," in *Issues in Pharmaceutical Economics*, ed. R. Chien (Lexington, Mass.: D.C. Heath and Company, 1979), p. 180.

22. Pharmaceutical Manufacturers Association, *Prescription Drug Industry Fact Book*, p. 35.

23. R. Schweiker, secretary, U.S. Department of Health and Human Services, Speech to the National Pharmaceutical Council, Washington, D.C., 23 June 1982.

24. O.H. Brownlee, "The Economic Consequences of Regulating without Regard to Economic Consequences," in *Issues in Pharmaceutical Economics*, ed. R. Chien (Lexington, Mass.: D.C. Heath and Company, 1979), p. 226.

25. W.M. Wardell, "The History of Drug Discovery, Development and Regulation," in *Issues in Pharmaceutical Economics*, ed. R. Chien (Lexington, Mass.: D.C. Heath and Company, 1979), p. 10.

26. Ibid. Also see "Drug Innovation Is Dragging its Feet," *The Economist*, 2 May 1981, p. 95. At the time of the writing of this book, patent-reform legislation was being debated in the U.S. Congress, which if passed, will extend the effective life of a patent, depending upon the amount of time lost through the regulatory process.

27. See Martin M. Eisman and William M. Wardell, "Incremental Time Study: An Analysis and Approval of Drugs for the U.S. Market," in *Economic Costs of FDA Regulations*, ed. Pharmaceutical Manufacturers Association (Washington, D.C.: Pharmaceutical Manufacturers Association, 1981), pp. 53-81.

28. See W.L. Casey, J.E. Marthinsen, and L.S. Moss, "Trade Secrecy and Patenting: Complementary or Substitutable Activities?" (Paper presented at the Atlantic Economic Society Convention, Washington, D.C., 13 October 1978). See also John J. Mahon, "Trade Secrets and Patents Compared," *Journal of the Patent Office Society* 50 (August 1978):536-553.

29. J.A. Miller, "Spliced Genes Get Down to Business," *Science News* 117 (29 March 1980):205. Reprinted with permission from *Science News*, the weekly news magazine of science, copyright 1980 by Science Service, Inc.

30. Pharmaceutical Manufacturers Association, *Prescription Drug Industry Fact Book*, p. 28.

31. See H.G. Grabowski, *Drug Regulation and Innovation: Empirical Evidence and Policy Options*, American Enterprise Institute, 1976, pp. 45-46; Harold Clymer, "The Economic & Regulatory Climate—U.S. and Overseas Trends," in *Drug Development and Marketing*, ed. Robert B. Helms (Washington, D.C.: American Enterprise Institute for Public Policy Research, 1975), pp. 137-154; and Louis Lasagna and William M. Wardell, "The Rate of New Drug Discovery" in *Drug Development and Marketing*, ed. Robert B. Helms (Washington, D.C.: American Enterprise Institute for Public Policy Research, 1975), pp. 155-164. For a statistical overview of R&D trends in the U.S. pharmaceutical industry, see "R&D Overview," *Chemical and Engineering News* 159 (27 July 1981):48-71; and H. Richardson, "What's Ahead for the Drug Industry, Pharmacy and Health Care in the 1980s?," *American Druggist* 184 (July 1981):79-80.

32. Barrie G. James, *The Future of the Multinational Pharmaceutical Industry to 1990* (New York: Wiley & Sons, 1977), pp. 78-79.

33. H.G. Grabowski and J.M. Vernon, "New Studies on Market Definition, Concentration, Theory of Supply, Entry and Promotion," in *Issues in Pharmaceutical Economics*, ed. R. Chien (Lexington, Mass.: D.C. Heath and Company, 1979), p. 48.

34. Ibid., pp. 48-49.

35. See Harold C. Relyea, "Businesses, Trade Secrets, and Information Access Policy Developments in Other Countries: An Overview" (Paper

presented at "Your Business, Your Trade Secrets and Your Government," a seminar on Protecting and Obtaining Commercial Information from the Government, American Bar Association, Washington, D.C., 11 May 1981), pp. 158-238.

36. P.J. Buckley and M.C. Casson, *The Future of the Multinational* (London: Holmes & Meier Publishers, 1976), p. 76.

37. See Louis T. Wells, ed., *The Product Life Cycle and International Trade* (Cambridge: Harvard University Press, 1972); and Raymond Vernon, *Sovereignty at Bay* (New York: Basic Books, 1971), pp. 64-112.

38. On the definition and use of the learning curve in managerial decisionmaking, see Gerald B. Allan and John S. Hammond, "Note on the Use of Experience Curves in Competitive Decision-Making," *in Readings in the Theory of the Firm*, eds. Laurence S. Moss and Donna M. Gagnon (Lexington, Mass.: Ginn Publishing, 1981), pp. 242-256.

39. W. Tsurumi, *Multinational Management: Business Strategy and Government Policy* (Cambridge, Mass.: Ballinger, 1977), p. 12.

40. Ibid., p. 79.

41. Pharmaceutical Manufacturers Association, *Prescription Drug Industry Fact Book*, p. 60.

42. "Innovative Japanese Drugs Move into the U.S.," *Business Week*, 10 May 1982, p. 150.

43. Telephone conversation, Robert J. Rice, Jr., consumer safety officer, Regulations Policy Staff, U.S. Food and Drug Administration, 19 November 1982.

44. Pharmaceutical Manufacturers Association, *Prescription Drug Industry Fact Book*, p. 62.

45. Telephone conversation, Robert J. Rice, Jr.

46. Grabowski and Vernon, "New Studies on Market Definition," p. 49.

47. Ibid.

48. E. Reis-Arndt and D. Elvers, "Results of Pharmaceutical Research: New Pharmaceutical Agents 1961-1970," *Drugs Made in Germany* 15 (1972):134-140; and E. Reis-Arndt, "New Pharmaceutical Agents 1961-1973," *Drugs Made in Germany* 18 (1975):123-130.

49. Grabowski, *Drug Regulation and Innovation*, pp. 49-51.

50. Grabowski and Vernon, "New Studies on Market Definition," p. 48.

51. Dr. Marion J. Finkel, speech to the American Society of Clinical Pharmacology, New Orleans, 19 March 1981.

8 Summary and Conclusions

Our research supports the claim that the Freedom of Information Act is being used for purposes other than those intended by Congress. While the intent of the act was and remains that of promoting a more open democratic society by exposing government policies, practices, and procedures to direct public scrutiny, the act, in fact, has both threatened the constitutional rights of individuals to their private property and discouraged entrepreneurial activity. The huge cottage industry of business-information seekers that has grown up to track and market business records in agency files serves as evidence of these disclosure practices. Those who support the act remind us that government's unlimited authority to maintain official secrets may undermine the very essence of a democratic society—namely, that government is the servant of the people and that the public has a basic right to know what their servant is doing and what procedures are being followed. It is evident, however, that the act has provided competitors in private industry with access to the corporate secrets of those firms submitting information to federal agencies.

The Freedom of Information Act has been interpreted as a disclosure statute by both Congress and the federal courts. While exemptions to disclosure exist, including the one designed to prevent the disclosure of trade secrets and privileged or confidential information of a commercial or financial nature, the 1979 *Chrysler* decision determined that information is exempted from disclosure only at the discretion of government-agency officials.[1] This means that information submitters have minimal constitutional protection against disclosure. For this reason, many managers believe that information, once in the hands of certain government agencies, is, for all practical purposes, published information. It is also the reason why corporate lawyers increasingly are advising their clients not to give "confidential business information to Federal government agencies if at all possible, and if [they] do, [to] take precautions to prevent it from being disclosed," such as requiring on-site inspection of business records, demanding subpoenas for information requested, insisting on the immediate return of submitted information, and severing all business ties with the government.[2]

In their day-to-day decisions on information requests, agency officials follow the broad guidelines laid down by the law and those specific guidelines established by their regulatory agencies. Because the Freedom of Information Act is superimposed over a myriad of other laws that have varying information-disclosure provisions, officials work within a framework of ambiguous and sometimes inconsistent rules and procedures. In some cases, there are stronger sanctions against those government officials who withhold information that should be disclosed than against those who disclose information that should be withheld. This asymmetry produces incentives for the transfer of economically valuable information from one business to the next through the intermediation of government. Agency officials face the difficult task of supporting the widely endorsed goal of providing for a more open government while at the same time protecting from disclosure information that is exempted. Conflicts inevitably arise because of imprecisions and overlaps in the legal definitions of exempted information. Given the fact that the Freedom of Information Act is a disclosure statute, it is not surprising that certain agency officials have adopted the general mantra of "when in doubt, give it out" rather than the more-prudent one, "when in doubt, black it out."

Of course, erring on the side of excessive disclosure may be viewed legitimately as the lesser of two evils, depending upon the requester's reasons for seeking the information. For example, the prevention of political corruption may be worth a billion dollars of released business information and the disincentives it creates. We are convinced, however, that the lion's share of information disclosures to past and present FOIA requesters has little to do with preventing the abuse of political power.

Historically, freedom-of-information legislation was intended to open government files to scholars, public-interest groups, and members of the press, who would use the information or the opportunity to obtain it in ways that would promote and preserve our democratic system of government. Yet, in reference to those major agencies that collect business information, such as the Food and Drug Administration, the Environmental Protection Agency, and the Federal Trade Commission, information requests emanating from scholars, the press, or even from public-interest groups are relatively rare compared to those emanating from business firms and their legal representatives or from market intermediaries.

For what purpose are these requests made? Based on interviews we conducted, statistical data we compiled, trade-journal reports, court cases, and scholarly texts, we conclude that businesses request information for the following reasons. Some requests by businesses are for policy procedures and new agency rules. These requests are a healthy aspect of the act's openness. However, other requests are admittedly fishing expeditions, motivated by a sense of curiosity or by the belief that, given the law of averages, if enough information is requested, something of value will predictably get caught up in the nets sooner or later. Monsanto's recent loss of its formula for its herbicide, Roundup, is a shining example of the success of legalized espionage by way of the government's take-out service. Other information requests are from firms for purely defensive purposes, the objective being, for example, to determine what portions of the records that they have submitted to government agencies typically are being released to third-party requesters. Acting through third-party intermediaries, these firms request their own previously submitted information in order to learn what is being released either in total or as fragmented bits and pieces. If such requests were submitted directly to government agencies, unpurged versions would be released.

Finally, many firms seek information from rivals through the Freedom of Information Act, knowing precisely what it is, where it is, and how to get it. Many companies formally budget espionage activities, and this high level of interest has spawned a number of FOIA intermediaries to facilitate access to this information. The cottage industry of FOIA intermediaries caters to this group of requesters by publishing information logs that serve effectively as menus for industrial espionage. It is not accidental that these market intermediaries have nurtured close relationships with those agencies that are concerned primarily with regulating business or acquiring information about business and that thereby possess the most valuable commercial information. Furthermore, our statistical evidence indicates that the rate of growth of FOIA requests from these business-oriented agencies is greater than in the case of others.

In our investigation of the impact of the Freedom of Information Act on the U.S. economy, we encountered a variety of horror stories about damaging information disclosure. Although relatively few in number in comparison to the total number of FOIA requests, these cases are the tip of an immense iceberg. Documentation of damaging disclosure, like the dimensions of the base of an iceberg, is difficult to obtain because perpetrators of acts of industrial espionage, who pirate information from government agencies, are able to cover their tracks with ease, particularly if information requests are channeled through third-party intermediaries. Once a leakage occurs, neither the information-supplying firm nor the information-requesting firm has an incentive to publicize the fact. Since information can be stolen without leaving the owner's possession, there is no empty barn to alert anyone that a theft has occurred. As discussed in chapter 7, there are strong incentives for both the thief and the victim to remain silent about such an incident.

A central conclusion of this book is that the Freedom of Information Act is an engine of legal industrial espionage and is discouraging innovation in the United States by making it more difficult for innovative firms to protect economically valuable information and thereby to capture sufficient returns on innovations over time to justify R&D outlays. In our investigation of the U.S. pharmaceutical industry, we noted some deep skepticism among managers of participating firms concerning the confidentiality of any information in the hands of government-agency officials regardless of how closely it may fit within the language of the trade-secrets exemption. We consider this type of business perception to be an important factor that companies weigh in the decision to commit resources to major inventions and innovations. Clearly, it is important for government agencies to be steadfast in protecting confidential information entrusted to them; it is likewise important for information-submitting companies to believe this to be the case.

Similarly, in the chemical industry, we saw how gaping holes in the confidentiality procedures of the Environmental Protection Agency have given rise to industry fears of disclosure. The claim has been made, of course, that business perceptions about the real or potential use of the Freedom of Information Act for purposes of industrial espionage are blatantly false and that legislative revisions should be based on fact, not fiction. We believe that business perceptions about the risks of information leakages from government agencies do indeed reflect reality. Admittedly, in the short run, fears may be exaggerated, but over the long run, the adjustment of distorted perceptions tends to occur spontaneously as businesspersons adapt their expectations to reality. In any case, business perceptions have remained deeply skeptical about government's commitment to respecting and protecting the confidentiality of corporate records. The statistical evidence we offer here lends credibility to these business perceptions.

We conclude that the extent of damaging information leakages from federal agencies, authorized by the Freedom of Information Act, has been understated significantly in the literature, the federal hearings chambers, and the courts. That is because the debate, to date, has revolved around the narrow definitions of trade secrets and privileged or confidential information as specified by the trade-secrets exemption of the act. Leakages of a broader type of business information are occurring with damaging effects on the entrepreneurial spirit and the willingness to innovate within the business community. We have labeled this broader type of information as circumstantially relevant business information. Included within this definition are all of those particular and sometimes localized bits and pieces of information that businesses generate. It is knowledge of particular times and circumstances that collectively provides innovative firms with competitive advantage over rivals. Often, this information is ephemeral and therefore not included in older, legal definitions of trade secrets. This particular type of knowledge leaks out of federal agencies not because of the ineptitude or indifference of FOIA officers but because it falls between the cracks of the exemption's defintions that do not recognize its importance.

Of what consequence is the leakage of circumstantially relevant business information? Its diffusion and dissemination would seem to promote the economist's idea of efficient resource allocation. Given the existence of this knowledge, the consumer will benefit predictably from its rapid dissemination throughout the economy. However, given the fact that businesses require incentives to create this knowledge, our position is that, if government were less inclined to promote its diffusion, the public interest would benefit from more discovery and application of information of this type. Business firms will not devote resources to innovative activities unless expected returns are sufficient to cover R&D costs. Returns are dampened through information dissemination by government to rival firms, thereby creating a strong disincentive to innovate.

We believe that the Freedom of Information Act, as it currently is written, gives insufficient protection to proprietary business information and, therefore, that it is operating as a threat to the future vitality of entrepreneurial and innovative activities in the U.S. economy. There are inadequate safeguards to prevent the damaging leakage of circumstantially relevant business information from federal agencies, and therefore, we conclude that legislative reform is needed.

Policy Recommendations

As economists, we are interested in providing a system that will allocate resources effectively and efficiently at any point in time and over the course of time. In its current form, the Freedom of Information Act does neither. Our recommendations are made in an effort to preserve the spirit of the act while at the same time showing greater sensitivity toward preserving legitimate property rights and toward more judiciously using precious tax dollars to serve the public purpose. Our recommendations can be classified into two major areas: (1) those related directly to the procedural and substantive aspects of the trade-secrets exemption and (2) those related to the proper allocation of government resources in fulfilling its responsibilities to the public.

The Proper Allocation of Tax Dollars

The allocation of resources to fill FOIA requests is a function of three parts of the act: (1) the time limitations for responding to a request, (2) the fee structure used to charge requesters, and (3) the requirement to segregate confidential information from nonconfidential information in agency files. The act requires that agencies respond to an initial request within ten days and to an appeal within twenty days.[3] These narrow time limits, for all intents and purposes, place FOIA requests at the top of an agency's priority list. The primary functions of an agency, such as approving a new drug that might prevent heart attacks or approving a new allergy cure, are placed on the back burner while these requests are filled.

In many cases, the requests are a tremendous burden to the financial resources of an agency. For instance, Phillip Agee, an author and self-proclaimed crusader to expose CIA officers, has submitted requests to the Central Intelligence Agency that have cost over $500,000 to fill.[4] Even the judge in Agee's case against the Central Intelligence Agency expressed amazement at the U.S. tolerance to bear these costs for such purposes.[5] Another (unrelated) request to the government was for information so extensive that it would fill 11,000 linear feet of file-cabinet space—a vertical distance that would dwarf the Washington Monument.[6]

In chapter 3, we documented the widely diverse cost-per-request estimates provided by a group of selected government agencies.

While the public interest is served by the timely disclosure of information in government files, a tremendous opportunity cost is paid for this benefit. It takes literally hundreds of labor hours of time and the use of highly qualified talent to identify requested documents and segregate the confidential from the nonconfidential information. Besides the $57 million in directly traceable costs to the act,[7] there are countless other costs as well— the most important of which is the sacrifice in public welfare by the under-employment and misallocation of government resources.[8] In return for these services, the agencies recover only 2 percent of the cost.[9]

We recommend that the fees charged for FOIA requests be raised to reflect more fully the marginal cost of fulfilling these obligations. Marginal costs should be charged for industry and third-party requests. We suggest a provision be enacted to allow for liberal fee waivers for requests that are clearly in the public interest. On the one hand, the problem with raising the fee to all requesters is that it discourages some requests that are clearly in the public interest but that do not meet the agencies' definition of that term. The benefit is that it weeds out requests for questionable purposes, like requests from students who use the government to write their term papers. On the other hand, the problem with eliminating the fee for all requests made in the public interest is that it encourages individuals who make such requests to overuse the government resource.[10] The benefit is that it intensifies the light of public review of agency action. Our suggestion is a workable compromise between the two.

Finally, the time limits in the act ought to permit some flexibility in regard to other functions of an agency. At present, FOIA requests are not budgeted separately. They have top priority by the time limits required, and thereby they displace other agency duties. We recommend that FOIA activities be budgeted so that there is a clear identification of the resources that are being used to fulfill requests and to permit Congress to indicate the resources it feels should be used in meeting these obligations relative to others.

Procedural and Substantive Changes
in the Trade-Secrets Exemption

We support the position that the trade-secrets exemption of the act be amended by Congress for the purpose of better protecting the property rights of information submitters. The current definitions of "trade secrecy" are too narrow. Using the *National Parks* test, information is exempt from mandatory disclosure only if its release is likely "to impair the government's ability to obtain necessary information in the future [or] . . . to cause substantial harm to the competitive position of the person from whom the information was obtained."[11] The *National Parks* test focuses only upon part of what constitutes proprietary business information. In its drive toward quantification and objectivity, this test systematically ignores valuable information that contributes to dynamic innovative efficiency.

Federal agencies are not protecting the rights of submitting firms adequately if trade secrets and confidential business information, narrowly defined, are the only information eligible to be withheld. As a rule, private business information, especially circumstantially relevant business information, should not be released unless the submitter agrees to waive exempt status or where the disclosure of the information is necessary to protect an overriding public interest like imminent health and safety dangers. For example, the report of a private pharmaceutical company, indicating possible carcinogenic elements in a new drug, should be made available to the consumer in a timely, informative way. Having said this, it does not follow that complete bodies of corporate records need to be disclosed in order to achieve this purpose. Careful attention should be paid, as it is done in the Common Market, to the volume and breadth of information disclosed when there is an overriding public interest at stake.[12] The public interest does not extend to the release of all data including what may relate only slightly to public health and safety.

Information to be exempt from disclosure under the trade-secrets exemption should meet four criteria. First, it should be information generated in the private, not the public, sector. One basic purpose of the Freedom of Information Act is to provide access to information generated internally within the government—information that is generated by tax money, not data loaned to the government for the purpose of helping the government make more-effective decisions. Second, the information must be truly confidential and proprietary. Ideally, any information already in the private sector should not be exempt unless it is organized or combined in such a novel fashion that the duplication of this information would be costly to a third-party requester, as the *Worthington* case provided.[13] Moreover, it should be exempt from further disclosure if it has been made public mistakenly through an unauthorized disclosure of a federal agency. In this extraordinary situation, all efforts should be made by government to recall the information, to prevent further dissemination, and to the extent possible, to prevent the recipient from using this information to gain government approval for a regulated product.

Third, the information must be of reasonable value to the submitting firm—that is, the type of information that the firms in the industry customarily recognize as proprietary. However, substantial competitive harm, resulting from its release, need not be demonstrated because often the amount of the harm, especially in the form of a lost entrepreneurial opportunity, is difficult to measure. Proof of competitive harm is difficult to measure for products that are newly developed, for information that could stir up labor/management problems, and for information that could lead to a loss of business goodwill. Finally, information, qualifying for the trade-secrets exemption, should not be of the type that would conceal unlawful activity, mismanagement, or violations of existing regulations or that would merely cause embarrassment to the firm.[14]

We believe that the procedures of federal agencies in managing information flows and the decision-making processes in releasing or withholding information should be altered to promote more consistency, uniformity, and efficiency. Specifically, we recommend the following.

Upon initial submission of its data, the business owner should be responsible for clearly identifying all information that it considers to be proprietary by stamping it confidential. Such a confidentiality designation would entitle the submitter to notification upon receipt of an FOIA request for that information. Businesses should not be required to substantiate their claims of confidentiality at this time unless they want a presubmission determination of the information's confidentiality from the agency to which they submitted the data. Since most documents submitted will never be requested, the necessity of justifying all claims of confidentiality at the time of submission would be costly and unreasonable. Thus, the government agencies should not be required ordinarily to rule on the proprietary nature of most information at the time of submission.

Decisions pertaining to documents for which no confidentiality determination was made should be done after a request for that information is received by the agency. Once a request has been received and timely notice has been made, the submitter should be asked to justify his claim of confidentiality at an agency hearing or through written testimony. The agency then will be in a position to decide about disclosure. If the decision is to disclose, timely notice must be given to the submitter to allow for judicial review of the agency decision in the federal-court system. To allow for this, the *Chrysler* decision should be overturned by Congress to provide a statutory basis for reverse-FOIA suits. Furthermore, the court decision should not be based solely on the agency record since the taking of private property is at stake. Review should be de novo—that is, it should be based on the merits of the agency decision, not just on a review of the bureaucratic trail left by agency procedures. This would be consistent with current provisions within the act calling for de novo judicial review of federal-agency decisions to withhold information.

In contrast, if the decision is to withhold the information, the requester should be given the same right as the submitter to argue his case before the agency. Should the agency reject the requester's claim, the present option of a judicial hearing with de novo review should be available. In either case, the decision to reject or accept an FOIA request should be made at the same agency level. Moreover, Congress should make the protection from disclosure through the trade-secrets exemption carry the weight of law. Information found to be within this exemption should be held mandatorily and not at the discretion of the agency.

There are cases where businesses would like the assurance of mandatory exclusion from FOIA disclosure prior to submission. In such cases, a petition should be made to the agency identifying the information that a business claims is confidential, and documents should be sent attesting to the perceived loss of value that release would cause.[15] Upon the evaluation of this petition and its support documents, the agencies should be able to grant or deny the request for mandatory confidentiality. A granting of this confidentiality status would result in a nondiscretionary obligation to withhold this information, an automatic denial of all requests made on such documents, and upon appeal by the requester, the burden of proof would then fall on the requester for demonstrating that the disclosure would be in the public interest.

What constitutes an adequate challenge to the submitter's confidentiality claims? The ideal situation would be one where the agency could divine the motive behind the request, distinguishing, for example, requests truly made in the public interest and those made by agents of industrial espionage. In such an ideal world, federal agencies would be able to weigh objectively the pecuniary harm to the information owner and the loss to the innovative process against the benefits derived from public scrutiny of the relevant data. Unfortunately, we do not live in a world where such a distinction can be made and where motives can be identified. While it seems reasonable to have a provision for an agency to override the confidential claims of an information submitter in cases where there are threats to public health and safety, it is difficult to imagine an agency procedure that could come close to providing this result. The agency is put in the impossible position of reconciling the legitimate rights of information owners and those obvious and legitimate rights of the public to obtain certain types of information.

Finally, the trade-secrets exemption should be expanded to include information submitted from nonprofit organizations such as universities and mutual insurance companies. With regard to universities, researchers often submit technical information in grant applications or in compliance reports. This information, in many cases, could be patented. However, U.S. law requires the patenting of a product within one year of public disclosure, and in many other countries, public disclosure prior to a patent application precludes such an application. Thus, FOIA disclosure could eliminate or substantially alter a researcher's plans for patent protection.

In the *Washington Research Project* case, the court found that:

> [a] noncommercial scientist's research design is not literally a trade secret or item of commercial information for it defies common sense to pretend that a scientist is engaged in trade or commerce.[16]

The funny thing about common sense is that it is not common. Over the past few years, we have witnessed the flow of scientists from academia to establish and work in biotechnology firms such as Genentech, Biogen, and Cetus. This plus the spectacular growth in the value of their stocks bear witness to the fallacy of the *Washington Project* decision and the need for the protection of proprietary information submitted from nonprofit organizations.

The protection for noncommercial information can be justified on the grounds of fairness. Many scholars devote countless hours to produce data banks and test results. Their reward is in being granted tenure, promotion, and salary increments. To have the government freely disclose this information to any requester would be to jeopardize the stream of benefits from this work.

Recommendations for Further Empirical Study

We believe that the need exists for empirical studies designed to trace the flow of information between private companies and government agencies, utilizing the meaningful and useful method of categorizing information that we offer in this book. In reference to the trade-secrets exemption of the act, the legalistic language devised to guide information processing in federal agencies is neither very useful nor meaningful. In the debate over information disclosures, too much attention has been focused on trade secrets and confidential business information, as narrowly defined. We proposed a more-expansive definition to include all forms of circumstantially relevant business information.

The failure to identify this broader category of proprietary business information has led to apparent contradictions in the empirical investigations of the Freedom of Information Act that have been conducted to date. On the one hand, some businesses complain bitterly about the loss of economically valuable information leaked from government agencies, and yet the search for horror stories has turned up precious few examples of leakages of trade secrets as defined by the *National Parks* case and its judicial progeny. In reality, a contradiction does not exist because businesses are concerned not only with trade secrets per se but also with a more-general type of business information, most of which lies outside the language and definition of the trade-secrets exemption.

What is needed, we believe, are new empirical studies, operating under a different set of definitions, undertaken for the purpose of determining to what extent business information submitted to federal agencies falls under the broader umbrella of circumstantially relevant business information; to what extent this type of knowledge is being released by agencies under FOIA authorization; to what extent this knowledge, if released, is ending up in the possession of rival firms; and what appropriate measurements are available to assess the economic impact this is having. The ideal approach would be to adopt the technique used by marine biologists in tagging whales or dolphins for the purpose of tracing migratory patterns. Unfortunately, information flows are not easily traceable. Information arriving at point B has not necessarily departed from point A; as a unique property asset, information may be sold or given away without the loss of actual possession. One cannot take inventory to determine whether a piece of information has been lost or is now in the hands of rivals.

It is possible, however, to identify the availability and disclosure of circumstantially relevant business information through the records of federal agencies. At several government agencies, detailed logs are maintained specifying the nature of information requested and released. The published logs, or menus, of FOIA intermediaries can serve also to identify the availablity, but not the dissemination, of circumstantially relevant business information. These companies will not release the names of clients requesting this or any other type of information because the guarantee of confidentiality is an indispensable feature of their marketing approach.

If the dissemination of circumstantially relevant business information by government agencies can be documented, the question of economic impact then arises. To what extent and in what ways are the competitive market positions of firms being compromised through the governmental release of this knowledge? Are there differences in impact from industry to industry? How are innovative or entrepreneurial activities being discouraged because firms are unable to prevent information diffusion and dissemination? We believe that answers to these questions would contribute significantly to the growing body of knowledge in the field of the economics of information. This book should be of value in defining terms, in outlining the problem, and in providing a historical and theoretical framework for further study.

Recommendations for Further Thought

There is little doubt that, if those who submitted valuable information to federal agencies were proprietors of small, family businesses and government was divulging their business secrets, the weight of legal authority would bend in favor of the individual firm's owner and not the ambiguous social interest trumpeted by the so-called public-interest groups. Privacy of individuals, even individual businessmen, might become a popular cause among political activists, especially those who support the disclosure of agency information. Of course, nearly every controversial case we have considered here and nearly every case brought to appellate review has involved a large corporation trying to maintain the confidentiality of its business records. For this reason, the moral and ethical issue of individual rights to privacy seems to be a nonissue since a corporation's privacy is not something recognized by law.

If government were confiscating the capital goods of small businesses and redistributing the proceeds to others, again it is predictable that sentiment would be on the side of the small man against the tyranny of government. In such cases, government would be hard pressed to justify actions that abrogate the property rights of individuals. Conversely, when large corporations lose information through government leakages, the hue and cry of privacy and individual property rights seems out of place. Since information is intangible, even the word *confiscation* seems to be an inappropriate term inasmuch as information can be taken from the owner without the owner losing the information—just the value of the information is lost. The loss of intellectual property is viewed somehow as being inconsequential. During this age of the modern, large corporation, concern with the issue of liberty and private rights to ownership seems archaic and misplaced.

It seems to us that, because the business corporation is a legal person, it does not follow that the organization should be subjected to an entirely different set of disclosure rules than if the organization were a small, privately owned business. Large-scale organizations survive because they are able to benefit from efficient, teamlike methods of production, housed within a single administrative structure. In our view, the imperatives of the entrepreneurial process do require government sensitivity to the proprietary nature of certain categories of corporate information housed in government. Without such a sensitivity, the powerful institution of corporate organization may lose valuable incentives to promote and further innovation.

The public does have a right to know about the workings of government, but need the public information flow out of government instantly with the only lag being the time it takes agencies to fill FOIA requests?

Perhaps we may look forward to the future when information is transferred to government agencies by way of computer telecommunications and accessed by all interested parties by a computerized information take-out service. With the time lag between invention and imitation reduced to microseconds, government probably will be extremely efficient and professional at managing an economy in the final stages of economic decline.

How do we combine the eradication of political bureaucratic secrecy with the secretive imperatives of the innovation process? This problem has been endemic to modern democracies. With the widespread and ever cheaper availability to data processing, storage, and retrieval mechanisms, the issues raised by the trade-secrets exemption to the Freedom of Information Act are liable to be with us for many years to come. In many cases, the legitimate interests of business and the economy must be weighed against the public-policy concerns surrounding health and safety. What we have tried to demonstrate in this book is that as long as the legal definitions of trade secrets and confidential business information are narrowly drawn to exclude circumstantially relevant business information, the balance will be struck to the disadvantage of the innovation process.

Notes

1. *Chrysler Corp. v. Brown* 99 S.C.T. (2d Cir. 1979).

2. U.S. Congress, House, Committee on Government Operations, *Freedom of Information Oversight*, 97th Cong., 1st Sess., 1981, p. 555 (testimony of Bert Braverman).

3. U.S.C. 552(a)(6).

4. U.S., Congress, Senate, Subcommittee of the Committee on the Judiciary, *Freedom of Information Act*, 97th Cong., 1st Sess., 1981, p. 638 (letter from William French Smith to George Bush).

5. Ibid.

6. Ibid., p. 82 (testimony of Robert L. Saloschin).

7. Ibid., p. 409 (testimony of Arthur R. Whale).

8. See chapter 5.

9. Senate, *Freedom of Information Act*, p. 78 (testimony of Robert L. Saloschin).

10. For a discussion of this problem, see ibid., p. 757 (testimony of Jerald A. Jacobs).

11. *National Parks and Conservation Assn. v. Kleppe*, 547 F.2d 673 (D.C. Cir. 1976); see the discussion in chapter 2.

12. Charles R. Wunsch, "Trade Secret Confidentiality: A Non-Tariff Trade Barrier in the Chemical Trade," *Cornell International Law Journal* 14 (Winter 1981):185.

13. *Worthington Compressors Inc. v. Castle*, 662 F.2d 45 (D.C. Cir. 1981).

14. For a related discussion of these issues, see the Administrative Conference of the United States, *FOIA Exemption (b)(4): Final Recommendation Proposed by Committee on Regulation of Business* (Washington D.C., 24 November 1981), pp. 2-3.

15. See the provisions in the *Toxic Substances Control Act*, 15 U.S.C. 2601-2629 (1976 ed.).

16. *Washington Research Project, Inc. v. Department of Health, Education and Welfare*, 504 F.2d 238 (D.C. Cir. 1974).

Bibliography

Books and Articles

Adams, Walter, ed. *The Structure of American Industry*. New York: Macmillan, 1961.

Advisory Subcommittee on Patent and Information Policy of the Advisory Committee on Industrial Innovation. "Draft Report on Information Policy." Washington, D.C.: U.S. Department of Commerce, 1978.

American Chemical Society. *Chemistry in the Economy*. Washington, D.C., 1973.

Arrow, Kenneth J. "Economic Welfare and the Allocation of Resources for Invention." In *The Rate and Direction of Inventive Activity: Economic and Social Factors*, vol. 1, edited by National Bureau of Economic Research. Princeton, N.J.: Princeton University Press, 1962, pp. 609-626.

Backman, Jules, *Competition in the Chemical Industry*. Washington, D.C.: Manufacturing Chemists Association, 1964.

———. *The Economics of the Chemical Industry*. Washington, D.C.: Manufacturing Chemists Association, 1970.

Barkley, Paul, and Seekler, David. *Economic Growth and Environmental Decay*. New York: Harcourt, Brace, Jovanovich, Inc., 1972.

Baumol, William J. "Contestable Markets, Antitrust and Regulation." *Wharton Magazine* 7 (Fall 1982):23-30.

Baumol, William J.; Panzar, J.C.; and Willing, R.D. *Contestable Markets and the Theory of Industry Structure*. New York: Harcourt, Brace, Jovanovich, 1982.

Bennet, Charles, P. "The Freedom of Information Act, Is It a Clear Public Record Law?" *Brooklyn Law Review* 34 (1967):72-78.

Bennett, James T., and Johnson, Manuel H. "The Political Economy of Federal Government Paper." *Policy Review* 7 (Winter 1979):27-43.

———. *The Political Economy of Federal Government Growth*. College Station: Center for Free Enterprise, Texas A&M University, 1981.

Berry, Peter C. "Accommodating Patent and Antitrust Law: Monopolists' Lawful Patenting Conduct and SCM Corp. v. Xerox Corp." *Boston University Law* 20 (1980):78-114.

"Biotechnology's Drive for New Products." *Chemical Week* (24 February 1982):47-52.

Blanchard, Robert O. *A History of the Federal Records Law*. Kansas City: University of Missouri, 1967.

Bouchard, Robert F., and Franklin, Justin, eds. *Guidebook to the Freedom of Information and Privacy Acts*. New York: Clark Boardman, 1980.

Bronson, Gail. "PRI Serves as Broker for Inventors, Firms Seeking Innovations." *Wall Street Journal*, 7 August 1979, p. 16.

Buchanan, James. *Cost and Choice*. New York: Markham, 1969.

_____ . *Freedom in Constitutional Contract*. College Station: University of Texas Press, 1977.

Burmeister, Edwin. "Synthesizing the Neo-Austrian and Alternative Approaches to Capital Theory: A Survey." *Journal of Economic Literature* 12 (1974):450.

Burtt, E.A., ed. *The English Philosophers from Bacon to Mill*. New York: Modern Library, 1939.

Cabot, Lynne O., and Fox, Ronald. "The Work of a Regulatory Agency: the EPA and Toxic Substances." *Harvard Business School Case Service* (ICCH 1-380-081):1-41.

Campbell, N.D. "Reverse Freedom of Information Act Litigation: The Need for Congressional Action." *Georgetown Law Journal* 67 (October 1978):103-205.

"Carter Plan to Spur Industrial Innovation Is Criticized for Its Lack of Tax Proposals." *Wall Street Journal*, 1 November 1979, p. 3.

Caruso, Charles M. "Industry Responsibility for Environmentally Caused Cancer under the Toxic Substances Act." *Rutgers Journal of Computers and Technology and Law* 213 (1979):216-217.

Casey, William; Marthinsen, John; and Moss, Laurence. "Trade Secrecy and Patenting: Complementary or Substitutable Activities?" Mimeographed. Paper presented at the Atlantic Economic Society Convention, Washington, D.C., 13 October 1978.

_____ . "The Relationship between Federally Sponsored Demonstration Projects and the Protection of Proprietary Information." Mimeographed. Paper presented at the Eastern Economic Association Convention, Boston, 12 May 1979.

Casson, Mark. *Alternatives to the Multinational Enterprise*. New York: Holmes and Meier Publishers, 1979.

"Catalysts That Can Slash Costs." *Chemical Week*, 20 October 1982, pp. 44-52.

Chandler, Alfred D., Jr. *Strategy and Structure*. Cambridge, Mass.: MIT Press, 1962.

_____ . *The Visible Hand: The Managerial Revolution in American Business*. Cambridge: Harvard University Press, 1977.

Chase, Marilyn. "Search for 'Superbugs': Industry Sees a Host of New Products Emerging from Its Growing Research on Gene Transplants." *Wall Street Journal*, 10 May 1969, p. 48.

"Chemical R&D: The Surge Continues." *Chemical Week*, 29 April 1981, p. 40.

Chien, Robert I., ed. *Issues in Pharmaceutical Economics*. Lexington, Mass.: D.C. Heath and Company, 1979.

Coase, Ronald. "The Problem of Social Costs." *Journal of Law and Economics* 3 (October 1980):1-44.

Cohen, Richard E. "Justice Report/New Information Law Gets Heavy Use from Public Business." *National Journal Reports*, July 1975, pp. 985-992.

Coleman, Jules L. "Efficiency Utility and Wealth Maximization." *Hofstra Law Review* 9 (Spring 1980):509-551.

"Confidentiality: Will Government Give Away Company Secrets?" *Chemical Week*, 10 December 1980, pp. 28-33.

Connelly, M.Q. "Secrets and Smokescreens: A Legal and Economic Analysis of Government Disclosures of Business Data." *Wisconsin Law Review* 1 (1981):269.

Council of Economic Advisors. *Economic Report of the President* [*Reagan to Congress*]. Washington, D.C.: U.S. Government Printing Office, 1982.

Davis, Kenneth Culp. "The Information Act: A Preliminary Analysis." *University of Chicago Law Review* 34 (Summer 1967):762-763.

Demsetz, Harold. "Information and Efficiency: Another Viewpoint." *Journal of Law and Economics* 12 (April 1969):1-22.

Dening, Mary B., and Eppy, Ali. "The Sociology of Rape." *Sociology and Social Review* 65 (July 1981):357-382.

Denison, Edward. *The Sources of Economic Growth in the United States*. New York: Committee for Economic Development, 1962.

———. "The Puzzling Drop in Productivity." *Challenge Magazine* 22 (May/June 1979):60-62.

Dominguez, George S. *The Business Guide to TOSCA*. New York: John Wiley & Sons, 1979.

"Drug Innovation Is Dragging Its Feet." *The Economist* 279 (2 May 1981): 95-96.

"Drug Disclosures Proposals Rapped Again by PMA." *Chemical Marketing Reporter* 202 (17 July 1972):1.

Earley, Pete. "EPA Lets Trade Secrets Loose in Slip Up, to Firm's Dismay." *Washington Post*, 18 September 1982.

Edwards, R.S. "The Rationale of Cost Accounting." In *L.S.E. Essays on Cost*, edited by J.M. Buchanan and C.F. Thulby, pp. 201-266. London: Weidenfeld & Nicholson, 1973.

"An EPA Blunder Spurs Move to Seal Data." *Chemical Week*, 19 September 1982, pp. 13-14.

"An Ex-CIA Man Is Now a Rising Star." *Chemical Week*, 21 April 1982, pp. 19-20.

Feldstein, Martin, ed. *The American Economy in Transition*. Chicago: University of Chicago Press for National Bureau of Economic Research, 1980.

Galbraith, John K. *The Affluent Society*. Boston: Houghton Mifflin Co., 1958.

_____ . *The New Industrial State* 2nd ed. New York: Mentor Book Co., 1971.

Gallese, Liz Roman. "Ideas for Sale: More Firms Buy, Sell the Fruits of Research to and from Outsiders," *Wall Street Journal*, 18 February 1976, pp. 1, 19.

Galnoor, Itzah. "The Politics of Public Information." *Society*, May/June 1979, pp. 20-32.

Gaynor, Kevin. "The Toxic Substance Control Act: A Regulatory Morass." *Vanderbilt Law Review* 38 (November 1977):1149-1195.

Gerth, H.H., and Mills, C. Wright. *From Max Weber Essays in Sociology*. New York: Oxford University Press, 1946.

Giagosian, N.H., ed. *Chemical Marketing Research*. New York: Reinhold Publishing Corp., 1967.

Giannella, Donald A. "Implementing the Freedom of Information Act: A Proposal for Uniform Regulations." *Administrative Law Review* 23 (1971):217-270.

Gilson, Roger P. "Administrative Disclosure of Private Business Records Under the Freedom of Information Act: An Analysis of Alternative Methods of Review." *Syracuse Law Review* 28 (1977):923-980.

Grabowski, H.G. *Drug Regulation and Innovation: Empirical Evidence and Policy Options*. Washington, D.C.: American Enterprise Institute, 1976.

Gruber, William; Mehta, Dileep; and Vernon, Raymond. "The R&D Factor in International Trade and Investment of United States Industries." *Journal of Political Economy* 75 (February 1969):20-37.

Hansen, Ronald W. "Comments on the Proposed Change in FDA's Trade Secrets Policy." *Journal of Pharmacy* 159 (September/October 1978):135-136.

Hayek, Friedrich A. *Individualism and Economic Order*. London: Routledge & Kegan Paul, 1979.

Helms, Robert B., ed. *Drug Developmental Markets*. Washington, D.C.: American Enterprise Institute for Public Policy Research, 1975.

Hershey, R. "Commercial Intelligence on a Shoestring." *Harvard Business Review* 58 (September/October 1980), pp. 22-30.

Hirschleifer, J. *Price Theory and Application*. Englewood Cliffs, N.J.: Prentice-Hall, 1980.

"Innovation Japanese Drugs Move into the U.S." *Business Week*, 10 May 1982, pp. 150-151.

Jackson, Barbara Bund. *The Value of Information: Course Module*. Boston: Division of Research, Graduate School of Business Administration, Harvard University, 1979.

Jager, Melvin F. *1982 Trade Secrets Law Handbook*. New York: Clark Boardman Co., 1982.

James, Barrie G. *The Future of the Multinational Pharmaceutical Industry to 1990*. New York: John Wiley & Sons, 1977.

Jewkes, John; Sewers, David; and Stillman, Richard. *The Sources of Invention*, 2nd rev. ed. New York: W.W. Norton and Company, Inc., 1979.

Kaldor, Nicholas. "The Economic Aspects of Advertising." *Review of Economic Studies* 18 (1950):1-27.

Kirzner, Israel. *Competition and Entrepreneurship*. Chicago: University of Chicago Press, 1973.

_____ . *The Perils of Regulation: A Market Process Approach*. Coral Gables, Fla.: Law and Economics Center Occasional Paper, 1979.

Kitch, Edmund W. "The Law and Economics of Rights in Valuable Information." *Journal of Legal Studies* 9 (December 1980):683-723.

Klein, Burton H. *Dynamic Economics*. London: Harvard University Press, 1977.

Koch, Charles H., Jr. "The Freedom of Information Act: Suggestion for Making Information Available to the Public." *Maryland Law Review* 32 (1972):189-224.

Lasagna, Louis, and Wardell, William W. "An Analysis of Drug Development Involving New Chemical Entities Sponsored by U.S.-Owned Companies, 1962-1974." In *Drug Development and Marketing*, edited by Robert B. Helms, pp. 155-181. Washington, D.C.: American Enterprise Institute, 1975.

Latovick, Paula R. "Protection for Trade Secrets under the Toxic Substances Control Act of 1976." *Journal of Law Reform* 13 (Fall 1979): 329-365.

Leonard, William N. "Basic Research and Lagging Innovation." Mimeographed. Paper read at the Eastern Economic Association Convention, Boston, 12 May 1979.

Little, I.M.D. *A Critique of Welfare Economics*. London: Oxford University Press, 1957.

Littlechild, Stephen C. *The Fallacy of the Mixed Economy: An Austrian Critique of Conventional Economics and Government Policy*. San Francisco: Cato Institute, 1979.

Lyon, Randolph N. "Auctions and Alternative Procedures for Allocating Pollution Rights." *Land Economics* 58 (1982):16-32.

Ma, Christopher. "The Paper Chasers." *Newsweek*, 21 April 1980, p. 104.

Machinery and Allied Products Institute. "Confidentiality of Information Related to Exports." *Executive Letter*, 17 November 1979, pp. 4-5.

Mahon, John J. "Trade Secrets and Patents Compared." *Journal of the Patent Office Society* 50 (August 1978):536-553.

Mansfield, Edwin. *Microeconomics*. New York: W.W. Norton and Co., 1970.

_____. "Contributions of R&D to Economic Growth in the United States." *Science* 175 (4 February 1972):477-486.

Mansfield, Edwin, and Rapoport, John. "Social and Private Rates of Return from Industrial Innovations." *Quarterly Journal of Economics* (May 1977) 91:221-240.

Mansfield, Edwin; Rapoport, John; Romeo, Anthony; Villani, Edward; Wagner, Samuel; and Husie, Frank. *The Production and Application of New Industrial Technologies*. New York: W.W. Norton & Co., 1979.

Markham, Jesse W. "Inventive Activity: Government Controls and the Legal Environment." In *The Rate and Direction of Inventive Activity: Economic and Social Factors*, vol. 1. Edited by National Bureau of Economic Research, Princeton: Princeton University Press, 1962, pp. 587-608.

Marshall, Alfred. *Principles of Economics: An Introductory Volume*. London: Macmillan, 1920.

McGarity, Thomas O., and Shapiro, Sidney A. "The Trade Secret Status of Health and Safety Testing Information, Reforming Agency Disclosure Policies." *Harvard Law Review* 93 (March 1980):837-888.

McKie, Edward F., Jr. "Developments in the Supreme Court." In *Intellectual Property Law Review*, edited by G. Rose, pp. 194-195. New York: Clark Boardman, 1981.

Miller, Arthur. *Death of a Salesman*. New York: Viking Press, 1949.

Mills, Julie Ann. "Spliced Genes Get Down to Business." *Science News* 117 (19 March 1980):202-205.

Mises, Ludwig von. *Bureaucracy*. New Haven: Yale University Press, 1972.

Montgomery, A. Thomas. *Managerial Accounting Information: An Introduction to Content and Usefulness*. Reading, Mass.: Addison-Wesley, 1980.

Moss, Laurence S. "Biological Theory and Technological Entrepreneurship in Marshall's Writings." *Eastern Economic Journal* 8 (January 1982):3-13.

Moss, Laurence S., and Gagnon, Donna M., eds. *Readings in the Theory of the Firm*. Lexington, Mass.: Ginn Publishing Co., 1981.

Murray, Chris. "Chemical Companies Wary over Toxic Substance Law." *Chemical and Engineering News*, 3 January 1979, p. 6.

Nader, Ralph. "Freedom of Information Act." *Harvard Civil Liberties-Civil Rights Law Review* 5 (1970):1-15.

_____. "New Opportunities for Open Government: The 1974 Amendments to the Freedom of Information Act and the Federal Advisory Act." *American University Law Review*, Fall 1975, pp. 1-83.

National Bureau of Economic Research, ed. *The Rate and Direction of Inventive Activity: Economic and Social Factors.* Princeton, N.J.: Princeton University Press, 1962.

National Science Foundation. *National Science Indicators.* Washington, D.C.: U.S. Government Printing Office, 1979.

––––––. *National Patterns of Science and Technology Resources: 1981.* Report NSF 81-311. Washington, D.C.: U.S. Government Printing Office, 1981.

"National Security and the Amended Freedom of Information Act." *Yale Law Journal* 85 (1976):401-407.

Niskanen, William. *Bureaucracy and Representative Government.* Chicago: Aldene Co., 1971.

Nordhaus, William, and Tobin, James. "Is Growth Obsolete?" *Economic Growth Fiftieth Anniversary Colloquiere.* New York: National Bureau of Economic Research, 1972.

"Now the General Drugs Can Be Look-Alikes Too." *Chemical Week,* 30 June 1972, pp. 41-42.

O'Reilly, James T. *Federal Information Disclosure: Procedures, Forms and the Law.* Colorado Springs: Shepard's/McGraw-Hill, 1982.

––––––. "Government Disclosure of Private Secrets Under the Freedom of Information Act." *Business Lawyer* 30 (July 1975):1125-1147.

––––––. "Regaining a Confidence: Protection of Business Confidential Data through Reform of the Freedom of Information Act." *Administrative Law Review* 34 (1982):263-313.

O'Reilly, James T.; Gaynor, Kevin A.; Carroll, David W.; and Cronin, Philip F., Jr. *Federal Regulation of the Chemical Industry.* Colorado Springs: Shepard's/McGraw-Hill, 1981.

Packard, Vance. *The Hidden Persuaders.* New York: Pocket Books, 1958.

Padover, S.K., ed. *The Complete Madison: His Basic Writings.* New York: Harper and Brothers, 1953.

Patten, Thomas L., and Weinstein, Kenneth W. "Disclosure of Business Secrets under the Freedom of Information Act: Suggested Limitations." *Administrative Law Review* 29 (1977):195-202.

Peltzman, Sam. "Toward a More General Theory of Regulation." *Journal of Law and Economics* 2 (August 1976):211-240.

Pharmaceutical Manufacturers Association. *Prescription Drug Industry Fact Book: 1980.* Washington, D.C., 1980.

––––––. *Economic Costs of FDA Regulation.* Washington, D.C., 1981.

Phillips, Patrick. "Are Trade Secrets Dead? The Effect of the Toxic Substances Control Act and the Freedom of Information Act on Trade Secrets." *Journal of the Patent Office Society* 62 (November 1980): 652-677.

Popper, Karl R. *The Open-Society and Its Enemies.* New York: Harper & Row, 1972.

Porter, Michael E. *Competitive Strategy: Techniques for Analyzing Industries and Competitors.* New York: Free Press, 1980.

Pracon Incorporated. "Study to Assess Impacts of Releasing Safety and Effectiveness Data on the Pharmaceutical Industry's Incentives to Invest in and Conduct Research and Development Program." Vienna, 1978.

"R&D Overview." *Chemical and Engineering News*, 27 July 1981, pp. 48-71.

Reekie, W., and Weber, M. *Profits, Politics and Drugs.* New York: Holmes and Meier Publishers, 1979.

Reis-Arndt, E. "New Pharmaceutical Agents 1961-1973." *Drugs Made in Germany* 18 (1975):123-130.

Reis-Arndt, E., and Elvers, D. "Results of Pharmaceutical Research—New Pharmaceutical Agents 1961-1970." *Drugs Made in Germany* 15 (1972):134-140.

Relyea, Harold C. "The Freedom of Information Act a Decade Later." *Public Administration Review*, July/August 1979, pp. 310-332.

"Reporting for the Toxic Substances Control Act. Can EPA Keep Data Secret?" *Chemical Week*, 1 February 1978, p. 41.

"Residents of Missouri Community Are Concerned, Confused by Dioxin." *Boston Sunday Globe*, 2 January 1983, p. 2.

Richardson, Hazen. "What's Ahead for the Drug Industry, Pharmacy and Health Care in the 1980s." *American Druggist*, July 1981, pp. 79-80.

Schief, Blanche. *Access Reports: A Bi-Weekly Newsletter on Freedom of Information and Privacy.* Washington, D.C.: Plus Publications, Inc., 1981.

Schmalensee, Richard. *The Control of Natural Monopolies.* Lexington, Mass.: D.C. Heath and Company, 1979.

Scnnapp, J.B. "Soichiro Honda, Japan's Inventive Iconoclast." *Wall Street Journal*, 1 February 1982, p. 20.

Schumpeter, Joseph A. *Business Cycles.* New York: McGraw-Hill, 1939.

_____ . *Capitalism, Socialism and Democracy.* New York: Harper & Brothers, 1942.

_____ . *History of Economic Analysis.* New York: Oxford University Press, 1973.

Seidel, Arthur H., and Panitch, Ronald L. *What the General Practitioner Should Know About Trade Secrets and Employment Agreements.* Philadelphia: American Law Institute, 1973.

Solow, Robert M. "Technical Change at the Aggregate Production Function." *Review of Economics and Statistics* 39 (August 1957):312-320.

Sowell, Thomas. *Knowledge and Decisions.* New York: Basic Books, 1980.

Stevenson, Russell B. "Protecting Business Secrets under the Freedom of Information Act, Managing Exemption 4." *Your Business, Your Trade Secrets, and Your Government*, 11 May 1981, pp. 102-106.

_____ . *Corporation and Information: Secrecy, Access, and Disclosure.* Baltimore: Johns Hopkins University Press, 1980.

Stigler, George. "The Theory of Economic Regulations." *Bell Journal on Economics* 2 (Spring 1971):3-21.

Taylor, Robert E. "Senate Unites, Backs Disclosure Safeguards for Sensitive Business Data Given to U.S." *Wall Street Journal,* 21 May 1982, p. 7.

"Trade Secrets." *Wall Street Journal,* 5 October 1981, p. 31.

Tsurumi, W. *Multinational Management: Business Strategy and Government Policy.* Cambridge, Mass.: Ballinger, 1977.

Unger, Stephen H. "The Growing Threat of Government Secrecy." *Technology Review,* February/March 1982, pp. 31-39.

Vernon, Raymond. *Sovereignty at Bay.* New York: Basic Books, 1971.

Weber, Max. *The Theory of Social and Economic Organizations.* New York: Oxford University Press, 1947.

Weidenbaum, Murray L. *Business, Government and the Public,* 2nd ed. Englewood Cliffs, N.J.: Prentice-Hall, 1981.

Wells, Louis T., ed. *The Product, Life Cycle and International Trade.* Cambridge: Harvard University Press, 1972.

Whale, Arthur R. "FOIA—For Our Inquisitive Adversaries." Presented at the American Patent Law Association of Rochester, New York, 4 May 1978.

"Where the Caribou Play." *Wall Street Journal,* 5 June 1979, p. 22.

Wiggins, James R. *Freedom or Secrecy.* New York: Oxford University Press, 1956

Williamson, Oliver E. "The Modern Corporation: Origins, Evolution, Attributes." *Journal of Economic Literature* 19 (December 1981): 1537-1570.

Wilson, James Q. *The Politics of Regulations.* New York: Basic Books, 1980.

Wolfe, Charles, Jr. "A Theory of Non-Market Failures," *Public Interest* 55 (Spring 1979):114-133.

"World and Chemical Outlook." *Chemical and Engineering News,* 20 November 1982, p. 50.

Wunsch, Charles R. "Trade Secret Confidentiality and Toxic Substance Regulation: A Non-tariff Trade Barrier in the Chemical Trade." *Cornell International Law Journal* 14 (Winter 1981):173-193.

U.S. Government Reports, Hearings, and Documents

U.S. Administrative Conference of the United States. "Protecting Busiess Secrets under the Freedom of Information Act: Managing Exemption 4." (Testimony of Russell B. Stevenson, Jr.). No. T-15706548 00.923.997510.251.

_____ . Letter to Confidential Business Information Mailing List from William C. Bush, staff counsel to the Committee on Regulation of Business. 24 November 1981 and April 1982.

U.S. Congress. House. Committee on Government Operations. *Administration of the Freedom of Information Act.* 92d Cong., 2d Sess., 1972, H. Rept. 92-1419.

_____ . *A Citizens Guide on How to Use the Freedom of Information Act in Requesting Government Documents.* 95th Cong., 1st Sess., 1977, H. Rept. 95-793.

_____ . *Freedom of Information Act Requests for Business Data and Reverse-FOIA Lawsuits.* 95th Cong., 2d Sess., 1978, H. Rept. 95-1382.

_____ . Special Subcommittee on Government Information. *Availability of Information from Federal Departments and Agencies, Part 1, Panel Discussion with Editors et al.* 84th Cong., 1st Sess., 1955.

_____ . Government Information and Individual Rights Subcommittee. *Freedom of Information Act Oversight.* 97th Cong., 1st Sess., 1981.

_____ . Committee on Interstate and Foreign Commerce. *Toxic Substances Control Act.* 94th Cong., 1st Sess., 1975.

_____ . Committee on the Judiciary. Subcommittee on Administrative Practice and Procedure. *Freedom of Information Act Oversight.* 91st Cong., 2d Sess., 1970.

_____ . Committee on Post Office and Civil Service. Subcommittee on Census and Population. *Confidentiality of Shippers' Export Declarations.* 96th Cong., 2d Sess., 1980.

_____ . Committee of the Whole House on the State of the Union. *Clarifying and Protecting the Right of the Public to Information.* 89th Cong., 2d Sess., 1966, H. Rept. 1497.

U.S. Congress. Senate. Committee on Commerce. *Toxic Substances Control Act.* 94th Cong., 1st Sess., 1975.

_____ . *Toxic Substances Control Act: Legislative History, Pub. L. 94-469.* 94th Cong., 2d Sess., 1976, S. Rept. 94-698.

_____ . Committee on Government Affairs. *Shippers' Export Declarations.* 96th Cong., 2d Sess., 1980.

_____ . Committee on Government Operations. Subcommittee of the Committee on the Judiciary. *Freedom of Information, Executive Privilege.* 93rd Cong., 1st Sess., 1973.

_____ . Subcommittee on Intergovernmental Relations. *Executive Privilege, Secrecy in Government: Freedom of Information.* 93rd Cong., 1st Sess., 1973.

_____ . Committee on the Judiciary. *Administrative Procedure Act.* 79th Cong., 1st Sess., 1945, S. Rept. 752.

_____ . *Administrative Procedure Act: Legislative History.* 79th Cong., 2d Sess., 1946, S. Doc. 248.

———. *Clarifying and Protecting the Right of the Public to Information and for Other Purposes.* 88th Cong., 2d Sess., 1964, S. Rept. 1219.

———. *Clarifying and Protecting the Right of the Public to Information.* 89th Cong., 1st Sess., 1965, S. Rept. 813.

———. *Oversight of the Freedom of Information Act.* 95th Cong., 1st Sess., 1977.

———. *Freedom of Information Act.* 88th Cong., 1st Sess., 1963.

———. Subcommittee on Administrative Practice and Procedure. *Freedom of Information Act Source Book: Legislative Materials, Cases, Articles.* 93rd Cong., 2d Sess., 1974.

———. Subcommittee on Patents, Trademarks, and Copyrights. *An Economic Review of the Patent System.* 85th Cong., 2d Sess., 1958.

U.S. Department of Commerce. Bureau of the Census. *Census of Manufacturers. Subject Series SR-9 Concentration Ratios in Manufacturing.* Washington, D.C.: U.S. Government Printing Office, 1981.

U.S. Department of Justice. *Attorney General's Memorandum on the Public Information Section of the Administrative Procedures Act: A Memorandum for the Executive Departments and Agencies Concerning Section of the Administrative Procedure Act as Revised Effective July 4, 1967.* Washington, D.C., 1967.

———. *Department of Justice Guidelines on Freedom of Information Act.* Letter from Griffin Bell, 5 March 1972.

———. "A Short Guide to the Freedom of Information Act." Compiled by Robert L. Saloschin, Thomas C. Newkurk and Donald J. Gavin, 1979.

———. *Memorandum from the Office of Information and Policy.* Prepared by Robert L. Saloschin, 15 June 1979.

———. *Memorandum to All Agency General Counsels.* Prepared by B.A. Babcock, 21 June 1979.

———. *Memorandum for Heads of All Federal Departments and Agencies.* Prepared by William French Smith, 4 May 1981.

———. *FOIA Update.* Washington, D.C.: Office of Information and Privacy, 1982.

U.S. Executive Office of the President. Office of Management and Budget. *Budget of the United States Government.* Fiscal year 1983. Washington, D.C.: U.S. Government Printing Office, 1983.

U.S. General Services Administration. *United States Government Manual.* Washington, D.C.: U.S. Government Printing Office, 1980.

U.S. Library of Congress. Congressional Research Service. "Press Notices on Disclosures Made Pursuant to the Federal Freedom of Information Act 1972-1980: A Compilation." Prepared by Harold C. Relyea and Suzanne Cavanagh.

U.S. Office of the Council of Economic Advisors. *Economic Report of the President [Reagan to Congress].* Washington, D.C.: U.S. Government Printing Office, 1982.

U.S. Office of Toxic Substances. *TSCA Information Security Manual.* Washington, D.C.: U.S. Government Printing Office, 1971.

_____ . *Toxic Substances Control Public Law 94-469, Reporting for the Chemical Substance Inventory; Instructions for Reporting for the Revised Inventory.* Washington, D.C.: U.S. Government Printing Office, 1979.

U.S. Patent Office. *Patent Activity Profile, All Technologies: A Special Report by the Office of Technology Assessment and Forecast.* Washington, D.C., 1979.

Court Cases

Abbott Laboratories v. Gardner, 387 U.S. 136 (1967).

American Jewish Congress v. Kreps, 574 F.2d 624 (D.C. Cir. 1978).

Amoco Oil Co. v. EPA, 541.

Audio Technical Services v. Department of the Army, 487 F. Supp. 779 (D.C. D.C. 1979).

Board of Trade of Chicago v. Commodity Futures Trading Commission, 627 F.2d 392 (D.C. Cir. 1980).

Braintree Electric Light Co. v. Dept. of Energy, 494 F. Supp. (D.C.D.C. 1980).

Bristol-Myers Co. v. Kennedy, Civ. No. 77-2122 (D.C. D.C. 1979).

Burroughs Corp. v. Schlesinger, 403 F. Supp. 633 (E.D. Va. 1975).

Chevron Chemical Corp. v. Costle, 641 F.2d 104 (3d Cir. 1981).

Chrysler Corp. v. Schlesinger, 565 F.2d 1172 (3d Cir. 1977), 412 F. Supp. 171 (D. De. 1976), *vacated and remanded sub nom Chrysler Corp. v. Brown*, 441 U.S. 281, 99 S. Ct. 1705, *on remand*, 611 F.2d 439 (3d Cir. 1979).

Citizens to Preserve Overton Park v. Volpe, 401 U.S. 402, 91 S. Ct. 814, 28 L.E. 2d 136 (1971).

Consumers Union v. VA, 301 F. Supp. 796 (S.D. N.Y. 1969), *dismissed as moot*, 436 F.2d 1363 (2d Cir. 1971).

Continental Oil v. Federal Power Commission, 519 F.2d 31 (5th Cir. 1975).

Diamond v. Chakrabut, U.S. 65 L. Ed. 2d 144, 206 U.S.P.O. 193 (1980).

Ditlow v. Schultz, 379 F. Supp. 326 (D.C. D.C. 1974), *decision deferred*, 517 F.2d 166 (D.C. Cir. 1975).

Dow Chemical v. Environmental Protection Agency, 605 F.2d 673 (3d Cir. 1979).

Eastland v. United States Servicemen's Fund, 421 U.S. 491 (1975).

Ethyl Corp. v. Environmental Protection Agency, 478 F.2d 47 (4th Cir. 1973).

Exxon Corp. v. Federal Trade Commission, 436 F. Supp. 1019, (D. De. 1977), 384 F. Supp. 755 (D.C. D.C. 1974), *remanded*, 527 F.2d 1386 (D.C. Cir. 1976), *on remand*, 466 F. Supp. 1088 (D.C. D.C. 1978), *on remanded review*, 1980-2 CCH Trade Cas. ¶ 63577 (D.C. Cir. 1980).

Federal Aviation Administration v. Robertson, 422 U.S. 255, 95 S. Ct. 2140, 45 L.E. 2d 164 (1975).

Firestone Tire and Rubber Co. v. Coleman, 432 F. Supp. 1359 (N.D. Oh. 1977).

General Services Administration v. Benson, 415 F.2d 878 (9th Cir. 1969).

Getman v. National Labor Relations Board, 77 L.R.R.M. 3063 (D.C. D.C. 1971), 450 F.2d 670 (D.C. Cir. 1974), *appeal for stay of order denied*, 404 U.S. 1204 (1971).

Grumman Aircraft Engineering Corp. v. Renegotiation Board, 425 F.2d 578 (D.C. Cir. 1970), *on remand*, 325 F. Supp. 1146 (D.C. D.C. 1971), *aff'd*, 482 F.2d 710 (D.C. Cir. 1973), *rev'd*, 421 U.S. 168 (1975).

GTE Sylvania v. Consumer Product Safety Commission, 404 F. Supp. 352 (D. De. 1975), 438 F. Supp. 208 (D. De. 1977), 443 F. Supp. 1152 (D. De. 1977), *aff'd*, CCH Cons. Prod. Saf. Gd. ¶ 75, 231 (3d Cir. 1979), *aff'd*, 598 F.2d 790 (3d Cir. 1979), *aff'd*, 447 U.S. 102, 100 S. Ct. 2051, 64 L.E. 2d 766 (1980).

Gulf and Western Industries Inc. v. U.S., 615 F.2d 527 (D.C. Cir. 1979).

Honeywell Information Systems v. National Aeronautics and Space Administration, Civ. No. 76-377 (D.C. D.C. 1976).

Hughes Aircraft Co. v. Schlesinger, 384 F. Supp. 292 (C.D. Ca. 1974).

Iron and Sears v. Chasen, No. 78-2372, U.S.D.

Johnson v. Dept. of Health, Education and Welfare, 426 F. Supp. 336 (D.C. D.C. 1978), *subsequent opinion*, Civ. No. 77-2013 (D.C. D.C. 1979).

Kewanee Oil v. Bicron Corp., 416 U.S. 470, 94 S. Ct. 1879, 40 L.E. 2d 315 (1974).

M.A. Shapiro & Co. v. Securities & Exchange Commission, 339 F. Supp. 467 (D.C. D.C. 1972).

Military Audit Project v. Kettles, Civ. No. 75-666 (D.C. D.C. 1976).

National Airlines v. Civil Aeronautics Board, Civ. No. 75-613 (D.C. D.C. 1975).

National Parks and Conservation Assn. v. Kleppe, 547 F.2d 673 (D.C. Cir. 1976).

National Parks and Conservation Assn. v. Morton, 498 F.2d 765 (D.C. Cir. 1974).

Open America v. Watergate Special Prosecution Force, 547 F.2d 605 (D.C. Cir. 1976).

Parkridge Hospital v. Blue Cross and Blue Shield of Tennessee, 430 F. Supp. 1093 (E.D. Tn. 1977).

Pharmaceutical Manufacturers Assn. v. Weinberger, 401 F. Supp. 444 (D.C. D.C. 1975), 411 F. Supp. 576 (D.C. D.C. 1976).

Pierce & Stevens Chemical Corp. v. Consumer Product Safety Commission, Civ. No. 75-410 (W.D. N.Y. 1977), *rev'd*, 585 F.2d 1382 (2d Cir. 1978).

Polaroid Corp. v. Costle, 11 Envir. Rep. Cas. (BNA) 2134 (D. Mass. 1978).

Porter County Chapter of the Isaak Walton League of America Inc. v. United States Atomic Energy Commission, 380 F. Supp. 630 (N.D. In. 1974).

Rural Housing Alliance v. U.S. Dept. of Agriculture, Civ. No. 2540-72 (D.C. D.C. 1973), *revised and remanded*, 498 F.2d 73, 78 (D.C. Cir. 1974), *on bill of costs*, 511 F.2d 1347 (D.C. Cir. 1974).

Soucie v. David, 448 F.2d 1067 (D.C. Cir. 1971).

Sterling Drug Inc. v. Federal Trade Commission, 450 F.2d 698 (D.C. Cir. 1971).

Superior Oil v. Federal Energy Regulatory Commission, 563 F.2d 191 (5th Cir. 1977).

Twin Coasts Newspapers Inc. v. U.S. Dept. of Commerce, pending, Civ. No. 78-0975 (D.C. D.C. 1979).

Union Oil Co. v. Federal Power Commission, 542 F.2d 1036 (9th Cir. 1976).

Washington Research Project Inc. v. Dept. of Health, Education and Welfare, 366 F. Supp. 929 (D.C. D.C. 1973), *aff'd in part, revised in part, and remanded*, 504 F.2d 238 (D.C. Cir. 1974).

Wearly v. Federal Trade Commission, 462 F. Supp. 589 (D. N.J. 1978), *rev'd on other grounds*, 616 F.2d 662 (3d Cir. 1979).

Wellford v. Hardin, 444 F.2d 21 (4th Cir. 1971).

Westinghouse Electric Corp. v. U.S. Nuclear Regulatory Commission, 555 F.2d 82 (3d Cir. 1977).

Worthington Compressors, Inc. v. Costle, 662 F.2d 45 (D.C. Cir. 1981).

U.S. Statutes, Regulations, Records, and Codes

Administrative Conference of the United States Act, Pub. L. No. 89-554, 80 Stat. 388 (6 September 1966).

Administrative Procedure Act, Pub. L. No. 404, 60 Stat. 237 (11 June 1946).

1 C.F.R. 305.82-1 (1982 ed.).

40 C.F.R. 2.113 (1977 ed.).

40 C.F.R. 2.201 (1977 ed.).

40 C.F.R. 2.203 (1977 ed.).

40 C.F.R. 2.204 (1977 ed.).

40 C.F.R. 2.205 (1977 ed.).

40 C.F.R. 2.207 (1977 ed.).

110 *Congressional Record* 17,086 (daily ed. 28 July 1964).

112 *Congressional Record* 13,644 (daily ed. 20 June 1966).

112 *Congressional Record* 13,661.1 (daily ed. 20 June 1966).

Export Administration Act of 1979, Pub. L. No. 96-72, 93 Stat. 503 (29 September 1979).

39 F.R. 44611.

40 F.R. 2.209.

40 F.R. 2.306.

40 F.R. 2.307.

42 F.R. 3094-3109.

43 F.R. 4599 (1978).

45 F.R. 74380.

45 F.R. 74378.

47 F.R. 46622-46666.

Government in the Sunshine Act, Pub. L. No. 94-409, 90 Stat. 1241 (13 September 1976).

Toxic Substances Control Act, Pub. L. No. 94-469, 90 Stat. 2003 (11 October 1976).

Pub. L. No. 95-396, 92 Stat. 819 (30 September 1978).

5 U.S.C. 22 (1964 ed.).

5 U.S.C. 552 (1976 ed.).

5 U.S.C. 706 (1976 ed.).

5 U.S.C. 1002 (1946 ed.).

7 U.S.C. 136 (1976 ed.).

13 U.S.C. 302 (1972 ed.).

14 U.S.C. 2613 (1976 ed.).

15 U.S.C. 2055 (1976 ed.).

15 U.S.C. 2601 (1976 ed.).

15 U.S.C. 2603 (1976 ed.).

15 U.S.C. 2604 (1976 ed.).

15 U.S.C. 2605 (1976 ed.).

15 U.S.C. 2607 (1976 ed.).

15 U.S.C. 2613 (1976 ed.).

15 U.S.C. 2618 (1976 ed.).

18 U.S.C. 1905 (1976 ed.).

21 U.S.C. 301 (1976 ed.).

21 U.S.C. 344 (1976 ed.).

21 U.S.C. 348 (1976 ed.).

21 U.S.C. 355 (1976 ed.).

21 U.S.C. 360 (1976 ed.).

21 U.S.C. 510-517 (1976 ed.).

33 U.S.C. 1251 (1976 ed.).

33 U.S.C. 1401 (1976 ed.).

42 U.S.C. 300f (1976 ed.).

42 U.S.C. 6901 (1976 ed.).

42 U.S.C. 1857 (1976 ed.).

42 U.S.C. 1858 (1976 ed.).

44 U.S.C. 1500 (1976 ed.).

Index

About the Authors

William L. Casey, Jr., is a professor at Babson College, where he teaches and serves as chairman of the economics department. Professor Casey received the Ph.D. in economics from Boston College and has held teaching positions at Boston College, Regis College, and Babson College. He also has been a consultant to government agencies, labor unions, and trade associations and currently is a senior partner in the Boston-based MCM Research Group, which specializes in policy analysis. Professor Casey is the author of numerous articles that have appeared in professional journals. His major research interests are in the fields of international capital movements, monetary policy, the economics of technological change, and the economics of information.

John E. Marthinsen is an associate professor of economics at Babson College and senior partner in the MCM Research Group, Boston. Professor Marthinsen received the Ph.D. from the University of Connecticut and has primary teaching and research interests in the fields of entrepreneurship, the economics of information, international finance, and monetary economics. At Babson, he chairs the Panel of Judges for the Academy of Distinguished Entrepreneurs. He has served as a consultant to the Army Corps of Engineers, the Department of Transportation, and the Commonwealth Research Group and is now working as an economist for the Handelsbank N.W. in Zurich.

Laurence S. Moss is a professor of economics at Babson College. He received the Ph.D. in economics from Columbia University and has taught at the City University of New York, Columbia, the University of Virginia, and The Fletcher School of Law and Diplomacy. Professor Moss is currently secretary-treasurer of the History of Economics Society and senior partner in the MCM Research Group, Boston. He is the author of several books including *Mountifort Longfield: Ireland's First Professor of Political Economy* (1976) and *The Economics of Ludwig von Mises: Toward a Critical Reappraisal* (1974). In addition, he has written many articles primarily in the field of economic theory and its history.